# Uprooted

A Memoir
of a Marriage

# Uprooted

## Esti Skloot

SHE WRITES PRESS

Published August 2019
Printed in the United States of America
Print ISBN: 978-1-63152-664-0
E-ISBN: 978-1-63152-665-7
Library of Congress Control Number: 2019939310

For information, address:
She Writes Press
1569 Solano Ave #546
Berkeley, CA 94707

Interior design by Tabitha Lahr

She Writes Press is a division of SparkPoint Studio, LLC.

Names and identifying characteristics have been changed to protect the privacy of certain individuals.

For my children: Tal, Shira, and Ori.

# Chapter 1:

# The Meeting

When I met Steve on the SS *Zion*, sailing from New York to Haifa, I never imagined I'd end up carrying his child. As an entertainment officer on the Israeli liner, which was part of the Israeli shipping company ZIM, I handed out my address to several young Americans who came to visit Israel. I was proud of my country, where I grew up watching our blue-and-white flag with the Star of David fluttering on top of buildings during Independence Day, where I marched along singing patriotic songs in boot camp during my army service. I liked having visitors and enjoyed showing them around. Besides, I believed it was part of my job to encourage tourists to stay in our country. Steve, who was going to volunteer on a kibbutz, was the only one of those tourists, however, who came to visit me in my hometown, Ashkelon, a small beach town on the Mediterranean, south of Tel Aviv.

When I first saw Steve, he was trying to get his big German shepherd to climb up a metal staircase leading to the main deck of the SS *Zion*. He wore a black V-neck sweater, blue jeans, and white sneakers. He dressed differently than Israeli guys, who walked around in shorts folded up to their hamstrings, undershirts, and sandals. I knew he was American right away since I had met other Americans on my previous trip to New York. He was young, in his early twenties, clean-shaven, and a few inches taller than my five foot five. I was surprised that he'd traveled all the way from New York with a dog, and it impressed me, though I wasn't particularly intrigued by him. In Israel, at the time, we used to make fun of Americans, whom we viewed as naive and square in their approach to life. I thought of him as just another passenger. As the ship's social director, it was my job to take care of him.

"May I help you, sir?" I said.

"No, thanks, I can manage." His tone was very matter-of-fact, and I moved on.

Crouching under the big dog, he shoved him forward with his right shoulder. "There you go," he said. He turned, flashed me a smile, scrambled after the dog, and disappeared.

Who was this strange guy with his huge canine? He must be a bit nutty, I thought, but I admired his devotion to his pet.

It was 1965, and I was on my second voyage on the large ship. At twenty-five I was proud to be the sole director of the entertainment program. I had attained that position after apprenticing with Victor Epstein, a veteran entertainment officer, for two voyages around the Mediterranean. I was glad the apprenticeship was over. He'd taught me the tricks of the trade but I had to do all the hard work, like manually blowing up fifty balloons for the Captain's Ball or getting up to lead morning gymnastics. The worst was when he asked me to iron his stiff white officer's uniform in his airless cabin. I obliged, believing he'd give me a negative report if I didn't. I was scared of people in superior positions, especially men. I came by it honestly after years of being told by my Jewish German father to do as I was told and not talk back to him. I'm the oldest of three siblings. My parents lived in England as refugees after fleeing the

Nazis in 1939. Once my siblings—Jeremy, a year and a half younger, and Rachel, four and a half years my junior—were born, my parents didn't have much time or energy for me. My father was raised by strict German parents and knew only one way to bring up his children: you obey, or you'll be punished, by a piercing look, a spanking, or being forced to skip a meal.

I met Steve again that afternoon. He appeared, with his dog tagging behind, while I was teaching Hebrew in the Carmel Lounge.

"May we join you?" he asked.

A German shepherd wasn't my idea of an ideal student. "What do you plan to do with him?" I asked.

"No problem, he loves to study."

Okay, so he's joking with me. I can handle that. Let's see where this will lead us.

"Does he know some Hebrew already?"

"No, but he just had his bar mitzvah."

I laughed. "Touché, you win."

This guy was like a big kid in every way—the way he looked, the way he joked around with his dog. He was so different from Israeli guys who at age eighteen had to enlist in the army and were serious and cynical.

He found a place on a side bench, patted the seat, and the dog settled down next to him.

"Where are you from?" I asked after the lesson.

"I'm from Queens, New York." Queens sounded like a regal place. I pictured mansions and stately gardens.

"Do you study there?"

"I finished my studies last spring—I majored in film at Boston University."

I was intrigued. As a teenager I went to the movies every single Saturday night. As I watched the screen, identifying with the heroes and heroines, the actors seemed to emit a supernatural light. I would run home, arriving breathless, heart throbbing, tears in my eyes. I'd be so taken by the romance or the historic epic I had just witnessed, convinced my life was meaningless and dull by comparison.

I sensed Steve's eyes moving over my body, gliding from top to bottom. The blood rose to my cheeks while I tucked my cream-colored blouse into my narrow, knee-length skirt. I felt uneasy, with him looking at me that way, especially since to me he was just another passenger, not an object of my romantic dreams.

He asked me how long I'd worked on the ship. I told him eight months.

"What made you go for this job?"

"I wanted to see the world and didn't have any money."

"You could have been a stewardess."

"And be a glorified waitress?" I sniffed. "No, thanks. Besides, I love the sea. And you, why are you traveling to Israel?" It was the standard question I asked passengers.

This was when he told me he was going to live on a kibbutz. He beamed, thinking it would impress me, and it did. For me, the kibbutz symbolized the Israeli spirit, communal living, equality, socialism, love of the land, and refuting capitalism and urban living. During my army service I spent time in various kibbutzim, where I'd made many friends. I felt a kinship with kibbutz members. I considered it the biggest compliment when someone asked me if I was a kibbutznick, someone born on a kibbutz.

"Which one?"

"Kibbutz Hazore'a," he said, adding, "near Haifa."

I couldn't help but feel a bit offended by him telling me where the kibbutz was. "I know where it is," I said coolly. I peeked at my watch; I had to run; I was in charge of the five o'clock music hour in the lounge. "Sorry, got to go. See you later."


During the ten-day voyage I bumped into Steve now and then, always with his loyal dog, O'Hara, at his side. One morning while

I chatted with some sun-tanning passengers on the upper deck, he joined in.

"How are you both doing?" I asked.

He nuzzled his dog. "O'Hara loves all the scraps everybody feeds him."

"Are you happy with the way things are on the ship?"

"Sure, you're doing a great job."

"Thanks." I felt a warm glow within. Steve's compliment made me feel good. My work was important to me; by nature I was a perfectionist and tried to excel in whatever I was doing.

At that point I decided to give Steve my address in Ashkelon. It was common for Israelis to invite tourists to their homes. We took pride in our small country and wanted to share our way of living with others. It might be part of the Middle Eastern culture, where it's customary to open one's house to strangers, much more so than in the States. In my capacity as social director on the ship, I felt it was a legitimate gesture.

I went below and scribbled my address on a piece of paper. "Here," I said, returning. "You're welcome to visit me."

He folded the note carefully and put it in his shirt pocket. I didn't imagine he'd follow up. I'd given my address to other foreign passengers and no one had ever shown up at my parents' house. Plus, my mind was elsewhere—on my work and on the affair I was having with one of the ship's officers.

A couple of days before landing in Haifa we held the traditional Masquerade Ball, where the passengers dressed up and prizes were given for best costume. I was nervous, wondering if I could manage to pull the whole evening off on my own. I was the sole person in charge of the ship's entertainment. I didn't have any team members to assist me.

I prepared the prizes—bottles of wine from Zichron Ya'akov and cosmetic products from the Dead Sea. I worked with the band director to coordinate drum rolls for the appropriate times, hung paper decorations, and announced over the loudspeakers that everyone should gather at 8:00 p.m. in the Galilee lounge. The passengers, dressed as gypsies, fairies, and cowboys, and the ship's officers in their sparkling white uniforms arrived in high spirits. On stage, in a décolleté sequined gold-green dress and white pumps, I welcomed everybody and introduced the panel of three judges. I felt very sophisticated in my fancy dress. I had bought it during a sale at Macy's when we stopped for a couple of days in New York.

The costume contest started with a drum roll. The dressed-up passengers paraded before the judges, who negotiated briefly before handing me their verdict on a piece of paper. Third place was a prisoner with a white beard, striped pajamas, and a number written on cardboard across his chest. Second place was a lovely fairy queen with a silken gown, a sparkling tiara in her hair, and a magic wand. And then finally, after a long drum roll, I announced the winner of the first prize: the Russian diplomat. A pudgy gentleman of medium height with a hefty belly, sporting a black beard with a monocle in his right eye, leaned slightly on a silver knobbed cane. Wearing striped black pants, a gold watch hanging from his vest pocket, he walked slowly toward me. Smiling, I stretched out my hand to shake his. He had a surprisingly firm grip.

"Congratulations," I said, playing the role along with him, "Where are you from in Russia?"

In a thick accent he answered: "I'm from Leningrad, a beautiful city."

His voice sounded familiar yet I couldn't place it. Later, when the dance music started, the Russian diplomat removed his beard, toupee, and monocle, after which he pulled a pillow out from under his shirt. Only then did I realize it was Steve.

At the end of the ten-day voyage, I received a letter with thirty signatures on it. In beautiful calligraphy letters it stated: *We'd like to thank you for your hard work, caring, and sympathy for each one of us. You gave us a sense of warm Israeli hospitality. The lively entertainment and your personal attention helped make our trip truly delightful.* The first signature, matching the handwriting of the letter, was Steven P. Skloot. I felt so grateful to him. I was surprised and honored. The letter felt like a warm hug to my ego.

Growing up, I never felt acknowledged. I worked as hard as I could polishing my father's shoes or cleaning his bike to a shine, but he never thanked me or said, "What a good job!" When I brought home a report card with straight As, he'd barely glance at it. I felt I could never get a good word from him. I grew up feeling I wasn't good enough, which made me try to excel in everything I did, to push myself to the utmost, but I was never satisfied with the results. When we first came to Israel, we slept on the floor of British barracks that served as an immigrant camp in the small town of Pardes Chanah. From there we moved to kibbutz Regba in northern Israel. My father hated communal living, so half a year later we moved to an old house in the midst of orange groves in Pardes Gan Chayim on the coastal plain of Israel. I loved playing with Elana and Aliza, two girls who lived nearby, among the citrus trees, inhaling the fragrance of orange blossoms. When, after two years, we left that home, my heart was broken.

I remembered being nine and a half, sitting with my little brother Jeremy on top of an open truck loaded with our household belongings: chairs, cabinets, boxes filled with pots and pans, metal bed frames and thin mattresses. Rachel sat in the cabin with our parents. We passed eucalyptus and orange trees while the warm wind blew in our faces, drying the tears trickling down my cheeks. I had to leave my two girlfriends—the only friends I ever had.

It had been the same during the war in England. My parents, who in 1939 had escaped the Nazis, moved often; they would pick up their kids and travel by train, tram, or bus to a new destination, where my father would work as a gardener while my mother served as a maid, cook, or both. From the time I was born in Gloucester to the time we immigrated to Israel when I was eight, we changed residences every year or so.

After docking in the northern port city of Haifa, I traveled home, to Ashkelon, where I stayed for a weeklong shore leave. I then returned to the ship for my next voyage to New York. Ten days later, after coming back from my trip, I walked along the path to our little home in Ashkelon, whistling our family arrival tune—the beginning of a German folk song. I looked forward to seeing my parents, especially my Mom, who liked to spoil me when I returned. My mouth dropped open when I saw Steve, O'Hara at his side, sitting on the doorstep.

"What are you doing here?" I asked. O'Hara raised his black ears as if I were addressing him. Steve grinned, displaying his perfect white teeth.

"Just visiting," he said. His pale, bony knees protruded from Bermuda shorts. I thought, only American tourists wear those shorts. As a young Israeli, I dismissed a kind of attire different than the norm in Israel. Except for the Orthodox Jews, we all dressed similarly, in the spirit of our new, pioneering country, the way kibbutznicks dressed; short shorts and undershirts or tank tops in summer, and simple, usually khaki, pants and cotton shirts, in winter

I brushed my hands over my pants, trying to straighten the creases. I hoped I didn't look too disheveled after traveling by bus all the way from Haifa. "How long have you been here . . . in my home?" I said.

"A couple of days." His deep-set blue eyes stared at me. I felt the blood rise to my face while I wondered if he'd waited around just because he wanted to see me. I also couldn't figure out how come my father let a total stranger stay in our home for several days.

"May I?" He took my valise and opened the screen door, spreading out his arm as though welcoming me home. "After you," he nodded.

My mother, busy in the narrow kitchen, an apron over her floral print dress, walked up to welcome me with a warm embrace. The way she looked at me, with her laughing blue-green eyes, I knew she was proud of her adventurous daughter. Her dark, wavy hair framed a gentle oval face tanned from years of working outside in a plant nursery, where she showed older women, mostly of North African and Yemenite descent, how to pot plants, transfer them, and take care of them.

"Estherlè, how are you? How was the trip?"

"Okay, *eemalè,* I'm fine, it's good to be home."

She nodded her head toward Steve. "It was fun getting to know your friend from the ship."

Is that how he introduced himself? I thought. "Well, he's not really—"

My mom smiled at us. "Would you like a cup of tea?"

Before we had a chance to answer, my father appeared, gave me a brief greeting—"Hello, Esther"—and turned to Steve. "You can join us for supper." Obviously, Steve has made himself welcome here, I thought.

I wondered why my father was being so nice to this American stranger. They rarely had guests stay over. I joined him in the kitchen, where he was retrieving bread from the breadbox.

"*Abba,*" I said, "it was kind of you to let Steve stay." He raised the corners of his usually closed, thin lips as he looked at O'Hara. My father had always preferred the company of animals to human beings.

"Well, if this young man traveled with his dog all the way from America, he must be a good person," he said.

As we sat down to a simple meal of white cheese, olives, salad, and soft-boiled eggs, my father poured himself a cup of tea from the teapot. He asked Steve how he liked Israel, and Steve, seeking my eyes, replied that he loved it, especially the kibbutz. Listening to them speak, I chuckled at their different English accents; my father, with his strong German diction, *Vot do you think about our country?* And Steve with his Yankee–New York accent, skipping consonants and turning vowels into diphthongs. I tried to teach the passengers Hebrew, but in such a short time none of them could learn to speak the language. My mother's smile deepened. She loved the company of people, especially from faraway places.

"How do you get along with the Kibbutzniks?" she asked.

"Great." Steve tapped his spoon to crack open the top of the egg. "They're so friendly, and material things don't mean a thing to them." His full lips closed over the spoon as he savored the egg yolk. Neither my father nor my mother asked him about his life in the US. Like most Israelis, it was more important for them to know what impression our country made on an American tourist. It would be nice if they asked him about his life back home. It would be more polite, I thought.

Steve finished the last bit of egg, scraping the inner shell with his teaspoon.

"This was delicious; may I have another?"

My father looked surprised.

"I'm sorry, but we only eat one egg at a meal, no need for more than that." He handed the bowl of olives to Steve. "If you like, have some olives; seven of them amount to one egg."

Steve glanced at me sideways, the half smile on his lips disappearing when he addressed my father.

"Very well, there's no harm in asking—right?" he said, winking at me. I peeked at my father, who sat poker-faced, not revealing his thoughts. I guess he thought Steve was a spoiled American who had no idea about food shortage or rationing, which we, refugees in England and new immigrants in Israel, knew so well. I wondered whether he picked up on Steve's humor, but I assumed not; my father rarely joked around.

After Steve helped clear the table, we sat on the patio, chatting and listening to the waves from the sea. I was tired from my long trip, so I said good night and went to bed in the little room under the terrace that my parents had added to our home. Steve slept in the living room on the old sofa. I lay on my narrow bed in my bunker-like room, my mattress just a few inches wider than my torso.

My eyes open, peeking at the garden lights through the narrow windows near the ceiling at the height of our garden lawn, I thought about our foreign visitor, this English-speaking guy with a huge dog. It appealed to my sense of adventure, yet I still didn't feel attracted to him; there were no sparks flying. I felt odd about him staying in our home, but part of me was excited, looking forward to getting to know this strange guy.

The following day Steve and I walked along the beach while he recounted the escapades of his "crazy family," as he called them. It was *my* beach, where every summer I spent hours swimming in the deep waters beyond the line of crashing waves, playing paddle ball on the silken sand, and watching fiery sunsets while crabs scurried sideways into their holes.

Steve's feet sank in the sand as he charged forward into the wind. He told me his grandfather and uncles loved gambling. I was surprised; gambling didn't exist in my world. My parents wouldn't dream of playing with money; they needed every penny for survival. The money I made just covered rent, food, and transportation. While studying in Jerusalem, I couldn't afford a bag of potato chips, and once, after purchasing deodorant, I tried to return it because I didn't have enough money for the bus. I looked at Steve but kept quiet; I didn't want to share my stories of poverty and need.

"They gambled even on the Sabbath," he chuckled, "when you're not supposed to touch money."

The white-crested waves come roaring down. The spray splashed in my face as I laughed with pleasure; I loved the salty air on my tongue. I felt free, light-headed, and alive. With Steve next to me I felt a sense of adventure; I touched his arm, feeling the soft fabric of his suede jacket, and a shiver of excitement ran through me.

"You know," I said, "my mother lights candles, but we don't really observe the Sabbath."

"How about Yom-Kippur? Do you go to the synagogue?"

"No; instead of praying, I pilfer guavas from our neighbor's tree."

Steve laughed. "You were pretty naughty, huh?"

That afternoon while my parents had their siesta in their small bedroom, I sat on our living room sofa watching Steve look at objects familiar to me: the small wooden coffee table, my father's desk stacked with magazines and newspapers he planned to read, my father's prized object—a record player on which he played the music of Brahms, Schubert, and Mozart—and the bookcase with books in German, English, and some Hebrew. Steve picked a hardcover book with gilded letters engraved in German on its cover, *Poems by Goethe*, and leafed through it. He turned to me. "Where are all these books from?"

"My parents brought them from Germany." I paused. "It's strange; I never really thought about it."

"The books must have meant a lot to them."

"I guess . . . I never saw them read those books; they were too busy working."

He walked over to the sofa, the book in his hand; he opened it and pointed to one of the pages. "Can you read this?"

I shook my head tentatively. "Just a bit." My parents never spoke to me in German. In England they never spoke it, since it was the language of the enemy, but once they came to Israel they resorted to their mother tongue. I learned German by listening to them.

Steve looked at me with wide eyes, mouth slightly open, absorbing every word I said. He was interested in me, in my life. Guys I'd met before didn't care about my history; I couldn't share much with them. A surge of warmth spread throughout my body. He's getting to know me, I thought, my home, my background, my world.

After checking out a few more objects in the room—a black-and-white wedding photograph of my parents and a delicate, painted porcelain fruit bowl, the only wedding gift they managed to bring with them from Germany—Steve came over to the sofa. He sat down next to me, so close our arms touched. When he spread them to make a point during our conversation, I could feel the silky hair on his forearms. My heart beat faster while I smiled and nodded without hearing a word he said. And then he stopped talking; it was quiet. I felt Steve's arm around my shoulder, gently pulling me toward him. I sensed my skin radiating heat under his touch. I looked at him. His eyes had a soft, imploring look, but he didn't say a word. I didn't react; the presence of my parents down the hall unnerved me; what if my father walked into the living room? But then Steve embraced me, holding me tightly, and before I knew it I found myself horizontal on the sofa with Steve upon me, his torso the length of mine. With my arms around his broad back, whatever resistance I had melted away. I relished his silken, smooth-shaven cheek, the scent of Old Spice, and the warmth of his body. When his lips, soft and gentle, met mine, I tasted fresh peppermint on my tongue. My body tingling, I closed my eyes, savoring the moment while the world around me, all sounds, colors, and scents, ceased to exist.

Suddenly a loud sound entered my consciousness; the bathroom door banged close. My parents were up! Steve hugged me tightly and then released me and got off the sofa. I jumped up, straightening my clothes as I opened the living room door. I inhaled deeply to calm myself down before going to the kitchen to put the kettle on for tea.

After drinking tea with oatmeal cookies my mom had baked, Steve thanked my parents for their hospitality and told them he had to go back to his kibbutz in the Valley of Jezre'el in northern Israel. My parents and I saw him to the door, where I promised to visit him. We watched as he walked down the garden path, O'Hara tugging on the leash, eager to go. I had mixed feelings about his parting; I enjoyed his company, but he was a foreigner, a world apart from everything I was accustomed to. I couldn't allow myself to take him seriously.

Steve opened the gate and turned left toward the bus station.

"Well," my father announced, "he seems a nice-enough guy, with good manners. However, four days is plenty." He cleared his throat to cite one of his favorite sayings, which he recited in German: "After three days, fish and guests stink . . ."

My mother smiled at me. "Yes, but I really like him."

The following week I visited Steve's kibbutz in the Valley of Jezre'el, with its green fields, cowsheds, and rows of chicken coops. Steve led me to his "home," a ramshackle wooden shack, one of those allotted to volunteers who work on the kibbutz in exchange for food and lodging. When the door creaked open, I was stunned. The room was immaculate—the blanket tucked in tightly, clothes folded on the shelf, and wildflowers in a glass jar on the rickety table.

I pointed at little figurines on the windowsill. "What are these?" He moved next to me. "I made them; they're my friends," he said.

I picked up a figure of a donkey, its torso a large cashew nut shell with toothpick legs, pistachio-shell ears, and a leather-scrap tail. Near it stood an old man made of acorns and twigs. They looked alive, as if they were waiting to act out a play.

"Steve, they're exquisite." I pressed his hand. "You're so talented."

I was impressed by the work that went into making those figurines; they were so delicate, so detailed. Only a man with an artistic bent and a sensitive soul could have made them. I'd never met anybody like that before. Steve must have seen the look of adoration in my eyes. He embraced me. I nuzzled my head against his neck, inhaling the scent of aftershave. I didn't know what it all meant, didn't know if I was in love. I didn't think about it, arms around his shoulders, my body radiating heat against his. I abandoned myself to his impassioned kisses and caresses.

The next day we traveled by train to Haifa. At the train station we planned to go our separate ways, Steve to pick up film equipment down at the port while I took a bus up to the Carmel to visit some cousins. I had return tickets for us both for six o'clock that evening, so we agreed to meet shortly before that at the station for our trip back to Ashkelon.

On my return, the sun cast a golden glow on the sea. As the bus lumbered toward the railway station I peered out the window, looking for Steve and O'Hara. A group of soldiers in khaki uniforms stood on the platform, combat boots and Uzis slung on their shoulders; two long-skirted Yemenite women, colored kerchiefs contrasting with their dark skin, gestured with their hands as they talked; a kibbutznik in shorts walked along, carrying a backpack, tanned legs, blond hair in a ponytail. My American friend was nowhere in sight. I approached the girl and asked the time. We still had ten minutes.

I paced the platform, my heartbeat quickening. I double-checked the time on our tickets. A loud whistle sounded, accompanied by the rumbling of a train. With a screech, it stopped, and passengers descended. Those on the platform collected their belongings and boarded while I gripped my pocketbook, praying for him to come.

I stood on the now-empty platform looking over my shoulder in a last desperate attempt to find Steve. The sharp train whistle blasted. A jolt passed through me. I watched my departing train thinking about what I would tell my parents, who would worry, not knowing what had happened to us. It was the last train to Ashkelon; I had no idea how we'd get home. Biting my nails, I started walking toward the depot. Gusts of wind twirled an old newspaper, raising a cloud of dust. A lean mongrel dog slunk by, dragging its lame leg. I was furious. I began to conjure ways to get back at Steve—giving him a black eye or a punch in the belly—when a dreadful thought crossed my mind: Could he be hurt? Hit by a car?

As if in response, I heard Steve's voice. "Esther!"

Wavering between relief and anger, I yelled, "Where were you? Why are you late?"

Pulling O'Hara, Steve rushed toward me, trying to catch his breath. "You're nuts," I snapped. "What happened?"

"I got hung up at the port waiting for them to bring the equipment." His voice was hoarse. "And then the stupid dog refused to go down the escalator."

"So what did you do?" My anger started to defuse.

"I had to carry him on my shoulders, so it took a while." He shrugged. "Sorry."

I hugged him, my eyes tearing. I realized I'd thought I would never see him again. My pounding heart quieted down, but there was hardness in my chest, a sense of uneasiness. I was happy he'd made it. I loved the way he cared about his dog, but what about his obligation to me? He agreed to be back for the six o'clock train! Walking next to them out of the station, I kicked a small stone, sending it flying.

Steve's three-month sojourn in kibbutz Hazore'a was coming to an end, and he was returning to the States. At the Ashkelon station, we parted; he to board the bus to Lod airport while I would catch a bus to Jerusalem. I had quit my job on the ship and was going to teach at an Ulpan, an intensive five-month Hebrew course for new immigrants. I hugged him briefly, my chest tight. I didn't like partings. The bus to Jerusalem arrived. I turned to Steve and said, "Have a good trip."

"Will I see you again?" He looked me in the face, trying to figure me out.

"Who knows?" I shrugged. He was going back to America, after all; it was on the other side of the globe.

"I'll write to you."

"Great, so will I." I felt awkward. I was sad he was leaving but relieved as well. I didn't want to get too attached—he was a foreigner, an American, and I was proud to be an Israeli. As my bus pulled out of the station, I waved to Steve—a forlorn figure standing on the dusty platform. I sighed and turned my head away from my friend.

A week later, I was in my cramped rented room in Jerusalem preparing lessons for my students when the door opened. Steve walked in, pale, gaunt, with stubble on his chin. I jumped up from my chair, almost bumping in to him. "Steve, my God, what happened to you?"

He smiled and plopped down on my bed as if his strength had left him. There were dark rings under his eyes. He had stayed for a while in Turkey, he said, but didn't feel well; it got very cold, and he missed me. I found out much later that he had contracted salmonella poisoning. Maybe he didn't want to alarm me by telling me about it at the time.

I put my arms around him, telling him I'd missed him too. I wasn't quite sure about it, but seeing him gave me a warm feeling.

That night, Steve shared my narrow bed with me. We made love for the five nights in a row that he remained in the country. His flesh smooth against my skin, I clasped his broad shoulders and surrendered, but never entirely; though I lost my virginity at age nineteen to my then Israeli–North African boyfriend, sex wasn't something I was comfortable with. I had picked up the message that I wasn't supposed to enjoy it. But Steve was persistent—almost clinging to me, hugging me tight, hungry for my touch. I enjoyed his closeness, let him caress me, enter me—yet I felt disconnected from my body. We never discussed any of it during the day, as if nothing happened, as if it were a dream, an apparition.

Growing up with my German father, I'd learned to cut myself off from my feelings in order to survive. I never heard the word "sex" in our home. As a teenager, my father once caught me staring at a picture of Rodin's *The Kiss* hanging on my parents' bedroom wall. The next day, it vanished. My mother used to tell me she had no idea how she gave birth to three children.

Still, I abandoned myself to Steve, engulfed in his desire and need. My body was uncomfortable in the narrow, Spartan bed. I wished I could get a good night's sleep; in the mornings I was bleary-eyed and barely had the stamina to teach for five hours at the Ulpan.

Then, he packed his suitcase and left. I was sad, bewildered, and frustrated at his coming and going, but this time I knew he was going back to America for good. I had no idea if I'd see him again.

## ❧ Chapter 2: ❦

# Decision

"Got your letter. Will come as soon as I can. Love, Steve." I read the cable typed on a thin slip of paper. I read it again, my heart pounding. It had been three weeks since Steve left. He's coming back to Israel; he'll help me figure out what to do. I don't have to decide on my own. Lying on the narrow bed in my room in Jerusalem, the cable on my belly, I stared at the high vaulted ceiling. I lowered my eyes to the desk where my Ulpan book and students' papers were scattered. I enjoyed teaching at the Ulpan, where the students were new immigrants from all over the world: Poland, Germany, Hungary, Romania, France, England, even South America. They were so eager to learn—they needed Hebrew for survival in their new country. In the classroom, I was completely immersed in teaching. Though I taught five hours every day, from eight in the morning until one, time flew by.

But now that I was pregnant, what would I do? The five-month Ulpan course would end in May, so I'd teach until then. I'd wait to tell my parents, brother, and sister; Jeremy was in Wisley near

London studying horticulture, and Rachel was in Seminar Levinsky studying to be a teacher, so I wouldn't see them soon. I would let my parents know when I got home, to Ashkelon. I wondered what they'd say. I felt I was going to let everybody down; I was so ashamed. How could I have let this happen? My reputation would be ruined.

A baby! This was the last thing in the world I wanted—a screaming, demanding little creature, entirely dependent on me. My only experience with babies was when I babysat to make money during my studies at the teacher's seminary in Jerusalem. The infant cried for what seemed like hours while I was afraid to lift him up from his cot. His parents hadn't given me any instructions before they left. Though I had a younger brother and sister, I didn't really remember them as babies. Growing up, the topic of bringing babies into the world wasn't spoken of. Though I was twenty-five already, I had virtually zero experience.

And would this baby mean I had to marry Steve? A chill passed through me. I didn't want a man bossing me around the way my father controlled my mother. Marriage had been the last thing on my mind leading up to this. And I'd known Steve for such a short time, six months only; I didn't know what to expect of him, and I had no role model for men in general other than my father. Would Steve be different?

I recalled an incident when he'd admonished my mother. She was in our home in Ashkelon, perspiring in the hot kitchen, an apron over her shorts and bra, boiling soup on the stove while she washed dishes in the adjacent sink. My father regarded her with disdain, his eyes narrow, his lips pressed together. "Look at you, how can you walk around like this? You should be ashamed of yourself." I was eleven or twelve at the time, and my heart cringed when I saw my sweet *eema*, her bright face crumpling like a plucked daisy. She didn't say a word, just slinked into the bedroom and came out with a blouse over her bra.

On another occasion, when I was about fifteen, I was sitting with my father in our living room while he showed me a letter he'd written to the local newspaper. I heard my mother come in from the kitchen. She had a wide smile on her face and started to tell us something. My father turned to her sharply and said, "Can't you see we're busy? Leave us alone!" I felt the bile rise up my throat. I wanted to defy him, to get up, walk with my mom to the kitchen, and hear what she had to say, but I didn't dare and so I remained glued to my chair while my mom turned on her heel and left without a word.

Not only did I not want to be subject to a man who would tell me how and what to do in my life; I had things I still wanted to do. I had traveled to Greece, Sicily, Scotland, New York, and Norway, but there were so many more places I wanted to see. I had never been to Africa, South America, or the Far East. I had performed in a military variety troupe, singing in army bases, kibbutzim, and concert halls. I wanted to continue singing, studying languages, performing, but all this would come to a standstill; I'd have to stay at home and be a nursing mother. It didn't dawn on me that I had other options. I couldn't even think about an acceptable solution; my mind was frozen, unwilling to deal with the dilemma I was in. I hoped Steve would come to untangle the mess. Even as my rational mind didn't want someone like my father, I expected and wanted Steve to tell me what to do with my body. My father controlled everything about my mother. He bought not only all her dresses, blouses, and skirts, but even her bras and underpants. She told me that when they started to date in Germany, he said to her: "I'm going to make a lady out of you." And I suppose I wanted that from Steve, or at least didn't know any better.

Steve hadn't told me when he intended to come, so I concentrated the best I could on my daily activities: I taught Hebrew in my new immigrant classes in the mornings, corrected my students' homework, and did a bit of shopping, cleaning, and cooking the rest of the day. I didn't go out much; I gained some weight and my breasts grew larger. I dreaded being found out; what would people say about me if they knew I was pregnant before getting married? I felt like some outcast.

One afternoon, eight weeks into my pregnancy, there was a knock on the door. When I opened it, there was Victor Epstein, the entertainment officer whom I had worked with on the ship. He looked at me with a big grin on his pockmarked face. I was used to being alone and had no close friends, so I was glad to see him, though I'd never cared for him much.

"What are you doing holed up in this room?" he asked.

"How did you know where I was?" I probably looked awful. On the ship I felt glamorous, wearing high heel, narrow skirts, and earrings. I wanted to run to the bathroom and change, but there he was, staring at me.

"I got your address from your parents. I happen to be in Jerusalem." He looked around at the scattered books, papers, and clothes thrown on the bed. I started to straighten up the mess.

"I didn't expect you . . ." I felt awkward, not at all the dashing figure I presented on the ship. I started walking toward the kitchen. "Would you like some tea?" I called out.

"No," he snorted, "let's go and have a drink somewhere."

Like this? I thought, With my shabby pants, old sweater and disheveled hair? I hadn't been to a bar since the time I worked on the ship, about eight months ago. It seemed like a dream.

"Okay, let me just change into something more presentable."

I grabbed from the closet a navy knee-length skirt, a light blue top, and a pair of stockings and dashed to the bathroom. With the change of clothes and dab of lipstick, I felt better. Once outside, inhaling the fresh air, I started to enjoy myself.

I turned to Victor. "Where are we going?"

"How about the King David Hotel? It's just a twenty-minute walk."

"Wow! I've never been inside; it's a real fancy hotel. All the diplomats and rich tourists go there."

He grinned at me. "Sure, let's go!"

When we arrived at the hotel, built out of beautiful Jerusalem stone, fronted with majestic cyprus trees, the concierge, dressed in a white uniform with gold epaulets, ushered us in.

We sat at a table in the bar while I looked through the large French windows and the dazzling array of rose bushes, jasmine, and shrubs. I was awed by the aura of solemnity; the gilded pictures on the wooden paneled walls, the hushed murmurs of a few other guests. Victor nursed a martini while I held a glass of soda water, pretending to pay attention to his prattle about his latest escapades. After a short while I excused myself to go to the restroom. When I returned, his eyes focused on my legs.

I raised my eyebrows. "Yes?"

He suppressed a smile. "You're wearing two different color stockings; one is tan and one is off-white. You should get a new pair."

I sensed the blood rushing to my cheeks—I needed air. I was embarrassed; I felt clumsy and unfeminine. I had to get out of there. I muttered, "Let's go. I need to get back."


During this time, I didn't make it easy for my little embryo. I tried everything to get rid of him. I stood on my head, did vigorous handstands and pushups, and skipped a rope until I had no air left. Once, while trying to force a miscarriage, with my legs up the wall, my hands pushing against the floor, Iris, my roommate, walked in.

She stared at me, her hands on her hips. "What the hell are you doing?"

"Nothing," I blurted, my eyes the level of her ankles, "just getting some oxygen into my brain." I bent my arms and brought my feet down with a thud.

The moment she left, I flopped onto the bed, burying my face in the pillow, my heart heavy. I tried not to think about what would happen if I had the baby. I couldn't accept the reality of my situation; I was in a state of denial. Taking a deep breath, and then exhaling with an audible sigh, I picked up my book, *The Earthquake in Chile*. The horrific scenes of devastation in the book matched my mood. It was all despair and darkness. I held the book but couldn't concentrate on the written pages. My mind wandered to the previous week, to the interaction I'd had with Nancy, my other roommate, a heavyset American girl with a pretty face—creamy complexion and hazel eyes adorned by flowing black hair. I'd bumped into her in the corridor and noticed she held a small box.

"What do you have there?"

"This?" she stretched her hand toward me. "It's the pill. I have it sent from the States."

"What's it for?"

She frowned, looking at me with consternation. "You don't know?"

I shook my head. "Never heard of it."

"You take them so you don't get pregnant." I detected a smirk behind her response. "That way you don't have to worry about being with a guy."

She was so smug, so self-assured. I hated her at that moment. I wished I had heard about that pill earlier, but now it was too late. Of course she had no idea I was pregnant. I didn't tell anybody except my sister; she was understanding and compassionate, but I decided to wait until after Steve arrived to tell my parents, figuring I'd know by then what I was going to do. I was too ashamed, too embarrassed. I kept it a secret while soldiering on, keeping a stiff upper lip, the way I was brought up. "You just get on with it" had always been my parents' unspoken message.

I turned over onto my back and crossed my arms under my head. Looking up at the ceiling, I wondered when Steve would appear, or if I'd hear from him again. With no telephone, and letters from America taking forever, there was no sign of life from him. I went through the motions—work, home, meals, shopping—trying to ignore the growing embryo within me, pretending my life was normal.

Steve finally arrived a week later. He burst into my room without knocking, finding me crouched over my notebook preparing lessons. He laid down his small brown suitcase and hugged me, his strong arms enveloping my body. In his dark navy blue suit, beige tie, and black patent leather shoes, he seemed particularly foreign. I passed my fingers through my hair, hoping I didn't look too bedraggled. I was happy to see him, yet annoyed; I wanted to look my best when he came. Steve seemed to always take me by surprise.

"Was it a long trip? You must be tired."

"Yes." His eyes centered on my belly. "How are you feeling?"

"I'm fine," I patted my still-flat belly, "just can't eat much in the morning. Here, I'll make you some tea." I filled a kettle with water, put it on a hotplate in the corner of the room, and sat beside Steve on the worn-out love sofa. "What shall we do?"

He lowered his eyes, staring at his feet. Then, he spread his arms, palms up, and looked at me. "I don't know. I can only stay for a few days. I have to get back to my job at Televideo, the one I wrote you about, in Manhattan."

I clenched my fist against my mouth. "Having a baby is such a huge thing. Besides, you live in New York and I'm here."

His hand covered mine. "Maybe we should not have the baby?"

I was shocked, hearing this come from him. Besides, I had become used to the idea of having the baby. Especially after my ten-week pregnancy check-up, when the young male doctor assured me with a big smile, "You'll have a fine little baby boy." I had no idea why he'd decided it was a boy, but at that moment, for the first time, I felt proud of carrying a baby.

"What do you mean—get rid of it?"

His face was pale and immobile. He didn't reply.

I didn't want to abort the baby; he was part of me; I couldn't do it. It would be unnatural to pry a living being out of my body. At the same time, I felt guilty. I should have been more careful. And what about Steve? He didn't take any precautions either. We never said a word to each other about contraceptives; it didn't dawn on me to ask him. I didn't dare tell him what I was thinking or feeling. In my family, nobody talked about such intimate things.

When the water boiled I got up to make tea. Steve's head was bent, his shoulders rounded; he looked defeated. He was only twenty-three. I couldn't saddle him with a baby. He wasn't any more ready to be a father than I was to be a mother. I put my arm around him. "Let's think about it," I said. I prepared our tea. We then drank it in silence.

The next morning Steve suggested we drive to the abortion clinic in Tel Aviv to talk to somebody there. I nodded. I didn't know what to say. I couldn't absorb what was happening to me. It was so unreal to be there. I had heard about women aborting their babies, but didn't know anybody who'd actually done it. It wasn't a subject for conversation—it was maybe only okay while gossiping with downcast eyes and furtive glances.

After we checked in at the clinic, we were told to sit down and wait. I looked around. There were about ten other women sitting on wooden benches, some with smooth faces and straight backs, others with wrinkled necks and worn-out hands, young and old, from different backgrounds. Most of them sat with downcast eyes or stared at a point in front of them. I wondered what their reasons were for an abortion: if they'd conceived by mistake, like me; if they were already overburdened by family; or if they were too poor to bring another child into the world. Drops of sweat trickled down my armpits. My heart felt as if it had turned from a living organ to a solid rock.

The air in the room was stifling and humid. It smelled of perspiration, cheap perfume, and fear. I turned to Steve.

"What do you think? How much longer do we have to wait?"

He pursed his lips and looked at an olive-skinned woman who got up and walked toward the white-clad nurse at the other end of the room.

"I . . . I don't know. I hope not too long."

Not too long! It felt as if we had been sitting there for a year. What would the doctor say? Would he ask many questions? Give advice? Reprimand me?

I glanced at my lover, his jaw muscles moving while his chin jutted forward. Our shoulders touched, but a deep chasm of fear separated us.

Trying to alleviate the tension, I put my hand on Steve's arm. "It's strange, I don't *feel* pregnant," I joked. "Can't we just forget about the whole thing?"

It wasn't really that much of a joke, though, since my body didn't feel that different, and I preferred to ignore reality, to put my head in the sand like the proverbial ostrich.

"Hum," he uttered without looking at me, "very funny."

Very funny, indeed! A lump settled in my throat. Why hadn't my mother, lover—*anybody*—told me about contraceptives? I turned to Steve, who was clenching and unclenching his fists. "I'm not so sure about this whole thing."

"What do you mean?"

"The abortion."

"Yes, I'm not sure either." His eyes had a soft expression in them; he sensed my fear, my silent plea. All of a sudden he stood up, his voice determined. "Let's get out of here. If it's all right with you, we'll keep the baby."

"What did you say?" I couldn't believe it. I felt as if a rock had been lifted off my heart.

"We'll keep him."

I was a bit taken aback by the pronounced gender. I recalled the doctor's cheerful announcement. I hadn't thought about the baby's sex, but I realized that Steve, wanted an offspring in his image.

Steve took my hand and pulled me up out of the seat. I hugged him, almost collapsing; my tears of relief and joy left a wet mark on his shirt. Though I feared having a baby, I realized I wanted it after all and that the prospect of an abortion seemed far worse. But I didn't dare express those thoughts. I felt so grateful to Steve. Stepping into the bright sunshine, I inhaled deeply. I had a reprieve—nature would have her way.

I turned again to him, put my arms around his shoulders, and kissed him.

"So, we'll get married?" I asked. The word "married" felt like glue in my mouth.

Steve squeezed my hand. It was almost as though we had been discussing marriage for months. "Of course; what do you think? We'll have to go to the rabbinate and let your family know."


The stone building at the end of King George Street loomed above us like some menacing God. It housed the chief rabbinate in Jerusalem, to which we traveled to get our wedding license. We sat in a room with a high ceiling and narrow arched windows. From behind a long table, three rabbis flung questions one after the other. They addressed Steve; after all, he was the man—*and the rib, which the Lord God had taken from the man, made he a woman, and brought her unto the man.*

"Where are you from?" The rabbi's scraggly beard moved up and down.

"The United States."

"How long have you been here?"

"This time? Four days."

The rabbi creased his forehead. "Are you Jewish? Have you been married?"

Steve nodded yes and then no.

"Who can vouch for you? Do you know anybody here?"

"Not really."

The rabbis turned and discussed the matter with each other.

"Why don't you call my rabbi in New York? He's known me since childhood."

"Is he Orthodox?"

"No, Reform."

I looked at Steve. He rolled his eyes and shrugged his shoulders as if to say, *Doesn't look like we're going to get much help from them. We're not religious, so what do they care?* I was relieved. My family was secular; we didn't like these long-bearded righteous patriarchs. I smiled at him; he was right. All they cared about were laws and rules based on the Bible. Reform rabbis had a more liberal interpretation of the biblical laws, but in Israel only the Orthodox approval was valid.

"That doesn't count then," said Scraggly Beard.

Steve's face was grim, and he pointed his chin toward the exit. I nodded, and we both got up.

"Thanks, we'll see you later," he said, and we left.

The next day after I finished teaching, I walked home. It was a spring day. The white Jerusalem stone sparkled in the bright sunshine, the indigo blue sky a backdrop for a couple of wooly clouds floating high up. I inhaled the pungent scent of the cypress trees that stood like a row of soldiers. Being pregnant, I soon discovered, made me see the world in more vivid, brighter colors. Maybe this heightened sensitivity was due to the new life I carried within me; maybe it was just all the hormones coursing through my body.

My stomach growled. I had eaten a couple of grapefruits in the morning, and later, at the Ulpan, some rolls smothered with jam. "You have a hearty appetite," one of the teachers had said. I felt the blood rush into my face, wondering if she could guess my condition.

I went through the corrugated iron gate and took out the key to the front door. It opened on its own to Steve, smiling broadly.

"I did it. I found a way to get around the rabbi problem."

"How?"

"I got a bunch of students from the Conservative Theological Seminary to vouch for me."

"But they don't know you!"

"Now they do! They discussed our problem in their Talmud class with their rabbi and came to the conclusion that it's okay to swear in vain in a case like ours."

"Really?" I lifted my arms, palms up, my eyes wide as saucers. "They're actually ready to take an oath that they know you? But you are complete strangers!"

Steve smiled; he was enjoying the trick he had played on the Orthodox rabbis. "So what? The students from the seminary are doing a mitzvah, a good deed."

He's right, I thought; the rabbis, who interpreted the bible, have decreed that if there's an emergency, you're allowed to act contrary to the law. After all, our situation was urgent; Steve had to leave in a few days, and I agreed to join him in NYC three months later, after I finished teaching the Ulpan course. For my parents' sake, we had to get married before Steve left. But the only way to get legally married in Israel was to have an Orthodox wedding, so having the students swear they know Steve, saying that he's Jewish and single, was okay!

Looking Steve in the eye, I laid my hand gently on his arm. "Good job, Steve; we'll get married, and I'll come to New York."

Yet I didn't feel so sure about it all. My heart was heavy. I was glad we found an acceptable solution, but it entailed such an upheaval! I'd have to leave my parents, siblings, friends, and country, everything I knew: I'd start from scratch with a new baby with nobody familiar to help me. However, being my parents' daughter, I banished those thoughts to the deep recesses of my brain, suppressed them the best I could while I dealt with the present, facing one moment at a time.

"Okay," I announced, "I'm going to the kitchen to prepare dinner."

Yet while the water boiled in the pot, my hands busy peeling potatoes, my mind raced; getting married because I'm pregnant, Steve having to resort to cheating the rabbis, the short time we had to organize a wedding, him having to leave the morning after—this wasn't a very auspicious way to start our life together. Taking a deep breath, exhaling forcefully, I reminded myself that things could be much worse; I had new life within me, Steve agreed to marry and keep the baby. I'm off on an adventure, I thought, to a different land with a new life in front of me.

I dropped the halved potatoes into the pot of boiling water, which splashed, causing drops of scalding water to scorch my fingers. Ouch, I thought, is this a sign for my future? I opened the tap, letting cold water run down on my outstretched hand.

### ◦⟨ *Chapter 3:* ⟩◦

# The Wedding

Our wedding took place at Samson's Gardens, a small pension just fifteen minutes away by foot from my parents' house. It was a clear day with a light breeze from the sea. The ceremony was to be outside, under two large palm trees.

As soon as my parents and I arrived, my sister Rachel rushed toward us. She was a veteran at weddings, having been married for a whole year. "Do you have rings?" she asked me with a worried look on her face.

"I don't know; I haven't even thought about them."

"How could you forget about that?"

"Believe me, Rachel. I have enough to think about."

"Okay, I'll ask David if he'll lend Steve his ring for the ceremony, and you can use mine." She ran off, silky hair flying behind her.

Rachel is four and a half years younger than me. Growing up, we hadn't spent much time together. When she started grade school in Ashkelon, I was studying in an agricultural boarding school an hour away. While she attended high school, I served in the army.

And by the time she was doing teacher training, I was traveling in Europe and working on cruise ships. I wondered if we'd be closer once I was married.

I leaned against a nearby ficus tree, enjoying the shade from its thick, rubber-like leaves and spreading branches. The rabbi and his assistant, two raven-like creatures in black coats and hats, appeared. For the chuppah, the wedding canopy, they picked up four wooden poles, which they attached to the corners of a large tallit—a white piece of cloth with blue and white fringes, a kind of prayer shawl that Jews wear in the synagogue. I could have used one of those prayers.

I couldn't believe I was getting married, so quickly, to a man I'd known less than six months. I'd once again have to leave everything—my family, friends, familiar surroundings—and start a new life in a foreign country.

Adjusting to life in Israel had been a difficult and painful process. I was eight when I emigrated with my family from England. The Israeli kids loved to tease me. I was fair, delicate, and polite. When we first arrived, we lived on a kibbutz. One day I was outside the dining hall, wearing a light floral print dress, when a boy came toward me. With his hands in his shorts pockets, feet in heavy work shoes, he shuffled closer to me.

"Are you *eizen beton*?" he asked, a sneer on his face.

I didn't understand any Hebrew, but *eizen beton* was a Yiddish expression. I knew it meant "fortified cement," an expression for "strong character."

I nodded timidly. "Yes."

Before I knew what happened, he kicked me in the shin with his steel-toed boot and ran away. I cried out in pain, but I also felt indignant and humiliated. I didn't deserve to be treated that way. I decided then that I needed to blend in, to become a sabra, a native Israeli—to be tough, tanned, and to speak Hebrew fluently with a guttural *ch* and *r*. Nobody was going to make fun of me anymore.

Soon the chuppah was ready. Steve and I would stand under its canopy, and I'd promise to be a good wife. I had no idea what that meant. Was it like my mother, tiptoeing around my domineering father, making sure all his demands were fulfilled? Was being a good wife an obligation to make my husband happy? I felt rebellious to think of it; that wasn't the vision I had of being married. A husband and wife should be good friends and respect each other. I didn't want to be like my mother. I had no idea what my relationship with Steve would be like, if he could be the partner I desired. I didn't think about it. By now, my future was cut out for me, so I figured there was no point in ruminating about it. I was in survival mode, putting one foot in front of the other.

My sister ran up to me again. The rings shone on her outstretched palm. Was I going to wear one of those? I recalled a bitter incident at home around the time I was eleven. I'd been twisting and turning a metal curtain-ring around my finger and now it wouldn't come off. The flesh, bulging above and below the ring, had a bluish tint to it. I cried out, "*Eema, eema*, help me." My mother rushed in, filled the sink with hot water, stuck my finger in it, and rubbed a soap bar over the ring, but nothing happened.

"Wait one minute, I'll call *Abba*."

My father came with a pair of pliers and snapped the ring open while I winced with fear.

"You silly girl, this will teach you a lesson," he said. And with that he walked away. I ran crying into my mother's arms.

"What are you dreaming about?" Rachel asked.

"Oh, nothing . . . thanks for bringing the rings." She smiled. "It'll be fine. Look, quite a few people came. Considering the short notice you gave, it's a wonder that more than ten people arrived."

I felt sad when I thought about my brother Jeremy not being there. Only a year and a half apart, we had always been close. I had sent a letter to England where he was studying horticulture, but I'd later find out that it didn't even arrive until after my wedding, it all happened so fast.

"You are an angel, Rachel," I told her. "I don't know how I'd manage without you."

She took out a handkerchief and dabbed the corner of my eye. "Come on, you can't have a red nose on your wedding day."

We clung to each other for a long moment. Then she held me at arm's length to get a good look at me.

"Is this the dress you told me about? It looks great."

"It's the one I wore to welcome the first-class passengers aboard the ship," I told her. "I sported arm-length gloves as well." I chuckled, but my mouth was dry. The dress had felt different when I wore it as an entertainment officer, holding a champagne glass, standing in line with other white-clad officers, shaking hands with first-class passengers.

"Can you see I'm in my third month?" I asked her, feeling suddenly self-conscious.

"No, you can't tell." Rachel shook her head.

I still hadn't told anybody outside my family about my pregnancy. I knew I had to tell my parents, as it explained our shotgun wedding. I assumed my mother would be fine with it, and I was relieved that my father accepted the news, too, with equanimity. "Okay, so you're going to have a baby," was all he said. He didn't ask me any questions or offer any comments.

I didn't expect him to say much else; we never talked about anything intimate or meaningful to me. He had very little idea of what went on in my life. Perhaps given all he'd survived—Nazis in Germany, extermination of their family, hardships in wartime England and Israel—my news wasn't so earth-shattering. Maybe I was just protecting myself, explaining away my wish for a caring, concerned father.

My mom, however, asked the crucial question: "Estherlè, do you love him?" I didn't know what to say; I was unsure of the answer. But seeing the imploring look on her face, her desire for things to be all right, I put my arm around her softly and smiled. "Yes, *eema*, I love him."

Now I heard a familiar voice behind me. "Hi, Esti, it's your big day."

It was Aliza, my friend, from the army entertainment troupe in which I had served for two years. She smiled at me with her green eyes.

"You sure surprised us."

Genuinely glad she came, I bear-hugged her. "I'll see you at the chuppah."

I looked around. Where was the rest of my family? My mother was chatting with Hannah, her second cousin. Tante Ruth, my father's only surviving aunt, who managed to escape the camps by going to Shanghai, sat with her son Klaus and his wife Tsila, on chairs set up for the wedding ceremony. On the other side sat Uncle Alex, a well-known doctor, and Aunt Lotte, my mother's relatives who lived in Jerusalem. I had often visited them when I studied at the teacher's seminary in Bet Hekerem, not far from their house.

I spotted my father, who stood alone with a frown on his face.

"*Abba*, is everything all right?"

"Where is Steve?"

Steve, the guy I was going to marry! Where was he? I asked Rachel if she'd seen him. She shrugged her shoulders in dismay. I kept searching and asked the few people who'd met him. Nobody had seen him. A knot formed in my belly. My mother approached me then, pointing to the path leading to the sand dunes.

"I saw him walking in that direction," she said.

"Can you get him?"

My mother dashed off, happy to be of help. She returned after a short while, waving at me. "He's coming; he's coming,"

"*Todah*, thanks, *eema*!" I called out. She'd always gotten me out of hard spots, and today was no exception.

Steve arrived at last, and I turned to him. With his tousled hair and grin on his face, he looked like a kid who'd been caught playing hooky. I felt the knot form again within me, irritated by this display of inconsideration.

I tried to keep my voice down. "Where have you been?"

"Oh, I went for a walk along the beach. You should've seen all the jelly fish on the shore." His white teeth gleamed. I inspected him. Grains of sand clung to the legs of his black suit.

"We were all looking for you." I reminded myself of how supportive Steve had been, how he was as blindsided by this whole situation as I was. He hadn't planned to marry so young and be saddled with a baby at the age of twenty-three. He agreed to marry a woman he hardly knew, from a different background and different culture. He made sure we'd have a wedding before he left. Steve was a gentleman, and I was grateful for that. Yet the knot in my belly refused to dissolve. A sense of uneasiness lingered within me.

"Where is the chuppah?" he asked.

"Over there," I said. Four male figures held the poles, two neighbors and two relatives. I knew that according to the Orthodox tradition only men were allowed to hold up the chuppah, the same way only men were permitted to take out the Torah from the holy arc. Women weren't allowed to participate in any of the rituals in the synagogue. I grew up with that knowledge and had to abide by it, but it always irritated me. Weren't men and women supposed to be equal? Yet, if I wanted to get married, I had to play by the Orthodox rules.

"Come on, let's go." I took his hand.

The rabbi grabbed Steve, motioning for him to sign the *ketubbah*, the Jewish marriage certificate stating that the groom is required to guarantee his wife a certain amount of money in case he divorces her or dies. The money, symbolically depicted with silver coins, guarantees that the husband will supply his wife with all her needs. The rabbi then turned to two male witnesses to sign the document as well. Each of them wrote his name at the bottom of the handwritten Aramaic text enclosed by decorated margins depicting Biblical fruits—figs, grapes, dates, and pomegranates—with the Wailing Wall figuring prominently in an arch on top. Steve wrote his name in immaculate handwriting, the English letters standing out like naked foreigners. I, the daughter of Ze'ev Epstein, was worth two hundred silver coins.

Ziggi, Hannah's husband, linked his arm in Steve's and led him to the chuppah. My sister accompanied me there.

Steve was on my right. He looked funny wearing a yarmulke on his head. The rabbi was talking to him, but Steve's face was blank. I knew he didn't understand any Hebrew. It had dawned on me that we wouldn't speak my native tongue together, which saddened me. I wondered how much of my culture—jokes, expressions, idioms—would be lost in translation. But at that moment our situation seemed comical. Though he came from a Jewish background and had a bar mitzvah, he didn't know anything about Orthodox Jewish customs. I nudged him.

"Steve, the rabbi's talking to you."

"What's he saying?" he whispered back to me.

I translated: "'You are hereby sanctified unto me.' You're supposed to repeat that after him."

Steve shrugged and looked at the rabbi, poker-faced. I couldn't tell what he was thinking, but he didn't seem to be taking the ceremony seriously.

Finally, the rabbi paused and stroked his beard. He stared at Steve as if he were a delinquent child. He didn't even glance at me, standing there next to Steve. Orthodox men are not supposed to look at any women besides their wives.

"*Nu*, why don't you say the blessing?"

"I don't understand Hebrew," Steve answered. The rabbi furrowed his brow, looking perplexed and annoyed at the same time. I guess he'd never dealt before with somebody like my future husband, someone who not only didn't understand any Hebrew, but a groom who seemed not to care much about what was happening in his wedding ceremony.

We each sipped some wine. Steve broke the glass under his foot, as tradition calls for, and slipped my sister's ring on my finger. The rabbi announced, "You are now husband and wife." And all present called out, "Mazal tov," good luck, and I figured we were married.

The ceremony didn't mean much to me; getting married wasn't something I had planned or looked forward to. I felt as if I were role-playing, going through the motions.

I heard a squawking sound and looked up. Two crows were perched on the electricity wire, gaping at me. One flapped its wings, took off, and landed on a thin branch of a guava tree, while the other screeched and flew in the other direction. I was too caught up in the day itself to take this as a bad omen.

For my wedding party we gathered around a long table, about thirty of us, and ate the modest pension food: a piece of chicken (as vegetarians, my family received a substitute), rice, eggplant salad, a green salad, egg-salad, hummus, tahini, and rolls, all kosher, no dairy—no milk in our coffee. Except for a few relatives, none of us were kosher, but in Israel, all public eating places had to be kosher in order to receive a business permit from the rabbinate.

After the meal, I played my guitar, singing out loud with the guests; my stringed instrument was my old friend that had accompanied me for many years through school, the army, and on my trips overseas. Strumming the guitar I could forget that I had just signed my life over to a man I hardly knew. I could pretend to be a guest at somebody else's wedding.

We sung upbeat Hebrew songs that I'd sung in my army troupe, then old English songs I knew well like "You Are My Sunshine" and "Oh Mary, Don't You Weep, Don't You Mourn," to which Rachel and I harmonized. We ended with German folk songs for the benefit of my parents; they both loved singing—my mother in a clear soprano and my dad in a rich baritone. When we finished, Rachel, beautiful in a dark blue dress, her black hair flowing over a décolleté, touched my shoulder.

"Where is the photographer?"

I looked at her, frowning. "I don't think we have one."

"What? Nobody arranged to have a photographer? It's your wedding!"

"So what?" I pressed my lips together in a bitter half smile. "This wedding wasn't exactly planned . . ."

Rachel tilted her head back in exasperation. "Don't you want commemorate it in some way?"

"I don't really care." I felt a heaviness weighing me down. "I don't feel like I'm married, so why should I bother with photos?"

In my mind I didn't want to face the reality of my wedding day. No wonder I hadn't planned to have a photographer or prepare wedding rings. But Rachel didn't give in. Smiling, she patted my arm.

"You'll thank me later on."

So, after the party, we dutifully joined Rachel in David's battered van. She insisted on taking us to Photo Moshe, a studio in the nearby Ashkelon's shopping center that consisted of little stores along a large expanse of lawn and ficus trees. Moshe, the Romanian owner, in a brown suit bulging over his stocky body, a gold tooth glistening in his mouth, pointed me to a straight-backed chair.

"Here, sit down." I did what he said. My short veil over my hair, feet in white pumps, I crossed my ankles and put my hands on my knees. I felt like a mannequin or a model for some wedding catalogue. Moshe turned to Steve and positioned him behind me.

"Put your hand on her shoulder. Smile!" Steve, with a serious face, obeyed. The photographer ducked under the dark cloth that covered the camera on a tripod, held the metal handle to the shutter, called out, "*Achat, shtayim, shalosh,*" one, two, three, and clicked. In the slick photo we are two young people frozen in time and space as if a sculptor had molded us out of marble. Steve, in a navy blue suit, brown hair neatly combed back, is standing very straight with a bewildered look on his face. He's gripping the back of the chair in which I sit, the hem of my knee-length white dress revealing demurely crossed legs. A shoulder-length veil adorns my short blond hair surrounding my face, onto which a forced smile is pasted.

That evening Steve and I spent our first night as a married couple on my parents' living room couch. It opened into a bed with a hard mattress and a gap in the middle where it folded into a sofa. We were exhausted and tense, and Steve was leaving for his job in New York early the next morning. We held each other like two lost children, Steve's arm around my middle.

"Will you be okay on your own?" he whispered into my hair.

"Yes, I'll be fine." I paused. "I'll manage."

That's what I'd learned to do all my life: to manage, to rise up to the occasion, to be strong and overcome any fears and uncertainties. But more than anything I'd learned not to *express* my anxieties. My grandparents, uncle, and aunt had all perished in the holocaust—and nothing could equal the emotional burden my parents carried with them. Whatever my troubles were, they shrank in comparison to what they had to bear.

Steve's body was warm against mine. Suddenly he moved, turning onto his back, then clasped his hands behind his head.

"You acted like an entertainer in somebody else's wedding," he said to the ceiling.

"You mean my singing with the guitar?"

"Yes, you hardly looked at me."

"I couldn't help it. We got married so quickly. I'm not used yet to the thought of being your wife."

Steve sighed and turned around. "Let's try to get some sleep."

No sex tonight, I thought wistfully. I nestled up against him, my arm around his waist. How could I get used to the idea of being married if he was going to vanish in a few hours?

Steve left first thing in the morning to catch a flight to New York. I had to stay to finish teaching at the Ulpan, the five-month Hebrew course for new immigrants. I would join him in mid-June. I remained behind with a baby within me, with my hopes and my fears.

A month later I went for a medical check-up I needed before leaving for New York myself. I was lying half-naked on an examining table in a large, half-empty room, the ceiling fifteen feet above me. A dull white light filtered through the opaque windowpanes onto a wooden table, a chair, and a partition with an off-white curtain. I was seeing an American doctor, and I expected his office to have more modern facilities, but it was in the city of Jaffa, in an old Arab building.

"I've got immigration papers for you," Steve had written in his latest letter in his immaculate handwriting. "You'll need to go for a check-up first."

I prayed the doctor wouldn't realize I was expecting. An irrational worry crossed my mind. What if the authorities found out I got married while pregnant and wouldn't let me into the States? I regressed into the little girl again who was afraid of being reprimanded for being "bad."

I shivered. There wasn't even a sheet to cover me up, so I crossed my legs, covering my belly with my hands.

The doctor—short, frail, with wisps of white hair on his head—appeared. I was relieved he was old; I figured his eyesight wasn't so good any more and he wouldn't notice I was pregnant. In my mind I had committed a sin, an unforgivable act, for which I was going to be punished. I hoped the doctor wouldn't observe the way I wiggled my toes, trying to suppress my feelings of being nervous and scared. An image of the doctor writing an official message to the American consul floated in front of me: *She is not fit to enter the United States.* Here was another man with the power to decide what would happen to me.

"Hello, young lady," he picked up a form from the desk. "So, you're going to America. Applying for a visa?"

"Yes," I stammered, feeling like a piece of meat on display.

The doctor took my pulse, checked my blood pressure, and tapped my knee. He stuck his stethoscope on my chest.

"Breathe in and hold." His cold fingers pressed my belly, probing. "Mmm . . ."

Inhaling, I tightened my muscles.

He peered at me over his thick, silver-rimmed glasses. "When did you last have a bowel movement?"

My pulse quickening, my mouth dry, I tried to swallow. No way was I going to tell him I was pregnant.

"Not for a while; I'm really constipated." I held my breath.

"You may get dressed now." The doctor's thin voice echoed in the room.

I jumped off the table, almost bumping into him as I rushed along the cold tile floor. Behind the partition, back in my checkered blouse, tan shorts, and sandals, I pressed my lips and let out a long "Phew . . ." When I drew back the curtain, however, the wisps of white hair reappeared behind the desk. He was scrunched over, scribbling something in his notebook. Tiptoeing in the direction of the exit, I heard his nasal drawl.

"How old are you?"

I clasped my hard brown pocketbook, the one I received when I began military service.

"Twenty-five." I covered my warm cheeks with my palms. As a girl, their roundness and red color had landed me the nickname "apple cheeks," and I was sure I'd be giving myself away in this moment if he were to turn and look at me.

"Do you work?" His eyes squinted behind the glasses.

I lifted my head and faced him.

"Yes. I teach Hebrew to new immigrants."

"Why are you going to America?"

"My husband's from New York." I made an effort to formulate the word "husband." I had never used that word in connection with myself. My mother had a husband. My sister had one, but me? The word didn't sound right, as if someone else were speaking through me.

"So, doesn't he want to live in Israel?" he asked.

Oh no, not that question again. As if living in Israel is so simple.

"He works in America."

I peeked at the door, hoping somebody would walk in. An overflowing wastebasket stood close to the entrance, where a diagonal dark crack sliced the wall.

"What a shame, a nice Israeli girl like you leaving the country."

He tilted his pointed chin in my direction like an accusing finger.

## ❧ Chapter 4: ❧

# Arrival

It was May 1966, the year of anti–Vietnam War demonstrations, peace marches, the Beatles, and free love,—and there I was, five months pregnant standing in the arrivals hall in JFK airport in New York. I felt sad and upset to leave my family and country, yet my adventurous spirit looked forward to the unknown. I wished Steve could have stayed with me in Israel after our wedding and not flown back to his job in New York. It had been three months since our wedding and three months since we had seen each other. It was hard to remember what I liked about him. I took out the black oval brooch I carried in my purse. About the size of a quarter, it had three little pearls embossed in it. On the back, under a glass frame, I had inserted a photo of Steve. Opening the clasp attached to the frame, I gazed at my husband: perfect arched eyebrows over beautiful eyes, aquiline nose, and a sensuous mouth. He looked so young and, in a way, unfamiliar. I had to remind myself that I was his wife, that I'd soon meet him and spend my life with him. It seemed difficult to grasp or internalize. I willed myself to feel some tenderness toward him. I had to love him, I reasoned; he was the father of the child I was carrying within me. I lifted the brooch to my lips and gently kissed it.

I had just spent a mini-vacation in England with my younger brother Jeremy, who invited me to stay with him for a few days in Wisley, the landscaping school he was attending, south of London. He was appalled by my pregnancy and hasty wedding. "How could you let this happen to you?" he demanded, shaking his head while gently patting my back. Jeremy had always put me on a pedestal, and my pregnancy smashed to smithereens his image of his clever, talented older sister. He quoted the all-knowing rabbis. "If the flame felled the cedars, what will the moss on the wall say?" If I, the mighty cedar, had fallen, who would complain about the actions of the lowly moss?

We were standing near a sculpted stone birdbath in the flower garden next to his dorm. Inhaling the fragrance of narcissus and primroses, I felt a twinge of sadness in my chest. His words hurt me, yet I felt I deserved his reprimand; I let my brother down; I disappointed him. I needed to clarify my situation, to have him understand and forgive me.

"Jeremy," I said, turning to him, "I didn't plan this."

"It's okay," he said, his lips pressed together in a forced smile, "no need to explain. What is done is done."

"But, Jeremy—" I tried again.

He cut me short. "Come, let's go." He took my arm, and we walked down the path.

He couldn't express his feelings; we never talked about anything intimate. When it came to personal matters, he clammed up. It was the way the three of us were brought up. I sensed he couldn't deal with my pregnancy—it was part of my sexuality, which made him uncomfortable, undoubtedly. His older, smarter sister wasn't supposed to get pregnant like that—unaware, no planning, before marriage.

We had a lovely time together in Wisley, strolling through the flowering azaleas and rhododendrons in various shades of peach, yellow, and orange. I smiled for his camera, my pink sweater blending into the floral background under an azure sky. We went to London to see *Dr. Zhivago*, where I cried watching Lara amid a sea of yellow daffodils. We joked around, recalling childhood episodes in Israel: when my father made us both sell bunches of flowers in Kfar Varburg, the neighboring village, how embarrassed we were to ask for money, or when Jeremy had borrowed my notebook to copy all the answers to the math questions.

He introduced me to Ray, a student friend of his. Jeremy extended his arm in my direction in a grand gesture.

"This is my sister," he beamed, "from Israel."

Ray wore a tweed jacket over square shoulders and had wide cheekbones, green eyes, and parted dark blond hair.

"Nice to meet you. How are you enjoying your stay here?" he asked, extending his hand. I loved his Queen's English accent.

I told him I liked the quiet, relaxed atmosphere, the polite, friendly people, the green countryside, and the soft, refreshing rain—quite a contrast to the heat and dry, brown landscape of my home country.

Ray looked me over. "Would you like to go for a walk?" he asked.

In my fifth month of pregnancy, with enlarged breasts and thickened waist, I didn't feel attractive, but perhaps my impending motherhood brought to my face a radiance of which I wasn't aware. Obviously he didn't realize I was married, and my bulky sweater covered my belly well enough.

On the other hand, I wasn't single anymore either. It might be nice to go for a walk with Ray, but I felt a bit odd. What if he started to ask me questions—like, Why are you traveling to the States? What is your work? I would be too embarrassed to tell the truth, and I didn't want to lie. I always had a strong need to be liked by people, to impress them. I wasn't brave enough to admit to my brother's friend that I was pregnant and had gotten married only three months earlier. I felt it was shameful. Besides, the weight of the baby was pressing on my bladder and I had to run to the restroom.

I turned to my would-be suitor. "Thanks, I'd love to, but maybe some other time."

I spent the rest of my short visit walking along narrow paths amid dark green hedges with white blossoms of flowering hawthorn, from which black-and-white magpies took flight. Being in nature always made me feel good, and with the new life within me, at that moment, I felt in perfect harmony with my surroundings. I lifted my face to the soft rain, glad to be alive.

I was happy I had decided to spend some time with Jeremy. Since we were only eighteen months apart, we had many shared experiences. Sitting in his room a couple of evenings before my departure, a nice cup of hot English tea in my hand, we reminisced about Jeremy's adventures in Ayanot, the agricultural school in which we both studied and worked. Jeremy, the joker in our family, loved to tell stories and act out the different characters in them. With a mocking expression, his lower lip protruding and his eyes narrowing, he faced me.

"You were known as an A student," he said. "So when I came along a year after you, the teachers expected the same of me. Boy, what a disappointment I was! Mr. Rulson, the math teacher, called you 'a genius.' I didn't have a chance."

We both doubled over in laughter. "Poor Jeremy," I finally responded, "it wasn't easy for you in Ayanot. At the end they kicked you out, right?"

"Yes," he chuckled, "Remember? I stole eggs from the chicken coop. They didn't like that."

On the plane over the Atlantic I silently thanked Jeremy for the gift of the lovely interlude we spent together, for my "honeymoon," as he called it. I hadn't had one with Steve. In my mind I saw my brother's grinning face and ruddy cheeks, heard the jokes that had cheered me up, and still felt the strong hug he gave me, expressing his caring and concern before I boarded the plane.

In the airport waiting area, pushing the cart with my luggage, I walked to meet my new husband and parents-in-law. I had stuffed whatever I could into my two suitcases: clothes, footwear, and the little bible I received as an outstanding soldier in boot camp. I also brought a corrugated iron hand-shaped *chamsa*—a charm for good luck I received as a wedding gift—and a photo album with pictures of my family back home, but not much else. What would the Skloot family think of me? How would they react? I had a sense of uneasiness, as if my innards were tightening into tangled ropes. Steve had written me that he'd announced his marriage at the family Passover Seder. I could see him in my mind's eye as he stated ever so matter-of-factly to his shocked family, "I got married to an Israeli girl." Steve loved the element of surprise.

I kept pushing my cart and looking around. A group of people approached me. They looked alike—short, the men in suits, the women in elegant coats over tailored skirts and high heels. The pervasive color was dark, black or gray. I slowed down, not sure what to do. There was a commotion, and the human-clump parted. One of the women came forward. In a perfectly coiffed hairdo, a golden chain adorning her black crew-neck under a fitted indigo jacket, she approached me with wide open arms as if to rescue me from a storm. Her red painted lips vocalized words I couldn't make out at first. When she came closer, I recognized the Jewish New York accent from the American films I had watched. Steve didn't have much of an accent; he had spent some time studying film in Europe, where he identified with the European way of life. He had a bit of an actor in him and downplayed his accent, preferring to sound more English than American.

Reaching just above my shoulders, the elegant woman hugged me tightly, her Chanel No. 5 perfume enveloping me. In Israel we shook hands, so it felt strange being hugged by someone I'd never met. Her words rang out: "Welcome to America!" I had a strong sensation of awe and bewilderment. Was she my mother-in-law? I looked behind her and saw Steve standing there, beaming, and enjoying the woman's performance. Raising my eyebrows, I shot him a quizzical look. He nodded his head as if to assure me that everything was all right while the welcoming-committee-of-one bombarded me with questions: "How was your trip? How are things in Israel? Are you happy to be here?" She must have noticed my confused face because she finally stopped and introduced herself in a low, raspy voice: "I'm your Aunt Carrie." It turned out that she was the oldest sister of my father-in-law, Milton.

Luckily, at that point I felt a warm arm around my shoulders, and Steve's voice melted away his aunt's buzzing questions. "Come, you must be tired." I was glad he was there next to me, protecting me, caring for me. He took my suitcase and led me to the rest of the Skloot clan. The next woman I met was similar to Aunt Carrie, but heavier and not quite as glamorous. She hugged me briefly, pecked me on my right and left cheeks, then stood back and looked at me from top to bottom. Her bright red painted lips parted in a deep smile while she shook my hand announcing, "I'm Gussie, your mother-in-law. I'm so pleased to meet you!"

I wondered whether she really meant it. I wasn't used to that kind of effusive language. At home, with a German father, none of us expressed much emotion. I wasn't sure what to say to my new mother-in-law. Even though I was fatigued and overwhelmed, I made an effort to respond in an enthusiastic manner.

"Thanks so much," I said, "it's a pleasure to meet you."

It took me a while to warm up to new people even though I appeared cheerful and outgoing. Maybe it was my unwillingness to be part of a new family, complete strangers who acted so differently and to whom I couldn't relate. I hadn't made yet the transition from my place and family in Israel, from my way of being there, from one culture to the other. Maybe I would never make it. I thought of my sweet *eema* back home. I didn't want a substitute mother, nor could Gussie ever be one; she came from a different world than the one I came from.

Steve introduced me to his father, Milton, his younger brother, Mike, and to the rest of his aunts, uncles, and cousins. We then drove to his parents' home on 108th Street in Queens. Sitting with Steve in the back seat of Milton's large black Chevy Impala, we sailed through a forbidding gray landscape consisting of tall brick buildings, store fronts, churches, and cemeteries. Steve's hand felt warm in mine while I tried keeping my tired, blurry eyes open.

"How are you feeling?" he asked.

"I don't know." I rested my head on his shoulder, my cheek against the lapel of his linen jacket. "I think I'm a bit out of it."

Steve laid his hand on my bulging middle. "How is he?"

"Fine," I chuckled, "except that my belly is so swollen, I feel like a stuffed animal."

I laid my head back against the headrest. Closing my eyes, I tried to relax, but thoughts kept swirling in my mind. How would I get along with Gussie? What an odd name she had, I thought. I had no idea what it would be like to have a New York mother-in-law. Would she be helpful? Strict? Demanding? I didn't know how I'd adjust to life in a small city apartment. I was used to living in a house, close to the ground. Would I manage to make new friends? I didn't know anybody in Queens; all my family and friends were back in Israel, on the other side of the globe. But soon the jet lag took over, and my thoughts slowed down until my mind, blissfully, clouded over while the wheels beneath me rambled along, carrying me to my new home, family, and destiny.

## ❧ Chapter 5: ❧

# New York, New York

I was in bed, eyes half-closed, body relaxed, when a familiar, mesmerizing sound entered my consciousness: the swooshing sound
of waves breaking against the shoreline. I smiled and breathed
deeply, picturing myself diving into the warm Mediterranean, my
body a lithe arrow, somersaulting with joy.

Lifting my head from the pillow and opening my eyes, reality
struck me; it was the sound of traffic rushing down below, along
the eight lanes of Queens Boulevard. I glanced at the wall calendar,
and the fog in my head cleared. It was June 27, 1966. I had left Israel
four weeks earlier.

I hated New York. Living in Queens was like purgatory. I
recalled one of my father's eternal German quotes: *Was man sich
macht, macht man sich allein.* "Whatever happens to you, you cause
it." I put my hand on my rounded belly. If it weren't for Steve and
the little baby inside me, I would never have come to live in New
York. The city was too much of everything: too much noise, crowds,
eternal gray skies, and, more than anything, loneliness.

In my light-green baby-doll pajamas, which showed my protruding belly, I walked out on the tiny terrace of our studio apartment. Steve had rented it on the seventh floor of Parker Towers, a large apartment building along Queens Boulevard. It was muggy and hot outside; it was pointless to try and breathe deeply—the air was heavy, motionless, and foul. Small flakes of soot floated down like black confetti scattered by the devil. Steve had mentioned the incinerators in which the garbage was burned, and, looking up, I could see smoke coming out of the smokestacks on top of high-rise apartment buildings. An image of Biblical sacrifices crossed my mind.

Yet, lowering my gaze, I smiled at the pretty coleus plants growing in the planter-boxes attached to the railing of our tiny terrace. Knowing how much I missed flowers, Steve had planted them for me so I'd have my own little garden. The sun came out for a minute and lit the array of contrasting colors of the plant's large leaves: maroon with a light green border, pale green with dark pink, and slender stems of small purple flowers peeping among the foliage.

A whine came from inside. O'Hara was pacing behind the door. The dog was part of the "deal," not that I minded having him. Steve left at eight, at times even earlier, and was usually gone until six or seven in the evening. Alone in the apartment, with no one to talk to or confide in, I often put my arms around the big animal, crying into his fur.

Now, I kneeled down at O'Hara's side. Stroking him, I whispered into his ear, "O'Hara, how is Rachel? Is she happy being married to David? How is *eema*? How will I cope when the baby is born?" I sighed. "I wish they weren't all so far away, on the other side of the world."

The phone rang. It was Steve.

"How are you feeling? Is the baby moving?" he asked.

"Yes, he's been kicking all morning."

"I won't be home for dinner."

I bit my lip. I'd been alone all day.

"I was just getting ready to go out with O'Hara," I answered in a forced, cheerful voice.

I wasn't going to plead with him. When Steve made up his mind, he stuck to his decision, and no pleading would help. Also, I didn't want to appear too needy and was afraid he'd get annoyed if I asked him to come home earlier. After all, he was the "breadwinner," so his work was important. Plus, this was the model I'd seen growing up: my mother hardly ever requested anything from my father; in fact, he was the one who made demands on her. If she tried to argue, he'd get angry.

I had slipped easily into my mother's role. Growing up, I had sworn I'd never be like my parents; I'd never give up my independence or take orders from my husband. Yet here I was, following in my parents' footsteps. I didn't dare to tell Steve that, at times, it was too much to have O'Hara with me all day, or that I didn't feel like making dinner or doing the dishes, that I needed him more at home. I was going to manage my role as housewife the best I could and make the most out of it.

I often thought of the time we'd go back to Israel. When I left, I had told my family and friends that I'd be back, that I was moving to New York only for a year or so. At that time, in Israel, anybody who left the country was considered a *yored*; a person who descends, someone who betrays her country. Israel is built on Zionism, with its basic tenet aliya, immigration to Israel. Many of my friends thought of me as a traitor, and in some ways I felt so as well. I promised them I'd come back. It was like a myth that kept me going.

I barely heard Steve's words on the phone. "I have to work late, but I'll come as soon as I can."

"I guess you're really busy," I said wistfully.

I wished he'd tell me more about his work at the television station. I knew it was stressful, but he wouldn't talk about it. I didn't ask him much about it either. I didn't want to nag him when he came home tired from work, and he always seemed so preoccupied. At times, for no reason, he'd get angry. It might have been job-related stress; it might have been more than that.

He'd been hired as a production assistant for a commercial TV station in New York, yet in reality he served as a gofer, getting the coffee in the morning, sweeping up at night, and doing whatever anybody asked of him during the day. When he applied for the job he was sure it would be the first step for becoming a filmmaker. He was an artist, so the reality of the situation frustrated him. Years later he would be accepted into the Directors Guild of America and become a well-known assistant director and production manager who worked on major motion pictures, such as *Love Story, Shaft, The Godfather,* and *Live and Let Die*. At the time he felt proud of his accomplishments, but eventually he tired of his relentless work managing and organizing timetables for the crew and actors, scouting for locations, and being blamed for anything that went wrong on the set. He had told me there were four worthwhile jobs in the film industry: director, actor, screenplay writer, and editor. He never got any of those jobs, and there was a sense from the beginning that he was sacrificing his creativity for the glory of others. I bore the brunt of that frustration.

"Got to run," he said. "See you tonight."

I put down the phone and turned to O'Hara, sighing.

"Okay, big beast, we're leaving."

O'Hara wagged his tail, stretching in anticipation. I dressed in drawstring cotton pants, a light summer top, and a pair of sturdy sandals. Grabbing the keys, I put O'Hara on a leash and left the apartment, making sure to triple lock it. Steve's words echoed in my head: "You're not in Israel; there are burglars around here." Back home, I never bothered with keys and bolts. I just closed the door and ran out of the house. Tears welled in my eyes. Why did I cry all the time? The walls of the elevator closed in on me as we rode down to the lobby. We slipped by the doorman, crossed the boulevard, and turned toward Forest Hills Gardens, the only place I could see some trees and lawns.

I enjoyed walking. It felt good: muscles working, lungs expanding, body moving forward, away from the confining apartment, the anguished thoughts, and the feelings of frustration. Passing green lawns adorning fancy red brick homes with not a soul in sight, I wondered why people bothered to have a lawn if they never used it. Back home, *abba* used to sit outside reading the paper, usually a week old. He was so thorough in whatever he did, he'd read the whole paper without skipping a word. *Eema*, my sister, and I used to do gymnastics on the grass with *abba* joining in when we got to the headstands. At times, a passerby could observe four pairs of legs sticking up in the air behind the hedge that fronted our garden.

I continued walking. Though I didn't have a watch it seemed as if over an hour had passed. Back among the spewing stone monsters and zooming cars, I was getting tired and thirsty; the little one within me weighed me down. O'Hara kept tugging at the leash, which didn't make things easier. But then, what was easy in America? When Steve first mentioned Forest Hills, I imagined rolling hills surrounded by vast green forests. Instead, I was surrounded by paved roads and line upon line of buildings blocking the horizon. My mind returned to the little white houses and golden, sandy beach back home.

Then I thought about the unfolded laundry strewn over our bed in our small studio apartment. The day before I had battled with the washing machine down in the basement, unable to figure out which coins the machine operated on. American money baffled me, all those different sizes. Why was the dime, worth ten cents, smaller than the five-cent nickel?

I looked down at my belly—at six months I was definitely showing. A car honked. I jumped aside, my heart beating. I hadn't seen the red light. Where on earth was Queens Boulevard? All the streets looked the same. I arrived at a main street but couldn't identify it. My legs started to ache. I wished I had at least some money to take a cab home. But why should I have taken money with me when I was just going out to walk my dog?

I looked at the cars zooming by, visualizing them to stop and offer me a ride. In Ashkelon, where everybody knew me, I always hitchhiked, but in New York? Not a chance. Still, I stuck out my thumb, something I had learned from Steve. In Israel, when I wanted a ride, I used to extend my arm and moved my palm up and down. I prayed some kind soul would have mercy and stop, but the cars just whizzed by. All of a sudden a patrol car appeared. I waved my arm from side to side like a drowning person. The car stopped. Two officers stared out of the window at O'Hara and me.

The younger-looking policeman exited the car. "Can I help you?" he asked.

He wore a meticulously ironed navy blue uniform, a wooden club, and a revolver attached to his belt.

"Oh yes, please! I'm lost . . . I can't find my way home."

"Where do you live?"

"In Parker Towers."

Before he could respond, I added, "I'm new here." I swallowed a lump in my throat. "Besides, I'm pregnant and tired."

I stroked O'Hara's head while the officers looked at each other with questioning eyes. The younger officer mumbled something to his older partner. I detected a note of sympathy in his voice and kept my fingers crossed. The first policeman turned to me.

"Okay, we'll take you home."

I couldn't believe my good luck.

"Wonderful, thank you." I pulled O'Hara's leash. "I really appreciate it."

But the older officer, who had a bulldog-like face, intervened.

"We can't take the dog. It's against the rules."

I felt as if he had knocked me down. Why was everything so difficult here? Just the previous week on another walk I rested on the lawn in front of a small church. A priest, wearing black robes, came out and angrily chased me away. "Don't you know the rules?" he yelled.

Tightening my fists, I looked at the younger officer.

"Please," I said, my voice quavering. "Couldn't you take us both?"

The older cop was talking on his radio.

"Hey, Tony, there's this young woman with her dog . . ."

He whispered something to his companion. The younger cop nodded, turned around, and with a large smile motioned for us to come up into the car.

"Thank you, thank you." I wanted to throw my arms around him.

He opened the door to the back seat. "Up, up," I said to O'Hara. Patting the leather upholstery, I tugged at the leash, and he lumbered in while I sank back beside him with relief. I wondered whether I should tell Steve about my escapade. Would he think I was out of my mind, or would he approve of my course of action? I didn't care. At that moment I was pleased with myself. The patrol car revved up, joined the traffic, and sped down the street. O'Hara, ears pointed, sat alertly behind the two officers.

## ❧ *Chapter 6:* ❧

# Summer of 1966

Steve was walking ahead of me holding his 16-millimeter film camera slung around his neck. It bounced against his white T-shirt while he walked with long strides alongside groups of people: shoulder-length-haired young men, young women in jeans and ankle-length dresses, colorful beads adorning necks and arms, wreaths of flowers highlighting their hair. Steve stopped and turned his head.

"Come on!" he yelled. "Stay with me."

"I'm trying to." I caressed my bulging belly. So what if I was six months pregnant? It was good for me to walk, I thought, exercise my body, and strengthen my muscles. Giving birth would be easier. Plus, by participating in the anti–Vietnam War rally in Central Park, I was making history. I was part of something bigger than myself.

"Are you okay?" Steve finally asked, face flushed, beads of perspiration on his forehead, as he waited for me to catch up.

"Yep, I'm fine." I clutched the rectangular tape recorder Steve had given me, its side nestling under my ribs. A new era was dawning in my life. I, the Israeli immigrant, was recording American war protesters. My job, according to the instructions Steve gave me the night before, was to record the noises of the environment so he could add them to the images he filmed.

I chuckled while thinking about Steve's ingenuity: after the recording instructions, he had handed me a plastic-covered nametag that read, "Mrs. Tom Paxton." I narrowed my eyes with suspicion.

"Why are you giving this to me?" I said.

"So you'll wear it."

"But why? That's not my name!"

"Of course not, but tomorrow you'll be Mrs. Tom Paxton, the wife of the famous folk singer." His impish smile deepened. "That way they'll let you enter the stage area. Only speakers, performers, and journalists are allowed in."

My eyes widened. "You mean, I'll pretend to be someone else's wife?"

"Yes. Nobody will know the difference."

I was incredulous. I felt as if someone were pressing hard against my chest.

"And what about you?"

"Me?" he pointed at himself while nodding his head. "I've got a journalist pass, so there's no problem."

Wow, I thought, he sure knows how to beat the system. I assumed he knew what he was doing, so I didn't ask any further questions.

Now Steve grinned at me. "Good, keep it up." And off he went, his camera poised to capture an image of a young man in colored baggy pants and dreadlocks.

It was a warm, muggy day; overcast skies, air filled with electricity, created anticipation akin to the coming of a rainstorm. Sounds of laughter and chatting were everywhere, set against the roar of chants coming from the distance, rising and falling, unintelligible at first, but then clear as they thundered in the air: "Make love, not war." "Bring our soldiers home." "No more fighting."

We walked in the middle of the road, moving with the crowd. Policemen in blue uniforms, brandishing clubs, revolvers snug against their hips, lined the sidewalks.

We entered the park. More people marched holding banners, placards, and handmade signs. On one of them, a narrow face sporting a wispy beard under a top hat in stripes of blue, red, and white, declared in bold black letters: *Bring Uncle Sam Home.* The thickening crowd pulled me along; policemen stood in a line, barring protesters from marching on. All of a sudden I was shoved aside together with the group of people next to me. The cops were yelling, "Move, move," as if they were directing traffic, motioning for us to move sideways, with one arm straight and the other bent, their forefingers pointing to a side path they had lined with yellow tape. With the masses pressing in on me, my chest tightened, and I felt as if I couldn't breathe. I started to panic. I couldn't see Steve. Standing on the tips of my toes, I strained my neck, uttering a high soprano "yoo-hoo," but the sound vanished into the general noise. My heart fluttered: Where was he? Had he just walked forward without noticing I was not next to him?

I understood that he was concentrating on filming; however, how could he be so absorbed in his work that he didn't even think about me? Shouldn't he be watching out for his pregnant wife? I called him again—no answer. I supposed I could go back to the park entrance and wait for him on the side where there weren't so many people. But then he might vanish. I shuddered; how would I find him in this crowd?

An image floated into my mind: I'm nine years old, walking along a dirt road in Israel. Behind me, *eema* is holding my four-year-old sister's hand. Rachel is tired; she drags her feet, pulling on my mother's skirt, holding her back. Jeremy is next to me, his round face flushed from the midday heat. He asks in a small voice, "When will we get there?"

*Eema* doesn't answer, and I don't know where "there" is anymore. Maybe it's the old stone building we call home, or the next village where we buy our milk and bread. Ahead of us, in the distance, is my father, a figure in shorts and a "dummy" hat, an Israeli cloth hat worn by the pioneers in the forties and fifties. He strides forward, oblivious to his family, not even glancing back to see how his wife and kids are doing. Rachel starts to whimper. *Abba* stops, turns around, waves his arm, and bends it toward his chest.

"*Komm schon,*" he yells, Come here, already. He waits a few seconds while *eema* rushes us along. "*Ich komme, ich komme,*" she calls out between breaths. She takes longer steps; Rachel and Jeremy try to keep up with her. I run to catch up with *abba*, but he has taken off. I stand, looking back and forth, like a puppy not knowing which way her master went. Then, I go back, smile at Jeremy. "Come on, I'll race you." But he's too tired, so I stay near *eema*, who hoists Rachel up piggyback while I shuffle alongside her, the words swirling in my mind: *I hate abba; I hate him.*

A warm hand landed on my shoulder. "Thank God I found you." I turned around. Steve's eyes were dark with consternation. He put his arm around me: "Okay, we'll stay together now." The lump in my throat dissolved. "I was worried," I told him. "Where were you?" I wanted to hug him, but resentment kept me back. Were his photographs more important to him than his brand-new wife?

I didn't dare ask him that. Though I realized it wasn't his fault we were separated, I felt abandoned, as if he didn't care about me. If he were more tuned in to me, he wouldn't have lost me. So when he stammered, "I'm sorry," I lifted my head defiantly, tightened my grip on the tape recorder, and started walking briskly. "Fine," I said, "just please don't leave me again here, alone."

After the Central Park episode, the days passed uneventfully, with Steve busy at work and me left to my own devices. Summer in New York was hot and humid. I felt restless. I was in my seventh month of pregnancy, spending too much time alone in the small apartment, thinking about my family in Israel and waiting for air letters from *eema* and *abba*. Besides walking the dog and doing household chores, I didn't have much else to do. All my activities had come to a standstill. Steve sensed my frustration. On Sunday, the only day he didn't go into Manhattan to work, we sat in our dining corner finishing off our dinner. Steve looked at my downcast face.

"What is it?"

"I need to do something, maybe find some work."

He frowned. "But you're pregnant; the baby is due in a couple of months."

"Just because I'm expecting doesn't mean I can't work."

"But you'll need a short-term job." He squinted, lost in thought. I could see his mind working, the production manager who was used to brainstorming and coming up with solutions for everything. "I can't think of anything now," he said. "I'll ask around."

The following evening he announced triumphantly, "There's a YMCA camp in Flushing Meadows not too far from here. They need a music counselor for the younger kids."

I pondered the suggestion. Teaching kids songs could be fun. But what songs would I teach them? I knew mostly Israeli children songs. I already felt in over my head. And soon I'll be in my eighth month, I thought, beginning to backpedal. Will I have enough energy to go back and forth to camp and work with little children?

I looked into my husband's questioning eyes, feeling unsure. "Do you think they'll hire me? What shall I teach them? How will I get to camp and back?"

Steve wrapped his arm around my shoulders. "You'll be great. You play the guitar and sing beautifully. I'm sure they'll love you."

Back in Israel, I had fallen in love with American folksingers. During my army service, I was stationed in Jaffa when I heard the pure, angelic soprano of Joan Baez pouring out of a boom box in the officers' clubroom. I was mesmerized by the sound, feeling a longing I hadn't felt before. Her plaintive ballads and gentle spirituals

spoke to my heart, lifting me away from the roughness and imme-
diacy of life in Israel. I practiced the guitar chords to "I'm on My
Way to Freedom Land" and "Oh Mary, Don't You Weep, Don't You
Mourn," so I could accompany myself. When friends remarked that
I sounded like Baez, I was elated, as if I'd received a medal of honor.

The next day I picked up my old guitar, the one I had bought in
Napoli during my travels in Europe. We had a long history together,
and I was in the habit of talking to it as if it were a person. Holding
the instrument tenderly, I muttered, "Do you think you and I can
make it? Will I get the job?" After Steve returned from work, we
drove to the camp director's home. I told him I was a teacher and
played a couple of songs for him: "Michael, Row the Boat Ashore"
and "Hava Nagila." The director, a young guy with curly hair, smiled
at me.

"Very nice; you have a great voice. Have you worked with
young kids before?"

"Not really," I hesitated, "but I was a counselor in the Scouts
youth movement in Israel."

"Could you start next week?"

Wow, I thought, did that mean I got the job? I glanced at Steve
with a triumphant smile. "Yes, of course, I can start straight away."

Outside the director's home, Steve put his arm around my
shoulder and drew me to him. "I knew you'd make a good impression on him. Mazel tov!"

Every day, for three weeks, I rode to camp with another counselor who lived in Queens. The first day I sat in a clearing in the
midst of eucalyptus trees while ten five- and six-year-olds sat cross-
legged on the ground, staring at me, this strange young woman with
the big belly. Smiling at them, I said, "Tell me your names."

The first to the left, a boy with curly brown hair and freckles, said, "I'm Charlie." A small girl with blond braids said shyly,

"Robin." I went around the circle until I'd heard all their names. Then I asked, "What songs do you know?" They didn't respond. A few shrugged their shoulders. "How about 'Michael, Row the Boat Ashore'?" I asked.

All I got were blank stares and a few giggles. I felt a pang of panic. I'd never worked with young children. How would I get them to sing? I started to strum my guitar. "Okay," I said, "clap your hands with the music. Go slow when it's slow and fast when it's fast." A couple of kids started to clap, and others joined in. As the tempo accelerated, they moved their arms faster, their bodies swaying, smiling faces flushed. "Great," I beamed at the children, "let's get up and dance." I felt light, buoyant, forgetting the size of my belly, the weight of the baby within me, my worries about giving birth, of turning into a mother with my own mother on the other side of the globe. I was in the moment, with those little American kids, as if floating in a hot-air balloon up in the clear blue sky.

After music the kids went to drama. They had mentioned munchkins, witches, and a wizard. I had no idea what they were talking about, so I asked the drama counselor, a tall athletic-looking redhead named Rosie, what play they were putting on. "Oh," she answered matter-of-factly, "*The Wizard of Oz*." I'd never heard of it. Back home we acted out bible stories connected with Jewish holidays. In third grade, when the holiday of Purim arrived, I was Queen Esther opposite wicked Haman. For Hanukkah we staged Judah the Maccabee, and for Passover, Pharaoh's daughter with baby Moses in the arc.

I wondered what songs I could teach the kids. Maybe I could use some recorded music of children's songs or musicals. I could even learn some new songs. At lunchtime I approached Rosie. "Do you know if they have any records here I could use?"

She pointed to a small wooden shack. "They might have some in there." On a dusty shelf I found a treasure: a small record player with several LPs and 78s. Looking through them I saw a record cover with a picture of a slender young man sitting in the middle of a circle of wide-eyed children. The title under it was *Hans Christian Andersen*. I felt my heartbeat quicken; I knew those songs, I'd heard them before! The following morning I told my group, "You're going to hear a song about an ugly duckling that grew up to be a beautiful swan." The kids loved listening to Danny Kaye's warm tenor. When the duckling went "quack, quack," we quacked with him, and when the swan soared, the children and I flapped our arms, soaring with it. In the evening, after dinner, I told Steve about my day at camp.

"I love it there. The counselors are really friendly, and I get to be in nature, away from the city."

Steve looked at me with a half smile, as if I were one of the kids at camp. Being born and raised in the city, trees, plants, and wildlife didn't mean that much to him.

"But being outdoors all the time, isn't it too hot for you?" He put a spoonful of chocolate ice cream in his mouth. "With no air conditioner to cool off, don't you get all sweaty and tired?"

"It gets a bit hot, but I'm in the shade, so it's okay. Besides," I chuckled, "you know I'm a tough Israeli."

Growing up in Ashkelon, nobody had air-conditioning. In the months of July and August, when the temperatures climbed close to a hundred degrees, *eema* would close the shutters before the sun rose, when it was still cool outside. We'd take a nap during the hottest time of day, between two and four, a common thing to do in Israel in the heat of the summer.

Once, while studying at the teachers' seminary in Jerusalem, there was a bout of *chamsin*—an easterly wind blowing in from the desert—and the temperatures went up to a hundred and ten degrees. To try and cool off, I took a shower every couple of hours; it helped for a short while, though since the pipes heated up, the water was warm. Finally, I soaked a bed sheet in the sink and hung it, dripping, on the window in my tiny dorm room. I stripped off my undershirt, shorts, and panties and lay without moving on my bunk bed. Any piece of clothing would cling to my perspiring body.

Steve's voice brought me back from my musing. He was looking at me with amusement.

"So when did you first experience air-conditioning?"

"On a ship, when I first traveled to Europe."

After boarding the Greek ship in Haifa, I entered the cabin I shared with another girl. The porthole window was closed, and the room was warm and stuffy. I opened the window to get some air in. It was a hot summer day, and the temperature in the cabin remained the same. At lunchtime I went to the dining hall two decks above us. When I returned a few hours later, the cabin was nice and cool. To my amazement, the window was tightly closed. I rushed out and asked one of the staff about the closed window and cool air. The white-clad man smiled broadly: "The air-conditioning works only if you keep the windows closed!" I felt my face turn crimson. What a strange concept—cool air coming from inside the room. I stored the knowledge in my mind with other discoveries I had made on the ship, such as flushing the toilet by stepping on a handle on the floor, or the phrase "on the rocks," referring to an alcoholic drink with ice in it.

"Wow," Steve said after hearing my story, "you must have learned a lot during that first trip."

"Yes. I felt so sophisticated when I came back home."

Steve took my hand in his. "And now you're learning again all these new things." I was grateful to him for acknowledging my efforts. I leaned over and kissed his cheek.

My three weeks of working at the YMCA camp helped to broaden my horizons. I got to be more familiar with American children's songs, plays, and games. In our final camp performance, I sang along with the counselors and campers: "We're off to see the wizard, the wonderful Wizard of Oz," and "Somewhere over the rainbow, way up high . . ." Somehow these songs expressed my hope for a positive experience in my new life in America. They related to the baby I was about to bring into the world. Maybe once I had my child, I'd make more connections, get to know other moms, have playmates for my kid. People are basically the same, whether in Israel or in the States. Yet a small voice within me doubted my optimistic view. Living in an apartment was so different from living in a house with a little garden; in a house, you could walk out and meet the neighbors, ask them to stop by for a cup of coffee. Or was it that the way of life in Israel was different? I had no idea; I hadn't experienced life in a small town in America. So far, in the couple of months I'd lived in the States, I didn't get to know anybody in our apartment building; maybe our big German shepherd, who usually accompanied me, scared people away. A couple of weeks earlier, I'd gone on some errands and left O'Hara in the apartment. When I returned, the doorman rushed up to me with an agitated look. "Mrs. Skloot," his voice was urgent. "You'll have to get your dog; nobody on your floor can get into their apartment!" I rushed to the elevator, and when the door opened to my floor, my eyes widened in astonishment. Five people were standing to the right looking in the direction of my apartment, which was near the elevator. I followed their gaze and my heart sank, but then, in spite of myself, I started laughing. O'Hara, in his majestic size, ears pointed, emitting a low growl, sat in front of our apartment, not letting anybody pass. I must have left the door ajar, so he got out and waited for me while protecting our home. After apologizing profusely to my neighbors (some way to meet them . . .) I took O'Hara into the apartment, gave him a treat, and put my arms around him. "Good job!" I whispered in his ear. Maybe I didn't have to worry about being alone; I always had my bodyguard.

*∗⟨ Chapter 7: ⟩∗*

# Tal

Steve and I nestled on the bed while the air conditioner, no match for the July heat, rattled in our studio apartment. Through the sliding door leading to our tiny terrace, leaden skies filled in the gaps between contours of high-rise buildings along Queens Boulevard. Steve, his arm around my shoulder, nodded at my abdomen.

"What shall we call the baby?"

"Erez." I circled my soccer-ball belly in a clockwise motion, avoiding my husband's eyes. I was concerned he might not like the foreign-sounding name.

"Erez . . . what kind of name is that?" Two deep furrows appeared between his eyebrows, as if he were trying to solve a difficult mathematical problem.

"It's a tree, a cedar, in Hebrew." I could see in my mind the biblical "Cedars of Lebanon," with their dark green foliage and majestic height.

"E-re-z, it sounds harsh." He tightened his lower lip over his teeth as he sounded out the last consonant. "Besides," he slapped down his trump card, "Americans can't pronounce that name."

Americans. That's what it boiled down to: how they talked, how they thought, how they acted. I was the person carrying the baby, the one who'd be taking care of it. I wasn't American, and names like Jim, John, or Joe didn't mean a thing to me. As Steve's wife, I had a green card, but the idea of obtaining an American citizenship scared me. I felt loyal to my country and family back home and couldn't bear to shed my Israeli identity.

The following Sunday, as usual, we walked over to my in-laws for a lunch of bagels, bialys, cream cheese, lox, beefsteak tomatoes, and red onions. I had never eaten bialys or bagels. Where I came from, "bagels" were twisted, salty crackers, the shape of the number eight, which I discovered were called "pretzels" in America. I never ate the lox. I didn't care for its fishy odor. Having been brought up vegetarian, I didn't eat any meat. Milton, my father-in-law, would pile up lox, tomatoes, and onion slices between two bagel halves, lift it up in admiration, and then open his mouth like a whale and shove it in.

On occasions when we went to the pizza parlor on Austin Street, I'd nibble on a large slice of pizza and sip from the tall glass of frothing milkshake Steve ordered. Back home, this would have been a meal for my whole family.

Living in New York, I fought the machines around me—plugging my ears while pushing the vacuum cleaner, searching in vain for what should have been the simple defrost button in our cavernous refrigerator, pulling stale-smelling sheets out of the hot dryer. My mind contrasted that with pictures of sheets flapping in the wind, smelling of sunshine; cool tiled floors, cleaned, splashed with water; and a fridge unplugged, its door left open to defrost, the ice melting in its own time.

One morning, Steve cornered me in our tiny kitchen while I opened a milk carton.

"When will you learn to open it on the correct side?"

He grabbed the carton, put it on the counter, and, with a

grimace, pinched the tattered opening. With a swift motion he formed a spout by pressing back the flaps of the unopened side.

"Here." He shoved it back at me, his eyes triumphant. He strode out of the kitchen while I stood frozen.

I had tried to put up with Steve's anger, though I wondered what was wrong with him. He was a different man from the charming, loving person I'd gotten to know in Israel. I had seen an inkling of his temper when I had watched him play Ping-Pong in the kibbutz, bent forward, legs apart, jaw muscles tight as he whacked the ball with a ferocity that sent an alarm signal to my brain.

Living with Steve, I followed my mother's example: internalize all feelings. Her messages, more modeled than spoken aloud, now rang in my head: "Do what he wants." "Don't complain." "He comes first."

My mother grew up in an orphanage and learned early on the art of obedience and acquiescence. She acquired household skills as she went along. As a refugee, she became a maid on a British estate where my father worked as a gardener. She cooked, washed, darned socks, ironed—all the while wishing she were on a farm, planting trees or milking cows. I realized that I'd become my mother. I was stuck in Queens in a small studio apartment in a high-rise building where nature consisted of a few trees in the sidewalks surrounded by cement. I learned by trial and error to be a housewife and please my pedantic husband. More often than not, I failed. Yet, luckily, I inherited my mother's cheerfulness and optimism, so I'd find solace in long walks with O'Hara or creating a tasty dish for Steve while daydreaming about my return to Israel.

One evening I was barefoot on the mustard wall-to-wall carpeting, bending over the ironing board in the middle of our tiny living room. The iron hissed as I pressed the steam button and smoothed out my husband's V-necked undershirt, making sure the sleeves overlapped. O'Hara, stretched out on the carpet, head on his front paws, followed my movements with his eyes. His ears perked up when I let out a loud "Ouch" as my pinky touched the hot iron. Sucking my finger, I kneeled next to the big dog, tears welling. "I hate this!" I cried out. His soft fur tickled my cheek. I clung to his neck, sobbing.

The next morning, when Steve got dressed to go to work, he opened the top drawer of the dresser and pulled out a fresh undershirt. With the undershirt hanging like a plucked bird from his fist, he strode to the closet and pulled out the ironing board.

"What are you doing?" I squeaked. "I ironed it already."

He spread the undershirt on the board and connected the electric cord.

"Maybe." He straightened the cloth. "But not the way I do it."

I wanted to crash the board over his head. Instead, hands in fists, I went to the galley kitchen and started cleaning the dishes from last night's spaghetti dinner. Tears in my eyes, I picked up plates, pots, and glasses without seeing them. A plate slipped and crashed. I knelt down slowly to collect the shards. The sharp edges glinted in the fluorescent light.

"What the fuck," Steve hissed. "Pay attention to what you're doing."

He appeared with a broom and dustpan, brushed me aside, and meticulously swept the floor. I scraped the remnants into the sink, put the plates in the dishwasher, and turned on the disposal, watching the blood-red tomato sauce snake down the opening.

The hot summer days continued. In the first week of August, I signed up for Lamaze classes. I enjoyed them and felt like I finally found something I liked in America. On Tuesdays I took the E train, switched to the F for Manhattan, and got off at the "Cheese-building"—the Museum of Modern Art, with its cement facade dotted with large, round holes. I lay on the floor with seven other women, bellies of various sizes: a watermelon, soccer ball, a helium balloon. I wondered who would give birth first, the pale blond on my right or the freckle-faced redhead on my left. I was due in October, so I had eight weeks to go. I had to figure out what to name the baby. I had no idea what its gender was, though the young doctor at the Hebrew University, his stethoscope on my belly, thought it would be a "lovely, healthy boy."

Hebrew names scrambled through my mind, their throaty sounds as natural to me as the fragrance of orange blossoms in an Israeli winter. Even though I wasn't back home, I decided I'd talk to my infant in my native tongue. I wouldn't give up that part of me. Since Erez was out, I thought of calling him Ofer, a fawn, or Tal, dew—the precious drops of water that revive desert plants. Jewish people pray for dew in the same manner they ask God for rain. King David cursed Mount Gilboa, where the earth was soaked with the blood of his beloved, slain friend, Jonathan: "Ye mountains of Gilboa, let there be no dew nor rain upon you."

"Breathe in, hold, tense your right arm," the teacher instructed, moving among us. "Breathe out, relax, let go." Her voice was like a nesting thrush. I contracted my muscles, inhaled, and exhaled. She was next to my head. "Good job," she said. I smiled and lifted my leg straight up, my muscles tightening. I would get an A in birthing, just like I did in math and grammar in school, always striving to be the best student.

I saw myself in the fifth-grade school gym, feet stuck under the last rung of the ladder, on my back, hands crossed behind my neck, knees locked. "Fifty-one, fifty-two," the gym-teacher's voice thundered above me. My cheeks burned and my forehead perspired as I lifted up my torso and brought it down to the wooden floor—up, down, up, down. The students' voices joined in a chorus: "seventy-eight, seventy-nine." My stomach muscles screamed while my whole body shook. I compressed my lips, hearing only the faint sound of: "ninety-eight, ninety-nine . . ." I gasped for air and forced my torso up. "One hundred." There was a round of applause. I'd won the contest, surpassed all my classmates. For the following week I couldn't walk straight and winced in pain whenever I touched my abdomen.

My goal in taking the Lamaze course was to give birth naturally, without medication or injections. I believed it would be healthier for me and my baby, so I tried to excel in it. Yet I also had an impulse to succeed, to prove myself, the way I did as a young girl growing up under my father's stern eye. If, as a kid, I could do a hundred sit-ups, I could now have a baby without any external intervention. My ambition was to deal with pain by breathing and relaxing my muscles, by utilizing my inner strength.

The baby grew as hot, humid days of August arrived in New York. My skin was taut, velvety to the touch, with fine spidery veins across the translucent surface. Lying on the bed, a pillow under my knees, I would sense a sudden movement in my belly, and when I pressed my hand on my abdomen, there would be a jolt, like a bucking goat against my palm. I laughed. The baby was talking to me; I marveled at the evidence of new life.

"Steve, I felt a kick." I would turn to my husband whenever this happened, though he was always engaged in something else— brushing O'Hara from head to tail with swift, precise motions, typing a letter, or working on a paper.

"Great," he would smile, "I bet you it's a boy."

"Whatever, as long as it's healthy," I would answer loyally, cupping both sides of my belly, wondering if the fetus, who might be a girl, was aware of the conversation.

"I've always wanted to be a young father," Steve had told me before we married, "so I could roughhouse with my little son."

Two years younger than me, he was only twenty-three at the time. He was certainly getting his wish.

It was late afternoon, the second of October. The high-rises were silhouettes against the magenta-streaked sky. My belly felt heavy; the baby pressed against my diaphragm, pushing down on my cervix. Gussie and Milton had come over for a light dinner of egg salad, coleslaw, onion rings, cold cuts, and thick slices of pumpernickel that they had picked up at the corner deli.

"Pass the mayo." Gussie, with her Spock-like penciled eyebrows raised in a constant question mark, stuffed a pickle in her mouth. She always seemed to have lipstick on her front teeth.

They were talking about subways.

"I hate to take the subway every morning," Gussie said, looking at Milton, her too-red mouth compressing into a thin line, over the pickle. "All those people breathing down your neck."

"Sweetheart," Milton said, wiping his mouth with a large paper napkin. "I can't help it if I have to take the car to work."

He bent over and picked up a fried onion ring, his large rhinestone ring flashing on a manicured finger.

"Let's see *you* take the train once in a while." Gussie tucked the napkin in the opening of her floral blouse, her bosom rising, her necklace heaving like a boat on high waves.

She turned to her son. "I need another napkin." She always needed another napkin.

Milton wiped crumbs from the corners of his mouth. "While you're at it, son, get me a drink." He smoothed his light sports jacket over his protruding belly, which, encircled in a black leather belt, held up perfectly creased gray pants. Steve pushed back his chair, clearly annoyed. He went to the kitchen and returned with a pile of napkins and a bottle of Scotch, which he plunked down on the table.

I felt his warm hand on the back of my neck. "Are you okay?"

This was the "other" Steve, the man who cared about me, who wanted to be a good husband and father. I loved it when the "good Steve" was around.

"I'm a bit short of breath." I covered his hand with mine. "I feel so heavy."

"Two more weeks and he'll be out of there." Steve touched the top of my belly, which stuck out like a counter top. "You might want to lie down a bit."

I sensed Gussie's and Milton's stares. I stood up, feeling the need to go to the bathroom. "Excuse me." I rushed to the toilet, but nothing happened; the pressure was still there. When I returned and sat on the sofa, Gussie and Steve were clearing the table and Milton, tumbler in hand, sat on the terrace puffing on a cigar. After ten minutes, I got up again. Steve raised his eyebrows.

"I have to go but I can't," I said. I waddled to the bathroom. Once on the toilet, I pushed, breathing forcefully. I gripped the seat. The black-and-white tiles whirled in front of me. I strained to no avail. Back on the sofa, I inhaled deeply. I was sweating.

Something was bearing down on my pelvic floor. I felt pressure, heaviness, and a stinging sensation. "I have to go." I caught my breath, "I have to go to the bathroom." My mother-in-law's eyes followed me as I hurried to the bathroom. "Don't you think you might be having your baby?"

An electric buzz crept down my spine. Gussie must be right; I was having my baby! She would know; she had two of her own. My body tingled with excitement. Yes, this was what was happening. I shuddered to think I could have had the baby in the toilet! I turned, as quick as I could, to collect my pocketbook from the bedroom.

"My God," Steve said. He picked up a traveling bag, a pair of shoes, and some toiletries, rushing around as if chased by a swarm of wasps. His voice rose two octaves, starting as a tenor and finishing at a high falsetto. "Let's go." We were at the door when he turned around and wagged his finger at O'Hara, who was looking at him with big brown eyes. "You stay here; I'll be back soon."

We all piled into a taxi. The driver leaned on his horn as we sped to Queens Hospital. Steve's face was pale. His fingers pressed into my arm. He barked to the driver: "Hurry, hurry!" I held my belly and breathed hard, trying to recall the Lamaze exercises. Buildings, stores, and pedestrians blurred as the world inside me heaved, churned, pushed, and poked. "Slow down, you're going to kill us!" Gussie yelled. Milton, in the passenger seat, his square shoulders rigid, was silent. The driver deposited us at the front door of Queen's Hospital. Panting, we crossed the lobby and squeezed into an elevator. The dark brown panels closed in on me. The musty air was nauseating. I groaned and bit my lip. Steve squeezed my hand. "Hang on—we're almost there." Milton chuckled nervously, "Whatever you do, don't have the baby here." I uttered a low moan.

The next thing I knew I was on a table, legs apart. Above me were white masks. Voices: "Baby's head," "cervix opening," "need to cut." I screamed as a needle was plunged into my vagina. There was no warning, and I had no idea what it was, but later I found out it was novocaine for the episiotomy. "Push." "Relax." "Breathe." I pulled myself up, holding on to the bed's sidebars, pushed until my whole body seemed to tear apart. My uterus burned. And then there was a sudden, immense pleasurable end of pain.

"It's a boy." The nurse, holding the slippery, blood-streaked bundle, smiled at me and then, incredibly, whisked him away. "A boy; that will make Steve happy," I murmured. But looking around I realized that nobody was there, neither Steve nor my in-laws. I didn't want them watching me give birth, but once it was over I bursted with a desire to share my joy, my sense of awe and gratitude. I wanted to embrace, hug, and laugh, but I was alone. Not even my baby with me. An orderly in a pea-green shirt wheeled me out of the delivery room, deposited me in the corridor, and left. I felt abandoned. Where was everybody? I looked up at the white ceiling. I wanted to share the moment of victory, let the world know that I made it. I had given birth to new life. Wiping the perspiration off my flushed face with a corner of my bed sheet, I emitted a deep sigh. My throat constricted, and I pushed back tears. I folded my arms over my soft belly, wishing Steve were there to hold me. After a while, my body worn out, I dozed off.

A cheerful voice woke me up. "Here he is! Would you like to hold him?" The young nurse handed me a tiny parcel swathed in white linen with only a face showing. She placed him gently in my arms. I pressed the baby to my heart, smiling and crying at the same time.

"He's so tiny!" I said to the nurse. I looked closely at my sleeping son's face. It was crumpled like the face of an old man. I chuckled, thinking, What a funny-looking baby. Then it dawned on me; he looked like a miniature Milton, my father-in-law. Shortly after, the baby, still sleeping, was taken to the baby ward. I was wheeled to the maternity ward, where I finally saw Steve and my in-laws who showered me with hugs, kisses, and flowers.

The following day, a nurse in a white, starched uniform, asked me the baby's name. "I . . . I'm not sure." I clasped and unclasped my fingers. "I have to double-check with my husband." She looked at me with care and nodded.

We left the hospital with a typed form—a blank over the line that read "Baby's First Name." In the apartment, cradling our four-day-old son in the rocking chair that was Gussie's present, I turned to my husband, took his hand, and stroked it.

"Steve, I'd like to call our baby Tal. Is that okay?"

"Tal . . . what does it mean?"

"Dew." I motioned with my fingers, dancing downward, like falling rain.

"Dew? For a boy?"

"Why not? Tal," I mouth the word. "It's easy to pronounce."

Steve rubbed his chin with his thumb and forefinger, the way a psychologist might when confronted with a patient's dilemma.

Hugging my baby, I tried to think of another way to convince my husband. I had to win. Please, Steve, I pleaded in my mind. Can't you see how important it is to me that our baby have a Hebrew name? I thought, communicated, and breathed in Hebrew, though I had no choice but to speak English. Addressing my son with a foreign name would be like cutting a piece out of my being; my baby would feel like a stranger to me. I pressed my eyelids; my mind churned trying to come up with another argument.

"There's Tal Brody, you remember? He was the American basketball player whose team won a gold medal in the Maccabiah. You remember, in the Israeli Olympics?"

I held my breath. Steve's eyes softened. A smile spread across his face.

"Okay, you win." He kissed me on my forehead, stroked the sleeping bundle, and went to the kitchen to make dinner.

I kept rocking my baby. Stroking his little arm, I marveled at his soft pink skin. My face close to his head, I inhaled the fragrance of talcum and Johnson baby shampoo. Inserting my pinkie into his tiny fist, I cherished the sense of warmth and contentment that pervaded my body. This is the essence of being a mother, I thought. As if by a miracle, my body, mind, and whole being adapted itself to the role of motherhood. I recalled my ambivalence in the hospital when a photographer of newborn babies wanted to take a picture of my son. "You'll love to look at it when he's older," he said. I had replied, "No, thanks, he's too ugly right now." But my maternal instinct told me that he'd grow to be a beautiful child.

Tal, my dewdrop. I said his name for the first time: T-ah-l. The name melted in my mouth like one of the golden ripe figs I used to pick from the trees in the Ashkelon sand dunes. The tip of my tongue was against my front teeth, curving down, gliding over the vowel, and landing softly on midpalate. It was a gentle sound evoking beads of morning dew sparkling on the grass after a scorching Mediterranean night.

### ❧ *Chapter 8:* ❧

# The Exam

Around the time Tal turned two, Steve was earning enough money for us to move to a larger, more modern apartment in Gerard Towers, a building in the same neighborhood. It had a small living room with two bedrooms, a bathroom, and a kitchenette, a vast improvement over our tiny studio apartment in Parker Towers. Every Friday I'd polish the wooden floors into a shiny buff and arrange flowers in the vases. Even though I grew up in houses where you opened the door and walked outside, our apartment on the eighth floor started to feel more like a home. Unfortunately, we didn't have O'Hara anymore—Steve found him a good home on a farm in upstate New York. We couldn't keep our dog since we had to stay at the Forest Hills Inn for a couple of weeks before we could move into our new apartment. I was sad to part from him, but it did make my life easier.

Steve, trying to make a name for himself as production manager on feature films, worked even longer hours. I was alone a lot, still waiting for the weekly air letter from my parents. There was an

Israeli family on the same floor, with a nine-year-old daughter. At least I could chat with Hannah, the thin-faced, brown-eyed woman married to Yigal, who worked at the Israeli Consulate in New York. When she opened her door she'd greet me with. "Hi, *ma shlomech.*" I'd tell her how I was, and we'd retreat to the kitchen, where she'd serve me *na'na* tea—fresh mint leaves in a glass cup—accompanied by Israeli Osem biscuits. Ilana, though much older than Tal, didn't mind playing games with him while her mother and I talked about our homes and family members back in Israel.

I was sad when Hannah told me that her husband's stint at the consulate was over and they were going back home. I envied her, wishing *I* could return to my country, to Ashkelon, to life near the sea. Though I had promised my parents we'd come back, Steve didn't show much interest in returning to Israel.

"When are you leaving?" I asked.

"Next month," she sighed, looking around and motioning with her arm in a wide curve. "I have to pack everything."

I put my hand on hers. "I know what it's like. I've been through this; packing a whole household isn't an easy task. Still," I looked her in the eye, "I'm kind of jealous. I wish I were returning to Israel. It's so sad that I can't share with my mom all these moments of Tal growing up. She's so good with little kids."

"How about Steve's parents?"

I shrugged my shoulders. "They adore Tal, but they're not around much. They're always at work. The only time we see them is on Sundays."

"Doesn't Steve's mom help you sometimes with Tal?"

"No, not really. She's not much of a grandmother type. Once, when he was a baby, we left him with her overnight and it was a disaster; he cried, had fever, and she didn't know what to do with him."

Hanna smiled. "I guess we can't choose our mothers-in-law."

Tal's ringing laughter came through the open door of Ilana's bedroom. I tilted my head in the direction of the room.

"By the way, how does Ilana feel about moving back?"

"It's difficult for her. We've been here for four years. She has friends and is used to her school. This is her home." Hannah shrugged, turning her palms upward. *"Mah la'asot?"*

"Yes, what can one do? This is life." Looking at her, I raised my eyebrows. "But I guess you're happy to go back."

"I *am* happy," Hannah replied, "but it won't be easy." She smiled at me. "I'll miss you. Make sure you come to see us when you visit."

I looked down at my feet, close to tears, finishing off my cup of tea.


The next day I took Tal to the supermarket. I bought products I knew Steve liked and grew up on. We shopped for Cheerios, Shredded Wheat, rye bread, bagels, Philadelphia cream cheese, and Smucker's blueberry jam. Per usual, Tal was my helper. "What cereal shall we get?" I'd ask him in Hebrew, the only language I spoke with him. He'd point to his favorite brand. *"Et ze!" "Ata rotseh et ze?"* Do you want this? *"Ken, ken,"* he'd nod his head, joyfully clapping his hands.

"Here, Tali," I'd say to him, "hold on to this." He'd sit in his seat in the shopping cart, a big smile on his face, clasping the box.

Back at our building, I took the elevator to our floor, entered the apartment, and went to the kitchen, where I started to unload the groceries, putting them away in the refrigerator and cabinets. Tal was playing in his room, or so I thought. When I went to check on him, he wasn't there. I dashed back to the kitchen, to the living room, and then to the bathroom, but he was nowhere in sight. I felt as if someone pushed me from a plane and I was free-falling. "Tal, Ta-a-l," I called, my voice shrill, but there was no answer. That's when it dawned on me. The front door was ajar; I must have forgotten to close it. My God, I thought, he went out. Heart pounding, I rushed to the hallway. I looked to the right and then to the left and back again, but all I could see were blank walls, with no sign of Tal. I turned the corner and ran through another hallway like a crazed woman, calling out my son's name at the top of my lungs. An acute pain lodged in my temples, as if my head would explode. I had to find Tal. He couldn't have vanished. He had to be somewhere. I ran to Hannah's apartment, the only person I could think of who might have seen him. I prayed against hope that perhaps he'd walked to her apartment, since we were there so often and he knew the way. In a panic I pressed the buzzer, holding it down for a while, and when nobody answered I banged on the door. Hannah finally opened.

"I'm sorry—" she started, but she stopped when she looked at me. "Your face is as white as a wall, *ma kara*?"

"Tal has disappeared!" My voice cracked. I looked at her with questioning eyes, my lower lip quivering. "I don't know where he is. Have you seen him?"

She turned her head from side to side. "No, but let me—"

But I couldn't wait. I dashed out of her apartment. Looking around, I noticed people coming out of the elevator. My mind worked frantically. Could he have taken the elevator to the lobby? Could he have somehow walked out of the lobby into . . . no, I stopped my thoughts. It was too horrendous. He couldn't be outside, on the sidewalk, near the cars zooming by on Queens Boulevard. He's so young; somebody must have noticed him. I rushed to the elevator and pressed the button. My fists were clenched, knees jerking up and down as if in a spasm while I stood in front of the metal door imploring it to open. "Come on, come on!" I repeated as I waited for the elevator to come. After an eternity, it arrived. I let a couple of people get out and was about to dive in when I witnessed a miracle. A tall man whom I'd seen sometimes on our floor emerged from the elevator holding onto Tal's hand.

"*Eema, eema*," Tal cried, prying loose from the man and running to me. Tears streamed down my face.

"Thank you, thank you so much. Where was he?"

"Down in the lobby. I thought he was your boy. I knew you lived on this floor, and I didn't see you." He smiled. "He's a cute little guy."

I clasped the man's hand, shaking it vigorously. Still out of breath, in a quivering voice, I thanked him again. "You saved my life; I don't know what I would have done without you!"

I crouched down and pressed Tal's little body to mine. Then, standing up, I took Tal's hand, holding it firmly. "Come, Tali, let's go home and eat."

That evening, after I put Tal to bed, I told Steve what happened. His face was stern. He compressed his lips while talking in a controlled voice, trying to suppress his anger.

"You should be more careful. We could have lost our son."

I swallowed hard. "It's something that happened, and he's fine, he's here. I nearly died when I couldn't find him."

"Well, make sure the door is closed, and . . ." He glared at me. "Don't, ever, again, let him out of your sight."

I lowered my head, recoiling from Steve's harsh words, just as I always had when my father admonished me. There was no use trying to explain to him how I felt, what I had gone through looking for Tal, or the fact that given my experience from earlier that day, I would never let it happen again and I didn't need him admonishing me. Steve was always worried that something might happen to his son anyway. He was a very protective father. It might have been better for both of us if I hadn't told him. But that wasn't the kind of relationship I wanted to have. I wasn't good at keeping secrets and wanted to share with him what was going on in my life. Yet when I told him something that wasn't to his liking, he'd criticize me.

I tiptoed into Tal's bedroom that night and watched my sleeping son hug his brown teddy bear, whom we named Doobie, "Teddy Bear" in Hebrew. I bent over and kissed his soft cheeks that felt like rose petals. "Good night, *laila tov*," I whispered.

A year after this incident at Gerard Towers, Tal turned three, and I figured I could return to teaching, at least part-time. Although I wasn't crazy about teaching little kids, I wanted to be useful, get out of the house, and earn some money. As a licensed teacher, I was sure it wouldn't be a problem getting a job at the Forest Hills JCC Hebrew School.

One evening, after the Jewish holidays of Rosh Hashanah and Yom Kippur, after we'd finished a nice eggplant-parmesan dinner I had prepared, I approached Steve with my idea.

He stared at me. "Are you sure? It's quite a commitment."

"It's only two afternoons a week and," I hesitated, "Sunday mornings."

"What about Tal?"

"I can get a babysitter for him, and on Sunday, maybe you could take care of him when you're home." I bit my lip. I wondered if I was asking for too much. Though Steve enjoyed spending time with his son, it was always on his terms, when he had the time and inclination for it.

Steve furrowed his brow, lost in thought. Then, to my relief, he smiled, nodding his head. "I guess it's okay. It will be nice to spend some time with Tali."

I hugged him, kissing his smooth cheek.

The following morning, armed with Steve's approval, I phoned the JCC office. I had mixed feelings. Per usual, the negative voices welled up and whispered in my ear. Will you be able to stand in front of a class of ten-year-olds? Will they listen to you? It occurred to me that it might be more discipline than teaching, but I forged forward nevertheless.

Clutching the receiver, a woman's voice answered. She had a strong New York–Jewish accent. "You're inquiring about teaching at the Hebrew school? Hold on, I'll transfer you to our education director." I waited, feeling more anxious now.

"Good day, this is Hyman Campeas. How can I help you?"

Swallowing, I repeated my request.

"Are you a licensed teacher?" he asked.

"Yes, I have a license." What did my accent sound like: Israeli? British? I knew it didn't sound American.

"Can you come tomorrow for an interview?"

"Sure," I said. But I didn't feel sure at all about being interviewed. I knew American Jews loved Israel, so there was a good chance they'd be interested in me. It was 1969, a couple of years after the Six-Day War, when the entire American Jewish community rallied for Israel. At the time, many young Americans flew to the holy land to volunteer for the war effort. There was an immense sense of pride in Israel's military achievement, winning the war against four Arab countries in six days!

The next morning, after depositing Tal at my neighbor's, I crossed Queens Boulevard and walked for ten minutes up the road to the JCC. Dressed in a smart black skirt and blue top, clutching my pocketbook with the Israeli teacher's license, I walked up the stairs and knocked on Mr. Campeas's office door. A tall, middle-aged man, slightly stooped, wearing a yarmulke, greeted me with, "So, you'd like to teach at our school." He motioned to a chair opposite his desk. "Come, sit down." He sank into his armchair. "Do you have a background in Judaism?"

I smiled. "Of course." My smile deepened. "I'm from Israel."

"At the moment we need a teacher for Jewish Studies." Seeing my raised eyebrows, he continued, "To teach Torah, Jewish customs, and holidays."

"I could do that," I said. Back home, we studied the Bible every year on a different level. I prided myself on knowing many verses by heart. I celebrated the Jewish holidays and knew all the customs. Or so I thought.

"Which teachers' college did you attend?"

With a clear voice I said: "The teachers' seminary in Bet Hakerem in Jerusalem." I waited to see the effect of my response. The name "Jerusalem" carried a special weight. Whenever I mentioned it, outside of Israel, the person I was in conversation with would open his or her eyes wide, acknowledging the uniqueness of that ancient, holy city. In my travels through Europe, I met a peasant woman in Denmark. When she asked me where I was from and I mentioned Israel, her face remained blank, but when I said Jerusalem, she nodded and her eyes shone.

So I was unprepared for Hyman Campeas's next question. "Is it a religious seminary?"

"No." I frowned slightly. "It's secular, accredited by the ministry of education in Israel."

He looked at me with kind eyes. "I'm afraid you can't teach here. We belong to the conservative movement." He pressed his palms together and lowered his chin in a contemplative manner. "In order to obtain a license to teach in Jewish schools in greater New York, you'll need to fulfill certain requirements."

My mouth dropped. "What do you mean? What kind of requirements?"

"You'll have to pass an oral exam on Jewish laws and customs."

"But I have already a teacher's license," I tried to protest.

"I know." He lowered his voice as if explaining a difficult concept to a child. "But you haven't studied Jewish religion at the seminary, have you?"

I felt numb. In Israel, I was Jewish just by living in my country. Everybody celebrated the holidays, we all observed Yom Kippur, and there were no buses driving on Shabbat, anywhere, in the whole country.

Spreading my arms, I took a deep breath. "Well, if I want to teach here, what am I supposed to do?"

He swiveled his chair around to face the bookshelf behind him. Searching for a moment, he pulled out a thin paperback book with a salmon-colored cover.

"Here." He handed it to me. "You'll have to study this. When you're done, you'll be tested on it."

I held the book. The black Hebrew letters seemed to bolt out of the cover page: *Pninay HaDat, The Pearls of Religion: A Condensed Version of Jewish Laws and Customs.* I had a strange, disquieting sensation, as if I had landed in a foreign galaxy. My belly hardened. I felt indignant. Was I not Jewish enough? What is the meaning of a conservative Jew? Why won't the Board of License in New York accept my Israeli teaching certificate? Yet I had decided I wanted the job, so I thanked Mr. Campeas and took the book from him. At least it wasn't very thick.

Once I got home and started to study the book, I realized how little I knew about Jewish prayers, customs, and laws. I had no idea what the *Amidah* prayer was, why one lit the Hanukkah candles before the Shabbat candles, or why one is supposed to say a blessing over *two* challah loaves on Friday night. I began my voyage of understanding the difference between living in America and in Israel, between being an observant American Jew and a secular Israeli. I found the material in the book rather interesting and regretted my cockeyed answer to the Hebrew-school principal.

Leafing through the book, I realized there are strict instructions for all activities during the day, from the time you open your eyes to the moment you fall asleep. There is a blessing for every bodily function, whether it's waking up or going to the bathroom. The reasons behind the instructions fascinated me. In the booklet, a quotation from the Jewish mystic book *Hazohar* explained that sleep is similar to death, and since a dead person is impure, the moment you open your eyes, you have to wash your hands to remove the impurity.

I started reading about the "Blessings of Pleasure," which related to food. Aha, I thought, the rabbis know what's important in life. The endless details tested my patience, however. There were different blessings before and after eating or drinking, varying according to the kind of food and its importance. Bread, which is the main sustenance, has its specific blessing—"Bless you, Lord, who brings forth bread from the earth"—whereas any kind of fruit grown on the tree, including olives or grapes, receives this blessing: "Bless you, Lord, creator of the fruit of the tree."

I chuckled when I read the chapter titled "Politeness During the Meal." Among a myriad of dos and don'ts, I learned that you shouldn't hold a slice of bread and tear a piece of it with the other hand; you shouldn't drink a whole glass of wine at once; you shouldn't start to eat or drink before a person who's older than you; and you shouldn't talk while eating because of the danger of choking. Then there was the edict I liked best: It's forbidden to throw away bread; even the crumbs should be collected and given to the chickens. The whole book, written in Hebrew, was bossy in tone and used only male pronouns. Whenever a person was addressed, it was the masculine "you," never the feminine. No wonder, since God was only addressed as "he" and male rabbis wrote the booklet I was reading.

I wondered why on earth I needed to know all these minute details. It didn't seem to have anything to do with teaching kids in Hebrew school. Yet since that was the only way to get the job, I persisted in studying the text. I tried to concentrate on the main prayers and customs for Shabbat and holidays. A part of me resisted the whole concept of religion, which involved following the commandments God dictated to his prophets and the interpretations the rabbis continued to dictate to us, the Jewish people. I grew up in a secular household, where we followed the Jewish tradition—celebrated holidays such as Rosh Hashanah, Passover, and Hanukkah—but we didn't follow the *mitzvot*, the biblical and rabbinical commandments.

When, in my teens, I asked my father why he didn't go to synagogue, would not fast on Yom Kippur, and didn't keep kosher, his reply was unequivocal: "Why should I? After all, my family was killed in the *Shoah*." With pursed lips and firm voice, he added: "There is no God." Anything that was religious, my father defied. The celebration of Shabbat and the holidays of Passover and Hanukkah had no religious meaning in our household; we followed the

Jewish traditions, the way my father's parents and grandparents in Germany celebrated them.

Three weeks later, after studying almost every night after putting Tal to bed, I felt ready to face the rabbis, more or less. On a cold, bright Sunday morning, leaving Tal with Steve, I took the subway to Manhattan to face my interrogators. Steve promised to take Tal ice-skating. He was an elegant, accomplished skater and had taught Tal to skate as soon as he could. Tal loved it and had lots of fun skating hand in hand with his father. Riding the F train, facing the gloomy faces of other passengers, I checked the notes I had taken. My chest felt tight. I wished the exam would be over already.

I recalled the high school matriculation exam I took while studying in Jerusalem; math wasn't one of my strong subjects, and I was sure I wouldn't pass. I crammed days and nights, covering several pages with numbers and equations. After the exam I walked around as if in mourning; I didn't believe I'd passed. A week later, after the results were posted, I saw that I received a good grade. That afternoon I ran down the pavement next to my school and did a little jig around each telephone pole.

Arriving in Manhattan half an hour later I got off the train. Clutching my pink book, I made my way from the subway station to the address I had been given: 426 West 58th Street. I entered the brownstone building into an anteroom, where the secretary ushered me into a room that at first glance looked like a library. Behind a large desk, rows and rows of books stood on shelves as if to warn me: this is the abode of learned people; you better be prepared for difficult questions.

Two men stood up and took turns shaking my hand. "I'm Rabbi Saul Barenboim," said the older-looking man. "And I'm Rabbi Daniel Kahan," said the other. "Nice to meet you," they chimed. I felt my face reddening. I didn't expect a rabbi to shake my hand *or* stand up to greet me. An Orthodox rabbi would never touch another woman except his wife. I remembered the rabbis in Jerusalem, dressed in black with long beards, who had questioned Steve before we got married. At the time I'd sat next to my future husband and they didn't even glance at me. Not once did they address me or acknowledge my existence. But these two men were a different kind of rabbi. They dressed in business suits, wore ties, and had clean-shaven faces. The only giveaway that they were observant Jews was the *kippa*, the skullcap they wore on their heads. So that's what conservative rabbis look like, I thought. In Israel, I had never heard about Reform or conservative Jews. My world was opening up. I was starting to embrace plurality, though I wasn't aware of it just then.

The rabbis returned to their seats behind the desk. I sat on the edge of the chair in front of them, my elbows close to my body, hands clasped. While they gathered their notes, I glanced at the highlighted answers on the sheet of paper I had prepared. I had a gnawing feeling in my belly, but I lifted my head and smiled at them. At least I would put on a good show.

"Shall we start?" asked the senior rabbi. I guessed he was in his midforties, which seemed quite old to me at the time.

I swallowed, wishing I had some water. "Yes."

"How many blessings are in the *Amidah* prayer, and what's the origin of its name?"

Good, I had memorized that. "It has eighteen blessings and is named *Amidah* because in Hebrew it means 'standing,' which is the position in which we recite the prayer."

They looked at each other and nodded. So far so good, I thought. Rabbi Kahan, the younger rabbi with smooth brown hair and glasses, asked the next question.

"When a Hanukkah night falls on Shabbat eve, which candles do you light first: for Shabbat or for Hanukkah?"

I smiled. At least this question had a logical answer. Since one isn't supposed to work on Shabbat, and lighting candles is considered work, the answer was obvious. "You light the Hanukkah candles first and then the Shabbat ones."

"Very well." His voice was solemn. "Here's another question: Why do we light the *shamash* in addition to Hanukkah candles?"

The *shamash*, the extra candle, hmmm . . . I'd wondered about that. I read that Hanukkah candles were lit in order to advertise the miracle that happened and shouldn't be used for regular light. "In addition to the eight candles, we light the *shamash* so we can use it in case we need light."

They asked me several more questions and seemed to be contented, though I couldn't tell from their blank faces and polite smiles if I gave the correct answers. After a while, perspiration trickled down my back, and my palms were clammy. The air in the room felt stifling. I seemed to be racing to a finish line. I realized suddenly that the room was silent; no questions hung in the air. Spreading his palms on the desk, Rabbi Barenboim cleared his throat. "Now, young lady, for the final question."

The way he introduced the question, it sounded serious, like a coup de grâce to prove to them my ignorance. The rabbi looked me in the eye, as if trying to estimate my general knowledge.

"Could you tell us who, in your opinion, paralleled Moses Mendelssohn in the Christian world?"

My heart sank. I wasn't prepared for this kind of question. Feeling the wheels turn and crank, I racked my brain for an answer. From my studies in the seminar, I knew Mendelssohn was a German Jewish philosopher who lived in the eighteenth or nineteenth century. I tried to retrieve any information I had in my gray cells about great Christian figures at that time. Mendelssohn had ideas of *Haskalah*, Jewish Enlightenment. Thinking, I bit my lower lip: Enlightenment, Reformation, German. Who could be his counterpart in the Christian world? Could it be . . . yes! That might be it. In a soft voice I uttered, "Martin Luther?"

The anxious faces of the two men relaxed into a broad grin, as if a weight had been lifted off their shoulders. "Congratulations! You got the right answer."

They stood up, motioning that the interview was over. Rabbi Barenboim extended his hand. "Thanks for coming. You'll get a letter within a week."

"Thank you so much." I almost curtsied before turning around and fleeing the room.

The letter, with the heading *Board of License, Hebrew Teachers Association of Greater New York*, arrived in the mail five days later. My heart beating with joy and pride, I read the printed Hebrew words: *Our hearty congratulations on being awarded an accredited Hebrew teacher's diploma. As a dedicated teacher you'll join our ranks and give your energy, time, and ability to strengthen and advance the fate of Hebrew Education.*

My first reaction was to share the good news with Steve; I was sure he would be proud of me, of my achievement. But I couldn't. He was away on location, filming. I'd have to wait a week or so until he returned. I couldn't phone him; I didn't even have a number where I could reach him. Once he went to work, he entered a different world—the world of films, in which he devoted all his time and energy into creating illusions.

I took the letter and went to Tal's room, where he was playing with his Mr. Potato Head. Waving the sheet of paper like a flag, I called out, "Look, Tali, *eema* got an important letter. It says I can now teach in New York."

Tal crinkled his forehead, not understanding why I was excited. But he saw how happy I was, so he hugged me, saying: "*Yofi, eema.* What will you teach?"

I held his warm body close to me as a tear slid down my cheek: "I'll teach Hebrew, silly."

# ❧ Chapter 9: ❧

# The Goat

I never knew what to expect of my husband. Would he come home stressed, distant, cursing his boss? Would he hug me? Would he be upset that dinner wasn't ready, or would he sit on the rug and play with his son? Being married to Steve was riding a roller coaster, up, down, up, down—wonderful music at five o'clock then angry words at five thirty; champagne dinners giving way to lonely weeks; mutual showers one day and slammed doors the next.

He confused me with his Jekyll and Hyde behavior. With a sense of humor, I might have been able to deal better with his tantrums, but growing up with a father who hardly ever smiled, I felt wanting in that area. *Abba* never fooled around, played games, or giggled. His stern bearing cast a shadow over our childhood. Steve was a prankster—he loved jokes, especially practical ones that left the other person confounded.

The person he most enjoyed surprising was his little boy. When Tal was about three and a half, Steve was working on a feature film called *Tomorrow* in Tupelo, Mississippi. "It was wonderful working with Robert Duvall; he's a great actor," he would later recount.

I tried to picture what it was like down there, in the South—probably hot and humid with lots of lush vegetation. On the other hand, I didn't want to think too much about Steve's work and whereabouts. As production manager and at times assistant director, he was busy on location. When he was away, he never wrote and rarely called. I felt shut off from a whole part of my husband's life; I knew very little about his work and almost nothing about any given film's crew, the people he worked with. At times he would spend twenty-four hours straight on the set, creating lifelong friendships with people I never met. One of these was with the producer of *Tomorrow*, Paul Roebling, whose grandfather engineered the the Brooklyn Bridge. Paul would only tell me that fact years later.

When Tal was four, Steve had been gone for three weeks leading up to Thanksgiving. I had no idea whether he'd even make it back for the holiday, but he called two days ahead of time and said, "I'll be back tomorrow." I skipped around the living room, humming to myself. I envisioned our meeting: I'd open the door and he'd sweep me into his arms, plant a kiss on my mouth and press me close, his body hardening against mine. I'd nuzzle my head against the small of his neck, inhale his Old Spice, and slide my fingers through his silky hair. I couldn't wait to see him.

"Come, Tali, let's clean up." I took Tal's hand and we went to the kitchen. Tal got his little broom while I pulled out the vacuum cleaner. We swept, vacuumed, and polished the wooden floors, dusted the bookshelves, watered the philodendron pots, cleaned the bathroom, scrubbed the Formica kitchen counter, and polished the chrome-plated kettle. I prepared a spinach quiche, and while it was in the oven, we ran down to Austin Street to pick up fresh flowers, which I arranged in vases on the dining room table, coffee table, and on our bedroom dresser.

When I finished, I went out to our tiny terrace. The sky was leaden gray above the traffic whizzing sixteen floors below. I didn't care; my husband was coming home. I'd hug his broad shoulders, feel his smooth cheek on mine, have a candlelight dinner.

Holding onto the railing, I bent my knees, stretching my back. As soon as I got back into the living room, I noticed my palms were black from the soot outside. Rubbing my hands, I realized that no matter how much I cleaned our apartment and decorated it with flowers, the reality was that I lived in a sooty, noisy environment in an urban setting.

My son hugged my waist and lifted up his cleft chin, his dad's chin exactly. "*Eema*, will *abba* bring me a present?"

"I would think so." I felt sad that Tal hadn't seen his father for so long. I resented Steve compensating for not being there for his son with presents. I hoped at least it was a good one!

Tal was as gentle and sweet as his name; he exhibited Steve's best characteristics. He was my constant companion when Steve was away. We went down to the Laundromat, where he helped me fold clothes. He walked to the supermarket with me, where he picked out his favorite brand of cereal. We played hide-and-seek in the park and sat on a bench eating ice cream.

The next day I got up early; I put on jeans, my blue T-shirt, Blushing Tulip lipstick, and a dab of Arabian musk while checking the clock every twenty minutes or so. It was noon when the doorbell rang.

"It's *abba*!" I shouted.

Almost slipping on the shiny floor, I rushed to the door and unlocked it. He was there in his beige Levi's jacket, skin tanned, eyes laughing. I stretched out my arms to hug him but then dropped them when I noticed something strange—a furry white muzzle and a pink nose peeked out of his folded arms. In his right hand he held a baby's milk bottle.

"What's this? Have you brought us a gift?" I joked. I wasn't ready for this kind of surprise—an animal. He couldn't be serious.

"Can't you see? It's a little goat for Tal. I thought he'd like a pet."

The goat wiggled his spindly legs while Steve tightened his hold on him. Steve squatted and motioned with his head to Tal.

"Come here, Tali." His voice rang with laughter. " Look what I got for you." Tal walked up and leaned on his father, his eyes wide, mouth open, trying to touch the goat's head with his small index finger. "Wow! Can I keep him, *abba*?"

"Sure, he's all yours!"

What was Steve thinking? If he thought this was amusing, he was wrong.

"Where did you get him?" I crossed my arms, pursing my lips.

"From one of the farmers in Tupelo," he said beaming, pleased with himself.

Only Steve could have come up with such a crazy idea. Although part of me thought it was funny, I also knew that I'd have to be the one to take care of it. I recalled from the goats I'd seen in Israel how messy and smelly they were. Having a goat in our apartment seemed altogether a crazy idea!

Steve must have been determined to bring Tal a special present. I wondered how he carried the goat all the way from Mississippi.

"How did you manage to put him on the plane?" I asked.

Steve's eyes crinkled with laughter. "I told the stewardess it was a dog, and when he started to bleat, I told her it had a cold."

The kid uttered a soft "me-e-e," and Tal laughed. Steve put down the little animal, and its hoofs slid on the polished floor. Tal ran after him, squealing.

I tried to rationalize in Steve's favor. I knew his history; he'd never gotten a pet as a child. Growing up in a small apartment in Rego Park, New York, his pleas for a dog, cat, or hamster were always turned down by Gussie, who would have nothing to do with an animal shedding and smelling up her neat apartment while she was at work. On one occasion Gussie relented, agreeing to let Rocky, a small pointed-ear boxer, into the apartment, as long as he was confined to Steve's room. Poor Rocky didn't last long—a few weeks later he was banished to the animal shelter after gnawing on the living room sofa, shredding its upholstery. Steve, eleven years old, refused to talk to his mother for several days. I didn't want to be like Gussie.

"What shall we do with him in the apartment?" I asked.

"You can take him for a walk." Steve took off his jacket and walked into the kitchen.

He didn't even ask me how I was, what had been going on with us while he was away. I needed a hug or a kiss; three weeks was a long time to be apart.

"Oh no—look." I pointed to the little brown pellets on the floor.

The kid trotted toward the bedroom, munching on a green philodendron leaf. "The plants! Get him away from the plants!" Tal ran after the goat, trying to catch him, but then I saw, from the corner of my eye, the kid collide with the coffee table. The wooden fruit bowl fell down with a crashing sound while grapes, apples, and pears rolled onto the floor.

Putting my hands on my hips, I faced Steve.

"Sorry, that's it. Take the goat away. I can't have him here."

"Where do you want me to take him?"

"Wherever." I collapsed on the sofa, holding back my tears.

Why didn't things ever go the way I planned? Was it a pattern in my life that every joyful event was marred, deflated like a party balloon? Or was it my husband, who, at twenty-six, refused to grow up, seizing life with the energy of a playful ten-year-old? I looked at his face. His eyes still twinkled while he sunk his upper teeth into his lower lip, shrugging his shoulders at Tal, as if saying, "It's not my fault you can't keep the goat." He strode to the phone, grabbed the phone book, and started leafing through it. I was alarmed. What was he up to now?

"Who are you calling?"

He didn't even look at me. "The zoo in Flushing Meadows."

Good, I thought, at least he's listening to me and getting rid of that goat.

"Hello?" Steve called, but there was no answer. They were closed for Thanksgiving.

"*Eema*, where will the goat go?" Tal held on to my arm and then looked at his father.

Steve grabbed the goat and the bottle and headed toward the door. "I'll see you soon," he said, and he was gone. A couple of hours later he came back without the goat. I was in the kitchen preparing dinner.

"Where is it?" I asked.

"In the children's zoo."

"How did you get in?" I washed the carrots in the sink.

"I climbed over the fence and knocked on the zookeeper's door." Tal's mouth was gaping. I started chopping the carrots.

"What did he say?"

"He wanted to know if it was for his Thanksgiving dinner." Steve stifled a giggle.

"And?"

"He's fine."

I took a deep breath. Placing the carrots in the boiling water, I turned to set the table. Would Steve ever stop shocking me? In fact, he wouldn't, and he didn't learn his lesson because I'd have to contend with pets such as a sea turtle and a duck while trying to raise our kids.

A few weeks later, we visited the children's zoo. Our goat was tied to a long rope near the zookeeper's home. He had a little pot-belly and a pointed beard; wisps of bright green grass protruded from both sides of his mouth. Tal went up to the goat, who wagged his tail then nuzzled Tal's lap. The zookeeper called the goat Cutie and told us that all the children loved him. I imagined the goat living happily ever after. If only my own life could be so simple.

## *Chapter 10:*

# Cejwin Camp

In late June 1971, we sat in the dining corner in our Queens apartment on an overcast, hot, and humid Sunday morning. I watched Tal, now four and a half, finish up his Cheerios, picking up the bowl and slurping down the milk at the bottom. I was six months pregnant with my second child. Spreading my hand on the side of my belly, I felt a little kick. It still amazed me that a living creature was inside my body. I turned to Steve. "The baby moved again."

Steve looked at Tal and ruffled his son's hair. "You'll soon have a little brother or sister."

I would have welcomed either, but I secretly hoped for a little girl, a daughter. Then there would be another female in the home. I sensed that the relationship with a daughter would be different than with a son, and I welcomed the idea of a mother-daughter bond like I had with my own mother. Steve stroked my arm. "Come, let's talk about the camp. I think it's a good idea."

Hy Campeas, my boss at the Forest Hills Jewish Community, had offered me a job in Cejwin Camp, a Jewish Leadership Training

Camp in upstate New York. I'd be the music counselor and stay there for a month. When he told me about the job, I was elated. But now doubts gnawed at me.

"Yes," I chewed on my lower lip, "but how will I manage? The camp is for teenagers. What will I do with Tal when I have to work?"

"I'm sure there'll be other young kids, children of the camp staff, and—"

"But where will we sleep? I won't have my own cabin."

With my big belly I needed to get up and urinate several times at night. I didn't know whether I'd have to use a communal bathroom.

"Look, we have to give Hy an answer. You can ask all these questions when you talk with him." I could hear the irritation in Steve's voice.

I had a heavy feeling in my chest. "I know, but how will the campers take to a highly pregnant counselor?" That was my real concern.

"Okay," Steve said, throwing up his hands in frustration. "What do you want to do, stay here in the hot city all summer? There's a lake there, trees, you'll have company."

Actually, he was right; I felt at home in nature and loved the outdoors. Queens, with its apartment buildings, pavement, and seven-lane road, turned into a stifling, airless place in the summer. I wondered why I was protesting; maybe, as a prospective mother of two, I worried more and tended to be protective of my son and my unborn child.

The fact that I'd be away at camp while I was seven months pregnant didn't seem to worry Steve. His attitude toward me was always that I was a tough Israeli and could handle anything. I guess that was the impression I gave; I had learned early on to appear strong and hide my fears and vulnerability. My parents, after all, had little time or patience for me. Complaining or crying wouldn't get me anywhere with *abba*. When we immigrated to Israel, we were a family of five, and life didn't become any easier. By the time I married Steve, I had perfected my facade.

Steve continued. "You and Tal will be taken care off." He looked me in the eye. "I won't have to worry about you while I'm away on location."

All of a sudden it dawned on me. He wanted me to take the job so he'd have peace of mind while he worked. If that's the case, I thought, I'll take the job. This fit a pattern I knew well—of my mother always being there for my father. Besides, it would be nice to escape from the routine and be on my own for a while.

I shrugged my shoulders. "Okay, I guess you're right, I'll call Hy tomorrow." I tilted my head. "Will you come to visit us?"

"Of course, I'll come up on the weekends." He paused. "I'll be there as long as I don't have to work."

Here we go, I thought. It was clear that his job came before me, his son, or his family life. Yet I realized that he was providing for us and he took that task seriously. I couldn't have known at the time just how driven he was, or how important it was for him to succeed in the film business. All of that would come later. For now I knew he worked hard but tried to be there for his little family as much as possible. Deep in my heart, I hoped his wish to become a film director would materialize, for both of our sakes.

On a bright summer day in July, I stepped out of our car onto the dirt parking lot at the entrance to camp. I inhaled as deeply as my belly would allow me. It was hot, but the air was dry and scented with pine needles. I took another breath. The smell of pine transported me back to Mt. Carmel in Haifa, where as a soldier I used to visit my relatives Hanna and Zigi. I loved their two-story house surrounded by tall pine trees, from which I collected large cones and savored their sweet, white-fleshed nuts.

Tal, cheeks flushed from the three-hour car ride from New York, pulled at my hand. "Come, *eema*, let's go." Like any four-year-old, he had a hard time sitting still.

"Sure, Tali." I caressed his hair. "I bet you're anxious to see our new home." I grabbed my bag from the trunk, took Tal's hand, and started to walk toward a wooden building with a sign that read, *Office.*

Steve followed us, lugging my old brown suitcase, in which I had packed Tal's and my belongings. Suddenly I heard a melodious bird call. "Look, Tal," I pointed to a small bird with an orange breast, "it's a robin. We don't get to see them at home." It was such a relief to be away from the roar of car engines, wails of sirens, grinding of buses, and shrieks of subways. I felt in my element, revived, like a wilted flower opening its petals after a light rain. I was glad Steve encouraged me to take the job.

When Steve caught up with us, I smiled at him, spreading my arm as if to encompass all the trees around us. "Isn't it great here?"

"Yes," he smiled back wearily, "but we better get going. I have to get you two settled in." He stopped to wipe perspiration from his brow. "I have to go back to the city tonight, remember?" I had forgotten it was Sunday and he had to work the next day. I didn't mind him going back to work, though, and I liked the idea of spending time in camp without any of the responsibilities of home: cooking, shopping, cleaning, ironing.

Camp would turn out to be wonderful. Hy got me my own cabin, a room with an attached bathroom and shower, so Tal could stay with me. I liked the room even though it didn't contain much: two narrow bunk beds, a cupboard for clothes, and a couple of chairs. Two windows covered with checkered curtains provided plenty of air. On the first day, looking at the barren wooden walls, I took an old calendar out of my suitcase. I had put it in there in case I wanted to decorate my room. I tore out its pages and taped them to the walls. Soon I was surrounded by snowy mountains, falling waterfalls, and picturesque villages. Feeling proud of my creation, I hugged Tal, exclaiming: "How do you like our new home?"

He looked around the room. "*Yofi, eema.* Can I go out now and play?"

"Of course you can; just be careful."

As I opened the door, a burst of sunshine illuminated the room. I laughed out loud in wonder, joy, and gratitude. In New York, I could never let Tal go outside on his own. I couldn't get up and breathe fresh air, or walk out the door and gaze at blue skies peering through green, leafy treetops. I hummed a tune—one of the songs I sang in my army troupe—while I put our clothes away. I had my own cabin, which I could decorate any way I wished and do whatever I wanted in!

It took me a while to fall asleep that night. My belly felt heavy, and it was difficult to find a comfortable position on the thin, narrow mattress. Luckily, Tal was sound asleep in his bed on the other side of the room. My thoughts turned to the songs I was going to teach and how I'd present them. Exhausted, however, I finally fell into a deep sleep. The sound of songs broadcast on the camp loudspeaker woke me up at 7 a.m.

"Come, Tali." I kissed my sleeping kid's warm cheek. "It's time to go to your play group." After depositing Tal with a counselor who supervised other staff children, I walked along the path to the dining hall. I enjoyed the fresh air, greenery, and absence of cars, but more than anything I had a strong sense of freedom, of being on my own. On the path, groups of campers, in twos and threes, passed by chatting and laughing. I wondered how I'd feel standing in front of them teaching Hebrew songs. Everybody was headed toward a large rectangular building, where I assumed breakfast was served. Entering the dining hall, I heard a din of voices as if I had landed under a tree full of squawking rooks. Campers and counselors sat at wooden tables, wolfing down pancakes and cold cereal. I found a seat next to a tanned, dark-haired woman.

I extended my hand. "Hi, I'm Esther, the music counselor."

"Nice to meet you. I'm the arts-and-crafts counselor, Hanna." She told me about the other specialty counselors: the drama counselor Roni, and Mike, the sports counselor.

"How do you like the camp?" I said.

"It's okay, kind of fun. The food isn't great."

But for me, the food was delicious, and I ate with gusto everything on the table. Being in the outdoors and having to feed the little one within me gave me a ravenous appetite.

I was ready to leave so I'd have enough time to prepare for my first group of campers when the head counselor called out, "*Birkat Hamazon!*" A hush fell for a second and then everybody began to sing the blessing over the food, emphasizing the lively rhythm by pounding on the tables. As I tried to pick up the melody, Hanna handed me a laminated page with the blessing printed in Hebrew and English. That's when I recalled Hy's description of Cejwin: "It's a conservative camp where the kitchen is kosher, Shabbat is observed, and blessings are sung after the meals." My study of the pink book, *Pearls of Religion*, which covered the rules and customs of Judaism, was coming alive. I chuckled at the irony of me singing the prayers. I didn't really get into it; it seemed as if I were playacting. In Israel I never said blessings before or after meals. I was a secular Jew with no religious background. The whole scene felt a bit weird.

The moment the blessings ended, everybody scrambled out of the hall. Walking back to my cabin, I passed the basketball court. A tall guy, in his early twenties, in a T-shirt, shorts, and sneakers, was aiming balls into a hoop. Turning around, he noticed me watching. Dribbling the ball he approached me, a wide smile on his face.

"Hi! Did you just arrive? I'm Mike Yoeli."

Yoeli, an Israeli name! Yet his accent was that of a New Yorker.

"Yes, I just got here yesterday." I couldn't resist the question. "Are you from Israel?"

The laughter lines near his eyes deepened. He threw the ball in the air and then twirled it on his finger. His light-blue eyes radiated kindness and compassion; he seemed amused at my question. He must have read the eagerness in my face. "My father is Israeli; I came here when I was two years old."

"Do you speak Hebrew?"

With his pointer above his thumb, he made the sign for "a little" and said, "*Ktsat*."

I stepped closer to him, beaming, and stuck out my hand. His handshake felt warm and reassuring. "*Yofi*! Great! I'm Esther, the music counselor." My nationality was such an essential part of my identity that I blurted, "I'm from Israel. Is this your first year in camp?"

"No, I've been here forever as a camper. My father's the camp doctor."

"That's great!" There was so much I wanted to ask him—about camp, about his father—but looking at my watch I realized I had to return to my cabin, pick up my guitar, and go to the first session. Also, I felt like I'd burst if I didn't get to the bathroom, since the baby was pressing on my bladder. "I've got to go; I'll see you around."


In spite of my trepidations, the first singing session with the teenagers went well. After it was over, I went to check on Tal. Even though I was aware of my belly, my step was light as I walked along the path, looking up at the tops of tall pine trees where shafts of sunshine filtered through the branches, creating a mesmerizing pattern of light and shade. I took deep breaths of tangy air, smiling, thankful for my beautiful son, the little one inside me, my ability to create and share music, the sense of freedom I had. Anything to do with Queens Boulevard, Gerard Towers, the apartment, or the supermarket, was far from my mind. I was grateful to Steve for encouraging me to go to camp. I didn't miss him. He belonged to another world, one in which I functioned only as a wife, mother, and housekeeper. In camp I was a person in my own right; campers and staff alike appreciated me for my contribution to their cultural life. I felt a sense of self; I wasn't just somebody else's appendix. Besides preparing for and teaching music sessions, I could do whatever I liked: rest, read, go for a walk, swim in the lake, play with Tal, or chat with new friends. For one glorious month, I didn't have to shop, cook, clean, or do laundry or any other household chore. I felt alive and free.

Approaching Tal's day care, I walked faster; I couldn't wait to see my little boy. Then I spotted him, standing near the building, shoulders rounded, a blue yarmulke on his head, teddy bear dangling from his hand. He looked dejected. I called out, "Hi, Tali, I'm here!"

He ran toward me. Flinging his arms around my legs, burying his head in my belly, he half sobbed, half groaned. "*Eema, eema*, I was waiting for you."

Bending down, I stroked his hair and kissed him. I pointed at his teddy. "How is Doobie feeling?"

Tal hugged Doobie and looked at me seriously: "He's not feeling well."

"I'll fix him." I held Doobie's snout and kissed it lightly. "Here, he's all better."

Hand in hand we walked into the activity room. I released his hand and gave him a little tap on his back. "Here, run along to your friends." But he grabbed my hand. His large, sad eyes made my stomach quiver.

"*Eema*, do you have to go? Can't you stay here a bit?"

"Okay, but just a short time." I walked over to the art table and started drawing a flower. I handed Tal a red crayon. "Here, Tali, can you draw something?"

While he started drawing with me looking on, the counselor came over and put her arm around Tal's shoulder. "You're doing a great job." Smiling at me, she nodded toward the door. I kissed Tal on his cheek and tiptoed away, hoping he wouldn't call me back.

In the afternoon, Tal and I read books, played games, and rested in our cabin. Then Tal went back to his group while I taught two more groups. At dinner all the specialist counselors sat together.

I was glad to see some familiar faces: opposite me sat Hanna, the arts-and-crafts counselor, and Mike Yoeli, in a fresh white T-shirt. A long-haired blonde, buxom young woman in a tight-fitting top sporting generous cleavage sat near Mike, laughing out loud and cracking jokes. Mike, who noticed me staring at her, introduced us. "This is Roni, the drama counselor." I waved and said it was a pleasure meeting her. Yet a strange feeling overcame me. Roni seemed so outgoing and sure of herself, and she was flirting with Mike. Here I was, seven months pregnant and jealous of another woman! But it was more than that: I was older than the other counselors and had a family and responsibilities, whereas Roni was single and carefree. I felt relieved when Mike asked me about my day and how classes went.

At one point I saw him looking around the table, holding a piece of toast. I picked up the butter dish and handed it to him. "Here, were you looking for this?"

"Yes, how did you know?"

I felt my cheeks flush. "I just guessed."

He smiled broadly, as if I had uttered the most beautiful words. "You know," his voice rose so that the other counselors turned to him. "When I marry, I'd like it to be to a woman like Esther who knows my inner thoughts."

Everybody laughed, including me. I felt acknowledged and valued. A warm feeling coursed through me as if I had bathed in bright sunlight. It could have been the attention I'd received, or maybe the hormones in my body. Or maybe it was the effect of being in nature, connecting with the growth around me—the trees, plants, and young people who joked and laughed. Back in Queens, I rarely had adult companionship. I spent most of my time alone or with Tal. I'd see Steve in the evenings and on weekends, and even then he was often busy with his film projects.

The next day after lunch, Tal and I walked down the path to the lake. It was warm and still outside. Nothing seemed to move. Suddenly a low, husky voice called out: "Hey, Esther, where you going?"

It was Mike. I turned around. "We're going to take a dip in the lake. It'll be nice and cool."

Mike pointed at Tal. "Is this your little boy?"

I preened like a mother hen. "Yes, this is Tal!"

Mike bent down, one knee on the ground so he came face-to-face with my son. "How old are you?"

Tal looked at Mike keenly, trying to figure out who that stranger was. He then turned to me, his eyes wide. But Mike, with a grin, spread his hand and lifted five fingers. "Are you five years old?"

Tal shook his head.

"Three?"

Giggling, Tal protested, "No, no."

Mike lifted four fingers. "Four?" Tal nodded while raising four of his little fingers opposite Mike's large hand. Mike then tousled Tal's hair. "Good. You're a big boy!"

My heart swelled with gratitude for Mike, for making Tal feel included and important.

"Tal, this is my friend Mike," I said. "He also works here in camp. He teaches sports. It's lots of fun."

We walked together contentedly. With his long legs, Mike had to make an effort to slow down and keep pace with our ambling along. Perhaps because Mike and I were talking animatedly, Tal began lagging behind. Mike turned around and, spreading his arms, called out, "Hey, Tal, do you want a piggy-back ride?" Before I had time to say anything, Mike lifted Tal up and strode down the path with my kid bouncing on his back. I wondered if Tal was scared, but he didn't even look at me. Before long, Mike stopped and hoisted Tal on his shoulders. He then started to gallop like a horse, calling out, "Giddy up, giddy up." Tal, hair flying, clasped Mike's forehead while his laughter rang in the air.

Watching the two of them, I was deeply touched. Silently I thanked Mike for the gift of warmth, a sense of security, compassion, and caring. However, I also felt a little sad. Steve rarely romped around with his son like this. I knew he loved Tal very much, but he was also often away, busy with work.

After a while, Mike deposited Tal on the ground. Looking up at his new buddy Tal, raising his arms, called out, "Again, again."

Drops of perspiration glistened on Mike's face and trickled down his wispy, blond beard. Lifting a corner of his undershirt, he wiped his forehead. "Don't worry, Tal, we'll play more tomorrow. I've got to go now." He waved at us, turned around, and jogged toward the cabins.

I took my son's hand. "Come, Tali, let's go swimming."


The days passed quickly. When the Sabbath arrived, the atmosphere in camp changed. A hush fell on everything: the cabins, paths, basketball court, dining room. I gave no music class. Campers and counselors dressed in white walked leisurely along the paths or sat in discussion groups on the lawn near the pine trees. The tone of the speakers was festive and subdued. You could feel the Sabbath descending, enveloping us all as the trees turned to silhouettes and the sky darkened.

One Sabbath, Steve and his parents came to see us. I had blocked thoughts of their arrival out of my mind. When Shabbat morning came, I prayed they wouldn't destroy the sense of calm I was feeling, that Steve wouldn't argue with his mother, and that Gussie wouldn't put Milton down. I wished they'd relax and enjoy being in nature, though I knew better. They were city people, and camp wasn't the most comfortable place to be in. Tal, though, looked forward to seeing his father and grandparents. He was so excited he couldn't fall asleep the night before, and he woke up on Saturday with the first chirping of the birds.

Midmorning, Milton pulled his large black Impala into the packed-earth parking lot near the dining room. We were walking along the path when I spotted them. I pointed to the car. "There they are, Tali." He let go of my hand and ran toward them, waving.

"Hi *abba*, hi grandma, hi grandpa!" he called out. He leaped into Steve's arms and leaned his head on his shoulder. Steve, handsome in new white sneakers, pressed jeans, and blue polo shirt, held Tal tight and kissed his head. Gussie and Milton, in turn, hugged Tal and planted a smooch on his cheek. Steve took out a white handkerchief and wiped the lipstick, a residue of his mother's affection, off Tal's face. Holding his son at arm's length, he looked at him with admiration. "My, my, camp food must be good, you've grown in one week!"

He turned to me. "And you, Esther." he wrapped his arms around my back, pressing me toward him, as much as my belly would allow. I guess being away from me made him more affectionate. I hoped he'd missed me. It was good to feel his body and smell. I had almost forgotten what it was like. "How are you?" he said.

I hesitated. I didn't want to admit how happy I was on my own. I wondered whether Steve would interpret my sentiments as me not caring for him, or managing better without him. I cherished the freedom to make my own decisions, to figure out what I really wanted, to listen to myself. At home I had obligations, duties, and Steve's expectations, or whatever I thought his expectations might be.

"I'm okay," I said, rubbing my belly. "It's getting a bit difficult to sit for a long time."

He pointed at my middle. "How is the baby doing?"

I smiled. "She's hearing a lot of singing."

In the meantime, Milton took a wrapped box out of the car, and Gussie presented it to Tal. "Look what we have for you. Here, open it." Tal tore the colorful wrapping paper and exclaimed when he saw the large red dump truck. He started pushing the truck around, then stopped and started to load the back with dirt.

Steve, adding a few stones to the truck, patted his son's back. "What do you say?"

"Thank you," Tal blurted, pouring dirt all over his pants.

Watching them, I smiled, inhaling deeply. I felt lightness, a gaiety within me. Tal was happy. Gussie and Milton loved their only grandson. But I also felt sad, missing my mother. When I took Tal the previous summer back to Israel, they'd had such a good time together; my mom, barefoot, in shorts and tank top, tumbled with Tal on the lawn, played paddle ball, rolled marbles, and stuck plastic pegs in a tic-tac-toe frame. My mother had grown up in an orphanage. With Tal, she became the child she never had a chance to be.

Gussie tapped me on the shoulder. "Isn't it time for lunch?" Gussie loved eating, especially Danish pastries, cookies, and ice cream. I'd suspected it was a substitute for many of the things she felt were missing in her life: money, success, and affection.

"Sure," I chuckled. "The four-star restaurant is open."

Steve touched his mother's arm, holding her back. "Wait a minute; let me give Tali his present."

He ran to the car and came back holding what looked like a broomstick, attached to a large bulging top wrapped in tissue paper. Tal's eyes widened as Steve undid the string tied around the top. A wooden head appeared with leather ears, a felt mane, and blue dangling reins. I clapped my hands. "A toy horse; isn't that great?" I was picturing Tal riding on Mike Yoeli's shoulders, laughing while Mike bounced along. Tal mounted the pole, one short leg on each side, and started galloping around and calling out, "Giddy up, giddy up." Steve stood near Tal, cheering his son on. Putting my arm on his sleeve, I smiled, though I would have preferred to see Tal riding on his father's shoulders.

I turned to Gussie. "Come; let's go to the dining hall." Suddenly I smelled the smoke from Milton's cigar. Oh, no, I thought, not here, in the midst of nature. Milton approached us, beaming, a large stogie stuck between his teeth. With his tightly pressed pants and sports jacket over his protruding belly, he could have belonged to Don Cor-leone's family. And yet Milton was the one I felt close to; whenever he saw me he'd give me a hug and ask me, "How are you, Esterka?" The present he had given me, a beautiful new guitar, was something I cherished more than any other gift I'd received in my life. At times I wished my father had some of Milton's warmth and generosity.

Gussie, in a flowered dress, panty hose, and pumps, looked the perfect match for Milton, but both were entirely out of place in camp.

Tal was pulling my wrist, trying to get my attention. "*Eema*, can I take horsy to the dining room?"

"Sure, you can give him a carrot."

Tal laughed. "No, I can't, he's not a real horse," he said, and he trotted off.

In the dining room we sat at the table with the rest of the staff. I introduced Steve and his parents to Mike Yoeli. He put down his fork and, grinning, shook Steve's hand.

"You have a great wife and kid."

"Thanks. How are they doing here in camp?"

"Wonderful! Esther gets the campers to sing all these beautiful Hebrew songs, and everybody loves your little son." He winked at Tal. "Am I right?" Tal, not sure how to respond, turned his head from Mike to Steve and frowned.

I wondered what Steve thought of Mike, whether he felt any jealousy, since it was obvious he'd spent time with us. Was he envi-ous of Mike's tanned arms and legs, blond unruly hair, and beard? Could he be jealous of the compliments Mike gave me or of my obvious attraction?

I recalled the summer of 1967, when I visited my parents when Tal was nine months old. Steve had planned to join us once he wrapped up his work on his current film set. In order to save money, he decided to travel on a cargo ship that was coursed to sail around Cape Horn. It took him two months to get to Israel. By the time he arrived, we had celebrated Tal's first birthday and Tal had started walking. Steve was devastated he hadn't witnessed his son's first steps. Since my parents' home was too small to accommodate us, we rented a little house not far from the sea. I had been looking forward to Steve's visit, wanting to show him how much Tal had grown and proud of the tan I had acquired. Yet on the second day of his arrival in the afternoon, he confronted me.

"Did you go out with somebody else while I was away?"

Shocked, I looked up to see if he was serious. I couldn't believe the question he was posing. I was married to him, loved him, and had his child. How could he think that way?

"Of course not," I swallowed. "Why would you ask that?"

"You seem remote, not caring."

I raised my voice. "But how can you ask such a question? It's insulting!"

"Well, I have the right to ask!" he yelled back.

I suppressed my tears. "No, you don't! You don't trust me. I've been alone with Tal for three months, waiting for you!"

"I had to work, to support you and the baby!"

I banged my fist on the table. "I wish I hadn't married you!"

Through my tears, I made my way to the unmade bed and flopped on the corner. The blood of my period had stained the sheet when Steve had tried to make love to me. Cupping my head in my hands, I sobbed. Steve stood above me, his face a pale mask.

"I don't fucking need this," he said, and he strode out of the house.

Back at the dining table at camp, Mike Yoeli's voice filtered through my thoughts. "So, what movies have you worked on?"

Steve smiled proudly. "*John and Mary*, with Mia Farrow and Dustin Hoffman, and now I've just finished working on a movie called *Love Story*."

"Wow! That's impressive. Who are the actors?"

"Ali MacGraw and Ryan O'Neal."

I felt a flush of pride when Steve said those names. I would have liked to be invited to the set once to see Steve in action, but Steve always kept his home life and work life separate. I wondered whether he tried to protect me from the "craziness of the film world," as he called it, or made sure he wouldn't be bothered by us during work. In any case, it wouldn't have been easy with a young child, and I didn't insist on it.

Gussie and Milton did enjoy the camp food: fish, potatoes, and salad. They both had seconds and then sat, a bit overwhelmed, while the campers belted out the blessing over the meal. We bade Mike Yoeli bye-bye, and, after a short stroll to the lake, Tal and I accompanied Steve, Gussie, and Milton to their car. I was happy that Steve got along with Mike but, more than that, relieved that the visit was over without any outbursts or arguments.

That evening, at dinnertime, I asked Mike what he thought about Steve.

Mike thought for a moment. "He seems like a real nice guy."

"In which way?"

"He has a nice way about him . . . a kind of aura that he conveys."

I was flattered but at the same time felt myself hardening, refusing to believe what I heard. "Really?" I blurted.

"Yes, he's charming." Mike raised his hand, palm outstretched as if trying to explain what he meant. "He seems kind of an easygoing, laid-back person."

"Wow! Thanks, Mike."

I'd seen before how people were drawn to Steve, and I knew he was charming too, but it was nice to have it confirmed by Mike. In company, Steve was soft-spoken, kind, and witty. Only with his family, with those close to him, did he let his demons run free. Sighing, I wistfully wished Steve were more considerate and charming at home as well.

After a month, camp was coming to an end. My belly had grown and I walked more slowly, but while I taught singing, I was completely absorbed in the music. *The little one within me will probably love singing*, I thought.

On the last day, Mike asked me, "So, what will you do after camp?"

I pointed at my belly. "I'll give birth, I suppose, in England."

His eyebrows shot up. "What?!"

"Yes, we're moving to London."

"How come?"

"Steve wants to try and work there, in film."

"I'll come and visit you."

I knew he meant it, and I was grateful to him. "I'd love it."

The next morning, I woke up to the sound of a familiar song coming from the camp loudspeakers: "All my bags are packed; I'm ready to go . . ." Looking at my sleeping son, at my suitcase in the corner, salty tears trickled down my throat. Caressing my big belly, I let out a heavy sigh, both of sadness and joy. I was sad to leave Cejwin, where I enjoyed being in nature, had my independence, sang with the campers, and spent time with Tal. Yet I looked forward to being with Steve, too, and having our family united. I was glad we were getting out of New York and moving to England, the country of my birth. With some trepidation I thought about giving birth in a new place, with no family around, but I smiled at the thought of my newfound friendship with Mike Yoeli. I knew he'd be a friend for life.

I walked over to Tal's bed and stroked his hair. "Come on, Tali, wake up. We're going home."

He stretched his arms and bolted up. "Yay! I'll get to see *abba*. When are we leaving?"

"As soon as we eat breakfast and pack our things."

After he dressed, we made our way to the dining room. Walking along, feeling my son's soft hand in mine, I lifted my face to the gentle morning sun, listened to the chirping of a robin, and inhaled the scent of pines. I thought of the new life within me, my hardworking mate, and my beautiful young son. Silently I thanked the universe for what it gave me.

*❧ Chapter 11: ❧*

# Shira

After my return from Cejwin camp, arrangements to move to London were already in the works. Steve's frustration at work had reached a boiling point as his dream of becoming a film director seemed to fall farther and farther away. It was August 1971, and we had lived for five years in Forest Hills. It looked like overseas might be the solution to Steve's problems. He could try his luck directing there. And I was desperate to get out of New York, so I was ready to go along with the plan, despite how heavily pregnant I was.

My chest expanded with sheer joy at the thought of leaving. And going back to England, too, the country of my birth.

"But can you work there?" I'd asked when he first proposed the plan.

"Why not?" he grinned. "I'm married to a British citizen, right?"

"Sure, but . . . won't there be a problem flying?" I rubbed my belly to prove my point.

"You'll be fine," he said, meaning I would rise to the occasion. His grin widened. "And if the airline gives us a hard time, I'll sign a release form."

It didn't occur to me to question him on this. We both were adventurous, though Steve was the one who initiated the moves, whereas I usually went along with his plans. This time, however, I was excited about the prospect of leaving New York and didn't mind Steve's doing things on a whim.

Right away I quit my part-time job teaching Hebrew at the JCC. We packed our kitchen appliances, pictures, books, and furniture for shipping, and we took off. After an uneventful flight, we landed in Heathrow, from where we took a bus to Hampstead, located in northwest London in the district of Camden. Steve had arranged with Greg, an American photographer friend (who, to my surprise, had a stash of marijuana in his closet), to stay at his house until we found our own place. Steve, Tal, and I shared a bedroom on the second floor, so I was glad when, a month later, Steve managed to rent an apartment in Heathcroft, part of Hampstead Court, not far from Greg's house.

I felt at home in our little red-brick ground-floor apartment that faced a circular rose garden enclosed by a low stone wall. Some unseen hand had guided me back to England, the country where I had spent the first eight years of my life. My senses reawakened, triggering memories of that time.

My nose quivered at familiar scents—sage, honeysuckle, and primroses; my taste buds rediscovered the sweetness of childhood—porridge with treacle and butter, raspberry-red Ribena, pungent Marmite, and crumpets with jam.

I was close to my due date when Steve, Tal, and I went for one of our weekend strolls. We arrived at the Heath, a vast expanse of green common land dotted with flowerbeds, not far from our home. Steve walked ahead with Tal, who was delighted at the sight of golden butterflies fluttering among stately, purple hollyhocks. I waddled behind them, belly bursting at the seams, ripe as the juicy, end-of-the-summer Mediterranean watermelons back home.

We walked through an archway covered with white roses.

Inhaling their fragrance, I marveled at the lawn area, where a group of English matrons played croquet. Dressed in midcalf gray and blue skirts, sturdy shoes, bonnets, and visors, they batted with swift, accurate shots, saying, "Go ahead, love," to each other. Their British accents titillated my ear; no matter what you say in Queen's English, even "I have to go to the loo," sounds dignified.

"*Eema*, where are you?" rang out Tal's boyish soprano. "Come see!"

I was too slow. Face flushed, hair flying, he ran toward me and grabbed my hand, pressing his little sweaty palm against mine. He pointed to a small balsa-wood glider in Steve's hand.

"We're having fun," Steve said, looking boyish as he tossed the glider into the air. His blue denim hugged his hips below his shirtless, tanned torso.

He was a different man, not the harried, tense New Yorker, the driven, overworked filmmaker who'd sit for hours in front of a large corkboard moving colored pins, coordinating the huge machinery of film production like a general planning a military operation. Back in New York, millions of dollars were at stake, but so were my husband's nerves and health. He'd often come home from a shoot during which he'd scarcely slept for weeks, his face pale, eyes bleary, and nerves on edge.

When it came to his work back in New York, nothing was negotiable between us, not even the use of our single bathroom, which he used as a darkroom. One hot, humid Saturday afternoon, I returned to our apartment pushing Tal in the stroller while holding on to O'Hara (before we had to find him another home). Sticky and perspiring, I rushed to the bathroom, only to find it locked, the doorframe covered by black duct tape.

"I need to go!" I called out.

"I'll be done soon," came Steve's muffled voice. "I have to develop these stills."

Now Queens was far away. Steve was more relaxed, more caring. As I watched my husband and son fly the glider, my belly suddenly felt heavier, the force of gravity stronger than usual. I inhaled deeply, uttering a sigh. Steve ran toward me, his forehead furrowed.

"Are you okay?" He took my arm. "Let's rent an armchair for you."

I leaned on him as we walked to the rental kiosk at the far end of the Heath. Tal and Steve took off running, chasing each other, while I sank into the chair. The air was warm and balmy, a special treat for British Isles dwellers. In the distance I watched a man walking his Irish setter. All of a sudden, I was jolted by a stab of pain. Everything blurred. Then a few seconds later, the shrubs, flowers, and the man with the dog came back into focus.

"Steve!" I shouted. I motioned downward. "It's the baby."

In an instant he was by my side.

Sliding one hand behind my back, he held my arm with the other. "We need to go to the hospital," he said. I resisted. "Not yet." The bright colors of the flowers framed by lush green and the corn-flower-blue sky were so beautiful I didn't want to leave.

But Steve didn't let go of my arm. He tried to keep his voice down, but I saw the pleading in his eyes. "We have to go. Now!"

"But we just got the chair!" I didn't believe I was about to have the baby.

Steve pursed his lips. "Do you want to give birth here?" He prodded me to stand. "You almost gave birth to Tal in the taxi, remember?"

I relented and let him lead me to the car. I wondered why I needed Steve to prod me, why I didn't listen to myself and decide on my own that it was time to go to the hospital. Had I handed over the decision-making to Steve even when it concerned my own body? I had nobody else to consult with—my mother and sister weren't around; it was just Steve and me. So I became dependent on him and let him call the shots.


I held my belly while Steve drove fast, arriving at Kings Hospital in half an hour. The sun was pouring in through the windows in the reception room. The curtains fluttered in the breeze. A cheerful receptionist with a ruddy complexion and cropped brown hair welcomed us.

"How are you, love?"

"She's ready," Steve said, his face pale. He squeezed my hand and then turned to Tal, who was watching us wide-eyed, the glider still clutched in his fist.

Steve laid his hand on his son's shoulder. "Come, we'll be back once *eema* has a baby brother or sister for you." Tal waved as they left hand in hand. Tears welled up in my eyes while I was rolled into the corridor.

Moments later I was on the examining table, legs spread apart. A nurse's bright voice reverberated above me. "She's fully dilated—puncture the water sack." Two hours later, at a quarter past 3:00 p.m. on September 12, 1971, my daughter slipped into the world. Her blue eyes, set in a pear-shaped face, smiled at me. I caressed the plumage of soft blond hair. I recalled Cejwin camp, where I sang for hours with the campers, the curves of my guitar matching those of my rounded belly, while she lay underneath my ribcage, absorbing the vibrations of the guitar, the strains of the melodies trickling through my skin, flesh, and veins to her ears—into her tiny being. That's when the name Shira, "singing" in Hebrew, came to me.

I was in the maternity ward with seven other women, the large room bustling with visitors who arrived with bouquets to greet the new mothers. An array of languages filled the hall—Urdu, Hindi, Arabic, and English—the tenants of the British Empire all here producing the next diverse British generation. I tried to detect sounds of Hebrew—after all, the British ruled over Palestine for many years—but could not. It would have been comforting for me right then.

I felt at peace though, with my baby sleeping on my chest, breathing gently. After a short while, with the exertion of having given birth, I closed my eyes. In what seemed like minutes later, I heard a soft voice. "Here, love, give me the baby. I'll take her to the baby ward so you can get some rest." I barely opened my eyes while the nurse picked up Shira gently and carried her away.

After a restless night, sounds of steps and chattering woke me up. I was groggy—it was five o'clock in the morning and the lights were glaring.

"Good morning, love." A white-capped nurse drew aside the partition while balancing a small tray in her left hand. "Here's a nice hot cup o' tea for the young mother." My crotch burned and my abdomen muscles ached when I turned over on my side. I sipped the sweet, milk-laced tea, savoring its warmth on my throat.

I remembered my father's exclamation as he imbibed his tea: "Mm . . . ah." What were my parents doing? I wondered. When would my mother see her granddaughter? Every summer during the New York years, I returned to Ashkelon to see my parents. My parents could never have afforded to visit us. My mother would play with Tal for hours, lying on the lawn, holding him like an airplane with her feet and arms in the air supporting his body. They'd both scream with delight.

In the year Shira was born, due to being highly pregnant, I hadn't gone in the summer to Israel. I was daydreaming about the following summer when I could take Tal and Shira to spend time with my parents.

"You may get up now." The nurse, smelling of stephanotis toilet water, with a small silver cross dangling from her neck, helped me gently off the pillows. In the bathroom I removed the sanitary pad and uttered a cry when the brownish-red blood gushed out of me. Gingerly I stepped into the bathtub, turned on the shower faucet, and let the warm water stream down my back. The blood washed down. The water cleansed and purified me. I felt lighter. Whenever I immersed myself in water—the sea, a pool, lake, or river—I was in my element. My body and mind relaxed, and my breathing became deeper, fuller.

Back in bed, on fresh linens, I devoured a breakfast of scrambled eggs, toast, marmalade, and coffee.

"Good morning, I'm Jenny." A young, dimpled-cheeked nurse with auburn hair stood beaming at me, my baby in her arms. "I've got something for you," she said. I pressed my newborn to my chest, throat constricting as I inhaled the scent of baby talcum and rose petals.

"You may nurse her," Jenny said.

I released my breast from the flannel nightgown, held the nipple between forefinger and middle finger, and brought it toward my baby's miniature lips. I could feel my uterus contracting while the blood thumped in my engorged breast. Shira stretched her neck like a little gosling while we both engaged in a struggle to adjust her tiny mouth around my pink nipple.

"It's all right." Jenny patted my arm gently. "We're feeding her sugar-water in the meantime."

I recalled it took me a while to adjust to breastfeeding Tal, so I wasn't worried about Shira. Having a second baby was much easier; I knew what to expect.

Exhausted, I lay back, closing my eyes while Jenny tucked Shira into a bassinette next to my bed.

I woke to a familiar voice saying, "Hello, sweetie." It was Steve. When he hugged me, I took in the scents of Old Spice and perspiration.

He peeked at Shira sleeping peacefully in her bassinette. "How is my little daughter doing?"

My heart swelled with pride. "Great! She's nursing, sleeping—a perfect baby. We're so lucky."

"Do you have a name for her?"

I knew by then that Steve realized how important it was for me to give my children Israeli names. I felt grateful for that.

"Yes," I smiled at him. "Her name is Shira, singing."

"Shira," Steve sounded out the name. "It sounds nice."

I held Steve's hand while he sat next to me on the bed. I missed my little boy and was sure he missed me. "How is Tal doing?"

"He's fine; I left him with the babysitter."

A muffled cry, like a cat's meow, came from the bassinette. Steve's eyes widened when the cry turned to a loud whine.

"It's the baby," I said. "Can you pick her up?"

Steve lifted the little bundle and, cradling Shira in his arms, pressed her close to his chest. Tears welled up in my eyes. He rocked her gently until she closed her eyes and then handed her to me.

"How are you managing?" I asked, eyeing the dark circles around his eyes.

"You know, there's a lot to take care off." He wiped his brow. "I'm also trying to get my work done."

I lowered my eyes to the sleeping baby in my arms. She was all that mattered to me at the moment. I wished I could be there for Steve, but he'd have to wait. When I looked up, I saw to my amazement Steve stand up, take off one shoe, then the other, and toss them aside.

With a jerk of his wrist, he yanked the curtain around the railing, and with a loud "aah," he plopped next to me on top of the blanket. He folded his arms on his chest, crossed his ankles, and after a few moments his jaw slackened while uttering a soft snore. I now had two babies at my side, a tiny one and a very big one. I was half-irritated, half-amused by Steve's ability to ignore hospital rules and act with such abandonment. I admired his capability to act according to his needs, so different from the way I functioned.

A hand slid the curtain slightly, and a blonde, round-faced nurse peeked through. I tried to catch her eye, but her gaze was fixed on my sleeping husband. Her eyes crinkled in amusement as she closed the partition and walked away.

I woke up the next morning, and my lower body parts were sore, my stomach soft and pudgy. I assembled a few pillows so I could sink my fleshy belly into the center as I lay facedown, hugging my head-pillow. Somewhere I had read that lying on the tummy after delivery helps to flatten it, to restore it to its original form. I recalled Steve's words a couple of months after I'd delivered Tal: "You better start dieting and get back into shape." I was shocked but not indignant; that would come much later. At the time I just nodded and started limiting fattening food—even though, as a nursing mother, I had a robust appetite.

Two months later, Steve administered the "pencil test."

"Here." He handed me a plain yellow pencil. "Put that under your right breast."

I raised my eyebrows but acquiesced.

"Now," my husband said, eying my naked bosom, "stand straight and keep your arms at your side."

"What's all this about?" I asked, but I obeyed. As I pulled back my shoulders, my chest rose, yet the pencil remained tucked between my breast and ribcage. I shivered with cold. It was winter and freezing.

"You don't pass the test," he said, seeming triumphant. With a cupped palm, he lifted up my breast, and the pencil fell to the floor with a thud.

I put my shirt back on, my muscles tense. What the hell was that all about? Was it some stupid game, or did Steve want to prove something? After nursing *his* baby he expected me to have perky, virginal breasts. I wished I had objected, but I always seemed to do what he told me to do; it didn't dawn on me to say no, to refuse to do something I didn't feel comfortable doing. He was my husband, and I grew up seeing *eema* do what *abba* asked her to do, no questions asked.

It was early morning, the third day of my stay at Kings Hospital. My daughter was nursing; her cheeks inflated and deflated while she sucked with little kissing sounds, her miniature hand stroking my breast, fingers with tiny pink nails clasping and unclasping to a hidden rhythm. Shira's half-closed eyelids fluttered in rapture as she drew out my milk. Enclosed in my curtained enclave, I blotted out the din of the maternity ward. Snuggling with my daughter close to my heart, feeling the heat radiate from her little body, I closed my eyes, inhaling deeply and retreating into our haven—the bit of heaven I shared with my little muse, my song.

Steve had visited me during the first and second day in the maternity ward but couldn't make it on the third day. I expected no other visitors and felt very much alone.

However, later that morning to my surprise, I did have a visitor, my next-door neighbor, Ruth Vecht. She arrived carrying a golden, fragrant cake. Strands of black hair appeared under her blue kerchief, tied in a knot on her nape.

"Mazel tov." She put the cake on the dresser and bent over to peck my cheek. "It's a honey cake." Ruth wiped her hands on her plaid skirt as if she had just finished baking. "Happy New Year."

"*Shana Tova*," I mumbled as tears welled up in my eyes. Rosh Hashanah had always been special and meaningful. At the hospital I'd forgotten when it was coming.

"What is it?" Her brown eyes looked at me with a moist, motherly gaze.

"I . . . I don't know," I choked. "I'm so alone; I miss my family— my mom, my sister."

"Here, here." Her veined, coarse hand covered mine. "Don't cry. You have a lovely baby." She motioned to Shira sleeping in the bassinette.

"Yes," I swallowed, trying to portray a stiff upper lip. "But it's Rosh Hashanah and I didn't even know."

As a young girl, in Ashkelon, I'd accompany my mother to the synagogue, which served as a town hall the rest of the year. Wearing a gray pleated skirt, white lace blouse, and a shimmering black-and-white scarf, *eema* would clasp her prayer book, intoning the words while drops of perspiration gleamed on her forehead. It was an Orthodox service, so the women worshiped separately from the men. The rabbis had long ago decreed that a woman next to a man would distract him from his prayers. I hated the stuffy women's section, enclosed by a cloth screen through which I peered at the men shrouded in white prayer shawls and yarmulkes, bobbing up and down like wooden toy chickens pecking at a board. After an hour I'd slip out and join my siblings. The three of us would then rush home to change into bathing suits, and twenty minutes later we'd be frolicking in the mirror-like sea, splashing at each other in the salty water.

Ruth, an Orthodox mother of five, wouldn't understand this kind of frivolity on a holy day. I couldn't tell her the memory.

I wiped the corner of my eyes with my knuckles. "Thank you, Ruth, thanks for coming."

On the fourth day at the hospital, I finally heard some Hebrew. A rabbi arrived wearing a black overcoat and fedora hat, under which dangled two side locks. He approached my bed with a brisk step, his shoes squeaking.

"Shalom," he nodded. "I'm Rabbi Solomon." Dark brown eyes set in a pale face with a dark beard peered at me. What on earth was he doing there? Who had sent him? It must have been that crafty Ruth.

I quickly buttoned the top of my dressing gown.

He stood at the foot of my bed. Removing his hat, he revealed a velvety-black skullcap. "*Shana Tova*," he said, "Happy New Year."

"So," he said, twirling his curled sideburns around his index finger. "You miss your family."

"Yes."

"Where are they?"

"In Israel."

"I see." He wiped his forehead with a crumpled handkerchief. "Do you have any friends here?"

"No, not really." As always, rabbis made me uncomfortable. I wished he'd go and leave me alone. For Ruth, an Orthodox woman, a rabbi's visit would have been welcome. For her he represented a spiritual leader who could comfort and console her. I was brought up in a secular household, so Orthodox Jewish religion was meaningless to me. Though the rabbi and I were both Jewish, he felt alien; I had no sense of kinship with him.

The rabbi kept talking. "Is it a boy or a girl?"

"A girl; her name's Shira." My down-turned mouth turned upward into a smile.

After chatting for a while longer, he picked up his hat, squeezed the front back into shape, and positioned it on his head. "Well, mazel tov, shalom, I'll see you again soon." He turned and left the maternity ward.

I felt worse after the rabbi's visit, more lonely and indignant. I realized it was a good-will gesture on his part, but his visit only emphasized my circumstances. Instead of a family member or friend, I had to put up with a person who didn't mean anything to me. I knew it was his duty to visit the sick and infirm or congratulate new mothers in his congregation, but to me he was a stranger.

Big, warm tears rolled down my cheeks when Jenny arrived later with my tea.

"It's all right." She stroked my hair. "It's the postpartum blues; it'll go away."

But it didn't. The following morning my eyes were red and puffy and I refused to touch my food. My mood lifted a bit when, in the afternoon, Steve announced, "You're out of here tomorrow." I was anxious to see Tal, to bring Shira home, and to get back to "normal." I smiled, envisioning Tal's face, framed by shoulder-length blond hair, and his bell-like voice chiming, "*Eema*, I missed you."

The following day, back in our apartment, I sat in the rocking chair with Shira in my arms. Tal was in his kindergarten at King Alfred School while Steve was out running errands. Lowering my head, my dark blond hair touching Shira's rosy cheek, I sang an old Hebrew song my mother used to sing. "*Noomee, noomee yaldati,* sleep, sleep my little girl, father went to work, he'll return with the rising moon . . ."

It felt good to be back in my home, yet the sense of loneliness gnawed within me. Finally, while I took Shira for a walk in the pram, a neighbor approached and peeked under the hood. She smiled at me. "What a lovely baby you have," she said. My whole being brimmed with gratitude; I wanted to hug her but figured it wasn't a British way of acting, so I smiled back, said, "Thank you," and continued walking.

## ❧ Chapter 12: ❧

# The Diaphragm

My life in London revolved around our family. It made a big difference having a second child; we seemed to have tripled in size. Steve used the car while I wheeled Shira's pram to pick up Tal from school, shop, or do laundry. It's strange how life repeats itself, revealing a hidden pattern. I was pregnant with Tal when I arrived in New York and had to adjust to a new way of life away from family and friends. When I came to London, Shira in my belly, I had to start all over again: to find a new physician, dentist, and pediatrician; discover the location of grocery stores, Laundromat, hairdresser, and bank—the mundane details of life that after a while become "par for the course," yet at first take so much time and energy.

Luckily, we lived near a nursing school, where I found a student who would babysit. Once a week I went to yoga or to a music lesson at the nearby church. I was content in my role as mother. Shira was a happy, outgoing baby, and Tal was a doting older brother. Steve, however, hadn't found work in the local film industry, which meant he was either away overseas, working as production manager for

American film companies, or sitting at his desk at home typing letters to British producers and actors, trying to raise interest in various scripts he'd written. Though he did receive a few positive responses, one even from Sir John Gielgud, his creative talents were still going largely unrecognized.

Our married life perhaps reflected Steve's frustration and was aggravated by the fact that we didn't communicate about the most essential issues: his work, the kids' upbringing, money, and our sex life.

Shira was eight months old when we were on our way back from Debenhams on Oxford Street after buying new curtains for the children's room. Tal was at school. We kept stopping and going as we drove through the narrow roads of Hampstead. Sitting in the passenger seat on the left side of the car, I actually pressed my foot against the floor when we curved around a stone wall. We'd lived in England over a year, but I still expected a car to come crashing into us. Steve gripped the steering wheel. Without turning his head, he hissed, "I might as well go to a whore." His words blasted my ear. I felt as if he had slapped my face, hard, with an open palm. Where was this coming from? An acrid taste filled my mouth.

"Why? What have I done?"

"It's what you don't do. We haven't made love for weeks."

I turned back to Shira, who was strapped in her car seat, gurgling. Breathe, I reminded myself, don't let this get to you.

Stroking my baby's plump leg, I turned my head to my husband.

"Steve, we're both tired at night—I'm busy with the kids and you with your work."

"You know it's not that."

"What is it then?"

"Figure it out."

We arrived at a stoplight. I turned to look at my husband. When I first saw him on the ship, his Roman profile, cleft chin, and square jaw had attracted me. His blue eyes, adorned with long dark lashes, beguiled me. I didn't know then about the pain those eyes would inflict on me when they turned steel-gray, when he'd slam doors or vanish without a word, leaving me alone with our young kids.

And now he wanted me to figure out why he was so angry with me. Maybe it was the diaphragm, that blasted rubber contraption I inserted before we had sex. I always waited till the last moment before dashing to the bathroom, but when I'd return to bed Steve wasn't in the mood anymore.

"I can't wait that long," he'd say. Now I had my answer. The damn diaphragm pissed him off, and he was harboring resentment about it. I guessed the solution would have been to insert the diaphragm every night before we went to bed, but I wasn't willing to do that. Still, maybe I could insert it earlier now and then. I hated that device, having to slather it with cream before pressing it between thumb and middle finger into my body, praying it would lodge correctly inside my cervix. When it didn't, and the hard rim bulged against my vaginal wall, I'd retrieve it with my forefinger, careful not to scratch the dome with my nail. Pursing my lips, I'd have to reinsert the diaphragm, breathing deeply once it slipped into place.

But what was the alternative? The pill didn't agree with me, and the thought of an IUD, a foreign body in my uterus, gave me the shivers. Steve would never wear a condom, and the thought of becoming pregnant so soon after Shira's birth gave me nightmares. Every month when my period arrived I'd feel like a reprieved prisoner.

We continued driving. We passed the turn-around approaching the little pond, about twenty minutes away from Hampstead Heath, the vast park near our apartment. Boys with knee-length socks and smart felt caps knelt alongside the water launching various vessels: wooden tugboats, fancy sailing boats, and little paper ships. They prodded the boats with long sticks, maneuvering them back to shore. Steve loved to go there and sail a model schooner with Tal.

The previous Sunday I'd sat there with Shira's pram by my side while father and son, eyes shining, acted out their dreams of being captains on high seas. Radiance filled my heart. I wanted to jump up, clasp my husband's face, and kiss him. But I didn't. What if he found it annoying, disrupting his activity with Tal? What if he ignored me? An image floated in front of me: I'm a young girl, walking with my parents, when my mother, laughing, throws her arms around my father. He pries her arms open, his voice stern. "Why do you always have to make a fool of yourself in public?"

We were getting close to home now. Hampstead Heath was to my left. A yellow Labrador chased a ball; a gentleman in a plaid jacket and knickerbockers tossed a stick to his lean greyhound. I inhaled the spring scents as we passed beds of yellow primroses, deep purple crocuses, and fairy-tale-like snowdrops. We turned into Hampstead Court with its two-story red brick buildings surrounding a circular rose garden. As soon as Steve parked the car, I released Shira from her car seat and we entered our apartment in stony silence. Why was I supposed to figure out everything? Was I a mind reader? Couldn't Steve tell me what bothered him? God knows I tried to please him. I took care of the household and let him do his writing while I looked after the children. I admired and encouraged his creativity. When a writer he was collaborating with visited us, I made sure they had coffee all day long, at regular intervals. Carrying the drinks to the men absorbed in their work, I felt useful, like I was contributing to the creative process.

Now, seating Shira in her playpen, I started folding the laundry that had piled up on our bed. Soon I'd have to pick up Tal from King Alfred School. Maybe Steve would come out of his funk when his son arrived.

The week before, Steve and Tal had decided to help me fold the laundry. I entered the kitchen juggling two woven straw baskets loaded with groceries and produce I had bought on Finchley Road. Tal ran to me, beaming, and grabbed my arm.

"We've put the laundry away, come and see."

"How wonderful."

After putting down the baskets, I followed my son to the bedroom. My jaw dropped when we got there—the wall opposite our bed was covered with clothing. Various items hung on colorful tacks—white bra, tan-colored panties, boxer shorts, woolen socks. I couldn't suppress a big smile; it was a hilarious sight.

"We're playing throw-the-clothes-on-the-hook. I'm winning."

Tal crumpled a sock in his hand and raised his arm. Steve sat cross-legged on the bedcover, grinning. He spread his arms, raising his shoulders and eyebrows.

"We're having fun."

I was glad to see them enjoy themselves. However, I was the one who'd have to fold the laundry and put it away.

"Yeah, right," I said, hands on my hips. I looked from one to the other. "You're a great help."

Tal came over and hugged my waist.

"It's okay, *eema*, we'll put it away." He looked at Steve, who winked at him.

Now, I folded the laundry while Steve sat at his typewriter and began pounding away. It was gray and wet outside. My husband's words echoed in my mind. "We haven't made love for weeks." It must be the diaphragm, I concluded. Maybe I could insert it before dinner, or at least before I started getting the kids ready for bed.

I jumped up and ran to the bathroom. Opening the medicine cabinet, I retrieved the round blue plastic container. When I lifted the lid, I felt the blood drain from my face. All that was left of the diaphragm was a round rubber frame, the size of my open hand. The latex had been sliced around the rim, leaving nothing but a gaping hole. I felt humiliated and indignant, and the violence of the act frightened me. But I couldn't bring myself to talk with Steve about it. Instead I went to Boots, the pharmacy around the corner, and bought a new diaphragm. Somehow, the act of destroying the old one had satisfied Steve or relieved his anger. Neither of us ever mentioned the episode, as if it never happened.

## ❧ Chapter 13: ❧

# Down South

In August, the summer of our second year in London, Steve announced: "We're going to New Orleans for three months." Looking into my eyes, his voice high with excitement, he added, "I got work on the movie *Live and Let Die*."

Wow, this was the James Bond movie he had being pining for. What an honor! But it also meant we'd have to pack up and go to the Deep South for three months. I felt I could handle that; it would be an adventure. I had moved many times from place to place, from one home to the other. I'd learned to delve into new experiences without preconceived notions, to dive into the deep end and start swimming. The children and I had just spent a month at my parents' home in Ashkelon, so our suitcases were barely unpacked. I started making a mental inventory of all the things we'd need: the children's toys, Tal's teddy bear, Shira's stroller, books, and my guitar.

"Where will we stay?"

"I've rented a place in the suburbs," he said. "It's nice and quiet."

"Is it furnished?" The last thing I wanted was to do was deal with getting any furniture for a three-months stay.

"No, but we'll get what we need there."

"What about school for Tal?"

"There's one nearby, within walking distance."

"Looks like I'll have to start packing again."

He gave me an impish smile, one I knew conveyed how happy he was having landed a job on such a big film.

"Yes," he said, "I'm afraid so."

A week later, we left London.

When we arrived at our new home I was surprised by the sight of a modern, two-story apartment-building complex with a patch of lawn in front of each building. I hadn't realized that the place Steve found for us was a half-hour ride away from the historic city of New Orleans. He thought it would be a safer place for me and the kids instead of being near the French Quarter, where most of the filming would take place. I figured it fit in with his notion of separating his work from his family life.

Entering our apartment, I was welcomed by the monotonous hum of an empty refrigerator, a sink and Formica counter, a bathroom smelling of Pine-Sol, and two empty bedrooms with mustard wall-to-wall carpeting. Off we went to Kmart to fill the shopping carts with plastic dishes, aluminum pots and pans, and a folding table and chairs.

Steve worked hard, at times spending as many as twenty-four hours straight on the movie set. The kids and I didn't see him often. On one rare Sunday off, he treated us to a canoe ride on the bayou. Tal, who was six by then, listened wide-eyed while his father described the scene in which Bond, maneuvering his boat along a meandering river, jumps over land from one tributary to the other, crashing into a wedding party on the lawn of one of the old mansions along the water.

"Look," Tal said, pointing to a dark object at the riverbank, "a turtle. A water-turtle." Steve steered the canoe toward a log covered with sunbathing amphibians. Some stretched out brown necks from their shells, beady eyes blinking.

"Isn't it something?" Steve said, bending forward, pulling on the oars.

The canoe glided through the bayou, its stern slicing the still water into two dark waves. Tal, on the center seat, looked at me, then at his father, and then with a frown back to me. He was hoping to get close to the turtles. While Steve maneuvered the canoe alongside the bank, Tal leaned sideways, a radiant smile on his face. "Look, there's a turtle with a red nose. Can I touch it?"

"Be careful; you'll tip us over," I warned. Steve veered the canoe alongside the log and then, to Tal's delight, he was picking up the turtle, gingerly holding on to the shell into which the animal had withdrawn. After a while the head emerged. Tal stretched out his hand and touched the reddish-brown leathery skin with a light tap. The turtle's head bounced back like a reverse jack-in-the-box. Tal jerked his hand away while Steve burst out laughing. Hugging Shira close to me, I smiled, savoring my husband's jovial mood.

I had hoped the adventure would rid me of the memories from the night before, but it didn't. We had gone to a party hosted by a local rich couple for the film crew members and their spouses. The vast mansion reappeared in my mind, the Southern belle hostess with bright painted lips, the movie crew milling around, cocktail glasses in hand, the cavernous wine cellar with rows of vintage bottles exuding a musty, heavy odor. I had walked around as if in a bubble, not able to insert myself into a single conversation or engage with any of the people who were bursting with laughter around me. My fingers pressed against the slender glass stem; shoulders raised, elbows pressed in, I forced a smile on my lips. I watched Steve sip his drink, his arm around Bill, the propman, a small, leprechaun-like guy who guffawed at a joke Steve told. I felt I didn't belong there, among those film people. I felt intimidated, like an outsider.

It was after midnight when we finally left the party. Steve drove fast, whizzing along the dark, narrow road. At a stop sign, he screeched to a halt and then lurched forward. The muscles in my body contracted. I hung on to the door handle. "Can you slow down a bit?" I asked, trying to keep the panic out of my voice.

"Now you're going to tell me how to drive?"

"Stop the car; let me out."

"What's your problem?" he said. "It's not my fault you don't know how to act."

"What do you mean?"

"To start with, you didn't have to ask the host that silly question about where all the wine bottles came from."

"What's wrong with that?" I said, my voice breaking. He didn't answer. The wind lashed through the open window while I lowered my head, clasping my arms around me, bracing myself. The tears trickled down onto my black velour dress. I pressed my lips tight, choking back the sobs.

Who was this man who changed colors from moment to moment? Would I even be sharing my life with him if it weren't for our children?

Now Steve and Tal had placed the red-nosed turtle back on the log. Flushed with excitement, Tal turned to his father. "Can I hold the other turtle, the little one?"

"Let me try and get him."

They were in their own world. I looked around. Strands of silver-gray moss drooped from oak branches, their tendrils hovering over the malachite-tinted water, creating a fairy-tale world of light and shadows. The air was humid, saturated with the sounds of chirring crickets. Shira started to squirm; she needed to be bathed and fed. Though I loved it on the bayou, I was glad when Steve announced, "Let's go back home." He pulled hard on the right oar and turned the canoe around. Tal waved bye-bye to his hard-shelled snoozing friends as we started to head back.

Looking at Steve, I wondered if our marriage was just a series of disjointed adventures, moving from one apartment to the next one, from one country to another in pursuit of Steve's vision to create his own movie and become a film director who'd leave his mark on the world. I, his wife and mother of his children, sailed along with him on his voyage, enjoying moments of calm seas followed by raging, turbulent waters.

The night before the party, knowing Steve would be home late—he had to finish shooting a night scene—I bathed and fed the kids, read them books, and tucked them in before going to bed myself and letting Vivaldi's *Four Seasons* lull me to sleep. When the phone rang at 2:00 a.m., I jumped up and turned on the light. Heart pounding, I grabbed the receiver.

"Go get my wallet." Steve's voice was flat. "It's on the kitchen counter."

"What happened?" I shivered under my light nightgown.

"Just go get the wallet." I recognized the strained tone. My husband was trying to control his temper. "Call a taxi and come bail me out of jail."

"What about the kids?" My heart sank. "What if they wake up?"

"Do what I say." I heard his quick, strained breathing. "You'll be back soon. Hurry." He hung up.

It was such a strange request. Why was he in jail? What had he done? How could I leave the kids—six and eighteen months old—on their own and go in the middle of the night to the police station? I swallowed. I could hear my heartbeat loud in my ears. Looking at the receiver in my hand, I waited for some explanation to make itself here, but there was only silence on the other end, echoing the hollow sensation in my belly. I felt I had no choice; Steve was waiting for me. I tiptoed into the children's room. A lump rose in my throat at the sound of their peaceful breathing. Where was my writing pad? I'd leave Tal a note, just in case. But would he understand it? Oh God! I began rushing around the apartment, getting my clothes, shoes, pocketbook. I called a taxi, who'd be there in a matter of minutes. While I waited, I slapped water on my face, brushed my teeth, my hair, retrieved Steve's wallet, and went out. I wondered whether to lock the door but decided against it, in case I needed a neighbor to check on the kids. I heard a single honk of a horn and plunged into the humid, dark night; I looked up at the faraway shimmering stars, the antiphonies of the cicadas resounding in my ears.

I huddled in the back seat of the taxi, pressing my knees together, arms crossed over my chest, clutching my pocketbook.

"Where to?" I sat up, startled at the sound of the driver's voice.

"To . . ." the words nearly refused to come out of my mouth, "the jail."

I wondered what the driver, his head erect on a thick neck and wide shoulders, thought of me, a housewife going to the police station in the middle of the night.

"You mean the downtown police station?" He eyed me in the rear-view mirror.

"Yes, I guess so."

Before I knew it we arrived at the station. The bright fluorescent light stung my eyes when I entered. An officer, clad in boots, light reflecting off the badge on his pressed uniform, walked through a glass door, revolver on hip, big wooden club bouncing against his knee. I approached the counter, where a policewoman talked on the phone. Feeling like a schoolgirl, I waited for her to finish, overhearing snippets of conversation: "Yes, bring him in." "No, no bail."

I cleared my throat. "Excuse me . . ." The policewoman lifted her forefinger, signaling for me to wait. I paced back and forth, clasping and unclasping my hands. She hung up the receiver.

"Yes, what can I do for you?" She stared at my tousled hair, T-shirt, old jeans, and sneakers.

"I'm here for Steve Skloot." I shifted from foot to foot, passing

my tongue over my dry lips. "I'm his wife." I felt as if I'd just identified myself as an accomplice to a murder.

"Just a minute." She lifted the black receiver.

A poster with mug shots of wanted criminals caught my eye.
The entire grouping of shots featured men with narrow eyes, drawn
mouths, and defiant looks. One face—large, sad eyes, mouth turned
down as if about to cry—didn't fit in; he looked so young. I wondered what crime he had committed. The minute hand on the white
clock pointed to 3:30 a.m. I'd already been there for almost an hour.

Finally, Steve, his face sullen, dark stubble on his cheeks,
appeared, accompanied by a tall officer. My husband stretched out
his palm.

"Did you bring it?"

I handed him the leather wallet.

He gave me a wry smile, but his eyes remained serious.
"Thanks for coming."

I sidled up to him while he waited next to the counter for the
policewoman to check out his papers. "What happened?" I asked.

"I'll tell you later," he muttered, "in the car."

After checking Steve's driver's license and car registration, the
policewoman returned the wallet to him. She announced in a flat
tone, "You'll have to post bail."

Steve looked grim. Pressing his lips together as if trying to avoid
uttering a curse, he opened his wallet and took out a credit card.
Sensing I'd be better off away from Steve, I moved from the counter
and sat on a bench near the wall. I knew he was indignant being at
a police station under those circumstances. Having me witness it
probably made him feel worse. I tried to keep my cool, though I was
tense and upset, especially when I though about the kids at home.

Once we were on the road, I turned to him.

"So?"

"I had an accident," he sputtered through clenched teeth, staring ahead.

"Are you all right?"

"I'm fine."

I touched his arm. "What happened?"

"Not much. After the shoot we had a few drinks. The road was narrow—I didn't see the motorcycle."

I gripped my seat, a wave of nausea rising in my stomach.

"How bad did he get hurt?"

"Nothing serious; he'll be okay."

"What's going to happen now?"

"I don't want to talk about it anymore." I knew Steve well enough to know that he meant we were never going to talk about what happened.

We drove the rest of the way home in silence. My chest felt like stone while my mind churned as I thought about the way Steve shut me out. First, he requested that I help him out and then he clammed up, unwilling to share anything with me.

Light streaks of gray appeared on the flat horizon, upon which silhouettes of farmhouses and solitary oak trees loomed like menacing monsters. My heartbeat quickened as we approached our apartment complex. Once home, I bolted out of the car and rushed to the children's room. Thank God, they were fast asleep where I had left them.

I plunked on our bed, my heart pounding. Why did I automatically obey Steve's requests even though they conflicted with my beliefs or needs? I acted like a robot conditioned to obey its master. My kids came first, so why did he put me in a situation that could have endangered them? Hands together, fingers intertwined, I pressed my palms so hard my knuckles turned white. If anything had happened to Tal and Shira, I would never have been able to forgive Steve or myself.

The day after our canoeing adventure, while Tal was at school and my daughter was napping, I leaned, cross-legged, against our bed, half listening to Vivaldi's *Spring*—the sounds of singing larks and bubbling brooks a welcome respite from the heat and loneliness. It was hotter than in Ashkelon, where at least there was a breeze from the sea.

It was the end of September—what date was it? I jumped up to look at the calendar, the one my parents sent me. The following week was Sukkoth, the harvest holiday. We needed a sukkah—a booth, a one-room hut, decorated with branches, leaves, and fruits that symbolized the ancient agricultural holiday and the makeshift dwellings the Hebrews erected during their exodus from Egypt. The previous year, in London, our Orthodox neighbor Ruth invited us to have tea and cake in her sukkah. It's customary to eat there for the seven days of the festival, so I sat with Tal and baby Shira in Ruth's evergreen-scented decorated sukkah, savoring every crumb.

I hadn't seen any Jewish people around. There was an Italian family next door who'd invited us once for spaghetti dinner, and the woman across from us had a German accent. There would be a sukkah in a synagogue courtyard, but there was no synagogue in sight. I felt isolated and cut off from my people and tradition. That night, in bed, I told Steve about my plan to build a sukkah so we'd have some feeling of the holiday of Sukkoth. I was hoping he'd help me with it but doubted whether he'd have the time or desire to do so.

"Are you crazy?" he said. "You need wooden poles, planks, branches; you need tools—a saw, hammer, nails. Forget it."

"I'll build it in the back courtyard, behind the kitchen, so I'll only need one wall. Tal will help me."

"Okay, if it's so important to you, go ahead, but you're on your own."

The following day, after cleaning up, doing dishes, cooking, and chasing my toddler around the house, I picked my son up from school.

"We're going to build a sukkah." I knew he'd be happy about it; he used to decorate a sukkah during the years he attended kindergarten at the JCC in Forest Hills. "*Yofi*, great," Tal said as he skipped beside me while I strode, pushing the stroller in which Shira sat, munching crackers.

"We'll need to collect green branches to make the roof."

"And we'll hang bananas and pomegranates." Tal jumped up and down; we had long ago nicknamed him Yo-yo.

I bent over and hugged him, feeling his soft, warm cheek next to mine. My son, my little friend; I could always count on him. "You remembered." I said.

My heart widened with a sense of gratitude; keeping the Jewish traditions alive meant a lot to me. Not just celebrating the main holidays of Rosh Hashanah, Yom Kippur, and Passover, but the lesser ones, such as Sukkoth and Shavuot (Pentecost) as well. They connected me with my roots, my culture, and my family back home; they anchored me in my new life in America. Passing those traditions down to my children was imperative to my sense of well-being, of wholeness. Just as I talked to them in Hebrew and gave them Hebrew names, I made sure we celebrated our holidays, no matter where we were.

Late that afternoon, red streaks crossing the sky, we walked to the far end of our housing complex, where tropical broad-leafed vines crept up an eight-foot broken-down fence, creating a tangled growth. Ignoring the deafening cicadas' chants, I took out my kitchen knife, an eight-inch glinting blade on a smooth dark handle, and started hacking at the gnarled wooden cords, tugging at the vines. Glossy spade-shaped leaves pelted my face; drops of perspiration gathered on my forehead, trickling down the arch of my nose and onto my lips, tasting like Dead Sea salt and bitter herbs. Tal ran around collecting the snake-like branches, holding them under his arm before adding them to the growing pile. After an hour or so, his face flushed bright red, he turned to me.

"*Eema,* can we go home? I'm hungry."

"Just a few more." I nodded toward the pile of vines. "In the meantime, you can push the stroller a bit."

I resumed cutting, pulling, and tugging until crimson welts formed along the soft, fleshy cushion of my palms. The physical exertion felt good. I was proud of myself for accomplishing on my own something I wanted to do. I didn't need Steve to help me.

When we had enough branches, I called Tal, and we trudged home under a heap of greenery.

The next day, while Shira napped, I erected the sukkah. I stuck a few branches in the ground, tied the vines to them, and then, using safety pins, I attached a yellow-print bed sheet. With the rest of the vines and branches I made a roof through which patches of sky could be seen. Tal and I hang up fruits and vegetables—green and red bell peppers, purple grapes, and yellow bananas. We dragged two kitchen chairs into the sukkah and had apple juice and crackers.

Tal gulped down the last of his juice. "Now what do we do?"

"I don't know."

"Can we have dinner here with *abba*?" My son's eyes widened with expectation.

"No," I bit my lower lip, "he's busy."

Tal lowered his head in disappointment. "Oh, I see."

I got up, walked over to Tal, put my arm around him, and tousled his hair.

"You know what?" I said. "It's fine to have just the two of us in the sukkah. You did such a great job helping me build it." I pointed at the ceiling. "Look at all the colors up there!" I bent over and kissed his soft cheek.

I felt content that I had finished the task I had set before me, even without Steve's help. I knew that, traditionally, family and friends would sit and eat their meals in the sukkah for seven days. But I didn't care; having Tal there, with me in the sukkah that we both built, was enough. I felt grateful.

### ❧ Chapter 14: ❧

# Going Home

In the spring of 1973, home from New Orleans and settled back in our London apartment, Steve still hadn't found work in England. Though we enjoyed the drives in the countryside, the picnics on the Heath, and the occasional drink in the local pub, he was getting more and more impatient and short-tempered. On a rainy day, while baby Shira napped, we sat in our small living room and talked about the situation. I was optimistic, but Steve was frustrated.

He smacked his fist into his palm. "I've had it. We're going back to the States."

"I like Heathcroft," I protested.

Through the drawn back curtains, a soft rain fell on flowering pink currant shrubs bordering a green lawn. The view from the window resembled a Monet painting.

"There's not much happening in the film industry here right now. I'm tired of commuting between London and New York."

I bit my lip. "Five years in Queens was plenty for me. There's no way I want to live there again."

"We could go somewhere else; America's a big country."

"Steve." I covered my husband's hand, caressing his slender fingers. I attempted to formulate the words rising in my heart. "You know . . . I've always wanted to go back to Israel."

"How can I work in Israel? Their film industry isn't worth shit."

"You could make some inquiries, maybe at the consulate," I pleaded.

He didn't respond. Scratching his head and rubbing his cheek, he stared at the floor at a point beyond me. My chest tightened.

"Steve, I've been away from my country for seven years already," I blurted. "It's only fair that I get to go back."

I held my breath, my eyes on my husband's lips. Above his head, in the painting of Aix-en-Provence, the lopsided houses piled one on top of the other seemed to topple over.

"I don't know," he said, "it won't be easy—the climate, language, finding a place to live."

"We'll manage; I'll help you."

Steve lifted his head; he smiled slightly but had a grave look.

"Okay. I'll contact the consulate. We'll give it a try."

"*Yofi!*" I threw my arms around him. "Do you really mean it?" Tears brimmed in my eyes. All my yearnings, hopes, and fantasies were packed into that moment. A flash of the last seven years rose in my mind—the daily aerogramme I'd sent home; the photos documenting my babies' growth; the birthday, anniversary, and holiday cards I'd mailed; and when I splurged, the long-distance phone calls, which were always too short, too abrupt.

I wrote my parents that very afternoon. "My dream is coming true. I'll finally be back in my country, my home. My children will get to know you. We'll be together again."

I longed to spend time again with my parents, sister, and brother, to see my school friends and army pals, yet when I thought of Israel, my mind pictured so much more. I visualized myself walking on the soft, yellow sand along the Mediterranean, diving into the blue, warm water, inhaling the fresh scent of the earth after the first rain, picking juicy oranges from the orchard near our home in Ashkelon, marveling at the display of wildflowers in the short springtime—yellow daisies, fiery red anemones, and fragrant white narcissus, which grew in clusters near citrus groves.

I recalled delicious salads with finely chopped tomatoes and cucumbers flavored with olive oil and lemon; small green olives; and an array of white cheeses and yogurts, which I loved and couldn't find in either New York or in London.

Israel was the place where I peppered my conversations with biblical references and everybody knew what I meant; when it was dark outside, I'd say "it's the darkness of Egypt," referring to the ten plagues, or when it was raining heavily, "it's a deluge," thinking about Noah's ark. In Israel, I could chat with strangers on a bus or on a train. Since the country was so small, we, the Israelis, felt close to each other; we had a sense of community, a sense of pride in our unique historical background and in our achievements in the modern-day world. Israel was where I belonged.

When I picked Tal up from school, I told him he'd soon swim in the Mediterranean; build sand castles with his cousin Gal; play games with his grandmother, *savta* Annie; and eat Aunt Rachel's yummy cheese cake. Hugging my waist, he asked. "When are we going?"

Two days later Steve contacted the emissary at the Israeli consulate, who was only too happy to assist us. There weren't many new immigrants from England, and the following week my husband walked in beaming.

"They offered me a job at the English department at the Israeli Educational Television Station in Ramat Aviv." He chuckled at the sight of my open mouth. "I'm flying over to check it out."

In May, when the primroses and crocuses bloomed again on the Heath, Steve returned from Tel Aviv with a positive response. I was elated as the preparations for our aliya got underway in earnest. I couldn't believe that it actually would happen. When Steve announced that our departure was set for August, I breathed a sigh of relief; a heavy weight lifted off me, like the pressure released when a cork pops out of a champagne bottle. My return to Israel was finally a reality.

I wheeled Shira across the cobblestone courtyard to my friend Cheryl's flat. Parking the pram at the bottom of the staircase, I carried her up three flights. Cheryl opened the door, her brown eyes welcoming, while her chubby baby boy clutched the long braid falling down to her waist. She was a farm girl from Minnesota, married to an Englishman. I felt secure and relaxed in her presence.

"Guess what?" I put Shira on the rug, next to Jason. "We're going to live in Israel."

Cheryl came out of the kitchen and handed me a mug of tea. I cradled it in my hands, slowly sipping the steaming hot liquid.

"When?" She took her tea and we both sank into the cuddly sofa.

"In three months."

"Wow! That soon." Cheryl hesitated for a moment, then smiled at me.

"Are you excited?"

"Can't wait."

"Good luck; I hope it works out." Her eyes clouded over, and I wondered if she was thinking about her family back in the States. I'd known Cheryl for a little over a year; she was one of the few friends I'd made in London. I didn't realize she wanted to go home, like me. Here I go, I thought, another person I'd never see again, another thread severed, another portrait in my mental album.

For the following couple of months I went through the motions of taking Tal to school, shopping at the greengrocer on Finchley Road, and wheeling Shira's pram alongside white picket fences with climbing roses. I walked around in a state of euphoria. At times I had to remind myself that it wasn't a dream, that we were actually immigrating to Israel, that I *was* going back home.

When the departure date approached, we packed our household belongings. Steve wrapped every cup and plate in sheets of newspaper, placing them inside large wooden crates. The wine glasses, with extra wrapping, he secured in a compartmentalized box with crisscrossed panels. It was the sixth move in seven years of marriage; we were experienced movers by now.

On a late afternoon in mid-August, the hottest month in Israel, we touched down at Ben Gurion airport. Hot air blasted my face, and the bright white sunlight almost blinded me as we descended the stairs from the plane onto the open tarmac. A backpack and large handbag weighing me down, I pushed the stroller, which I had packed for our trip to Israel, leaving the pram back in England. As I hurried along, Tal hung on to the stroller, trying to keep up with my pace. Steve was ahead lugging two suitcases. The shimmering heat from the asphalt seeped through my shoes while we walked to the bus that would bring us to the terminal. We shoved our belongings onto the bus, hoisted up Shira's stroller, and clung to the vertical hand bars while the doors shut behind us. Several people stood between Steve and me. He raised his eyebrows, making fanning movements with his palm, while I lifted my shoulders in response. In the din around me I picked up parts of conversations, jokes. My ears pricked up at the familiar sounds, the guttural consonants and staccato vowels of Hebrew. I took a deep breath. I was back in my element.

This strong sense of homecoming accompanied me to the immigration line, when all of a sudden I had a strange sensation of double identity. I was a returning citizen but felt like a new immigrant. Though I'd visited almost every summer, it seemed to me I was different. I'd been away for so long. Had my accent changed? Did I still look like a sabra—tanned, energetic, with a natural appearance? I'd always been proud of being considered a native. When I first arrived in Israel from England at age eight, the kids made fun of me. Since then I'd worked hard to sound and act like a person born in the country. I was so successful in my attempt that during my army service, when I performed in the variety group, the audiences would invariably think that out of the four women soldiers, I was the authentic sabra, born and raised on a kibbutz.

I waited for Steve, who had been summoned to a side office. Tal sat on one of our suitcases, his chin cupped in his hands, while I held Shira on my lap. He looked at me with his light blue eyes.

"*Eema*, when will we see *savta* Annie?"

"When we go to Ashkelon, but first we're going to our new home."

"Where?"

"It's near Tel Aviv, not too far from here."

"But why aren't we going first to Ashkelon?"

"Because they don't have enough space for all of us," I answered. I caressed his soft hair, not telling him that my father had never been fond of young children, that he was worried his own grandchildren might mess up his house or disturb his sleep.

"Where's *abba*?"

"There." I pointed to Steve, who was waving his hands at an officer with a navy blue cap and brass-buttoned uniform. My husband turned around and strode over to us, his lips pursed, brow furrowed.

"That idiot says I'm a new immigrant." He wiped his forehead. "I tried to tell him that I've registered in the consulate as A1, a temporary resident. I've no intention of settling forever in this godforsaken country."

I wanted to yell at him, to say, we've just arrived and you're already talking about leaving, spoiling everything! But I knew better—if I said something, he'd fly into one of his rages, just like my father did when I came home late or dared to ask for some spending money.

How would Steve manage to deal with things here in Israel? The authorities weren't going to end with airport personnel. Israeli officials—from bank to government clerks—were not going to kowtow to Steve in spite of his American accent and haughty demeanor. They were the bosses; he wasn't. Would my husband be able to adapt to my country? Tal had moved to my side, and I felt the warmth of his arm against mine. I wondered how much the children absorbed of their father's tantrum.

Once we were done with customs, Steve having secured his A1 status, we walked out to the waiting area into throngs of people yelling, laughing, hugging, slapping each other's backs, and embracing. My head held high, I turned it like a mechanical doll to the left, to the right, and to the left. My heart sank—where was my family? Then I heard my name, "Esther, Esther!" There, at the end, where the mass fizzled out, I saw my parents. My mother, tears rolling down her cheeks, threw her arms around me, pulling me toward her. She was smaller than when I'd last seen her, yet her arms were so strong. I felt my ribs when she hugged me. She held me at arm's length, studying me.

"You're so thin; have you lost weight?" she asked.

The strands of gray in her black hair and my father's lined face reminded me they were getting old. My father, who could have competed in his vanity with Oscar Wilde, hid his bald head under a smart hat. We all waited on the curb for the Jewish Agency van, which was coming to pick us up and take us to Ramat Aviv. I turned to my father.

"Are you coming with us?"

"No, we have to go back."

Steve frowned. It would have been nice to have some help settling in, but I don't know why I'd expected that of them. They both had to take off from work and drive on mostly narrow roads for a couple of hours. My father could only afford his first car when he was in his fifties, after he received reparations from Germany. He wasn't a very secure driver. My mother never learned to drive. It was a big effort for them to get to the airport.

I eyed my mom holding Shira, bouncing her up and down in her arms while making funny faces at her, poking out her tongue and wiggling it from side to side. Shira giggled, and Tal laughed out loud. My *eema* would be a great help with the kids, but my father would no doubt cause more anxiety than we could stand. He was used to giving orders. My mother, Rachel, Jeremy, and I always catered to him and his needs. Steve and I were tired and tense, and my father, quick to condemn, slow to praise (if ever), would make the situation worse. He and Steve were both strong-willed, stubborn men, and sparks were sure to fly.

After about an hour wait, the Jewish Agency's van arrived. We hugged my parents good bye, got into the black van, and headed north for the half-hour drive to Ramat Aviv.


Our new home was a five-story building called Bet Milman, which served as temporary housing for new immigrants who were academicians, mostly from the Soviet Union, a few from England and the States. We were crowded in a small one-bedroom apartment on the fourth floor. Two metal-framed beds with thin mattresses issued by the Jewish Agency lined the walls in the bedroom. In the kitchen/dining area, four straight-back aluminum chairs surrounded a square Formica-topped table. The walls were stark, with no pictures or prints. Holding Shira, I sat on one of the beds—the mattress sank; the coiled springs squeaked. While Steve and Tal went out shopping, I explored the tiny kitchen. Shira whimpered; she needed her bottle. I opened the cabinet doors until I found a couple of tin pots.

A week passed. Steve left in the mornings for the TV station, where he helped produce programs in the English department. Or that's what I assumed he did, since we never discussed the details of his job and I didn't press him. I went out of my way to avoid being the nagging wife. I followed my mother's example: if your husband doesn't want to talk, let him be. Don't upset him, and especially don't contradict him. When Steve was at work, I took Tal to school; then I went shopping or to the playground with my little daughter.

I was glad we'd come back to my home country, but I felt disappointed; I thought it might be better. I didn't have a car or a phone. If I wanted to make a call, I had to go to the public phone on the street, near Bet Milman. My parents worked during the week, and there was no public transportation on Shabbat (it was forbidden, according to Jewish religion). It was a trek for me to travel to Ashkelon with the kids. I couldn't stay over, since my parents' house was small, but more than that, my father didn't invite us. I knew he wouldn't tolerate two small children in his home, even if they *were* his grandchildren. Before we moved back to Israel, when I had visited during the summers, It was only me and Tal. Even one grandchild was a lot for my father, but we managed.

As for friends, they lived in Ashkelon; I didn't know people in Ramat Aviv and wasn't familiar with the surroundings.

I did some yoga and taught Israeli songs to new immigrants, which made me feel useful, but on the whole I felt alone, in the place where I had hoped to be welcomed and feel at home.

On the third week after our arrival, we were on our tiny balcony facing the street, having supper. The air was heavy, but after sunset it wasn't quite as hot outside. Steve sat across from me, next to the table laden with a finely cut salad consisting of tomatoes and cucumbers, a container of soft white cheese, a bowl with small green olives, yogurt, fresh-sliced dark bread, and two bottles of treacle-colored malt beer. He stared at me.

"So, what's with your family?"

"What do you mean?"

"Why don't they come to see us?" He cut a slice of bread into two even pieces. "We always have to schlep to Ashkelon."

"Rachel has the two little ones and . . ."

"Your parents?"

"They're busy working."

"So what? Your father could get off his ass and visit his grandchildren."

"But it's not easy." I hadn't told Steve how I'd already observed what little interest *abba* had shown in Tal or Shira.

"I don't care! We came here so you'd be with your family." He slammed the table with his fist and went inside. Yes, I thought, but there's more to it than just my family. It's residing in the country where I grew up, where I had hiked up in the Galilee and down to the Negev (the desert). Israel was the place where I came into my own as an army entertainer, the place where I experienced my first love.

I could understand his resentment. I too wondered why my parents didn't make more of an effort to come see us. Steve was right, but his anger wouldn't solve anything. I couldn't change my father; he'd never been much of a family man. My mother, who'd do anything to see us, was dependent on him, not only for transportation but for every move. She wouldn't have dreamed of taking off from work in the plant nursery, getting on a bus, and leaving her husband behind.

The following Shabbat my parents arrived in their small Renault. It was only their second visit since we had come to the country a month earlier. Tal helped me arrange the table. We set out biscuits, raspberry juice, soda water, a sparkling bunch of grapes, and slices of juicy red watermelon. I placed paper napkins—a rare commodity in Israel—next to each plate. Steve was in the shower when there was a knock on the door. My parents were dressed in festive outfits—my father in his red-checkered shirt and beige slacks, my mother in her summery blue frock. They walked in, smiling.

*Eema* looked around. "Where's the baby?"

"She's napping."

"Good." She took Tal by the hand. In a minute they were on the floor, rolling a ball to each other. My father sat at the table, removed his homburg, and mopped his forehead.

"It's hot in here." He looked around—at the sofa we got from my sister, the semi-shuttered windows, and the potted plant. I was glad I'd tidied up and swept the floor. I was a married woman, a mother of two, yet I still got stomach cramps anticipating my father's disapproval. He turned to Steve, who had joined him at the table.

"So, how's life in Israel?"

"Not easy."

"How's your job?"

"So-so. The people at the TV station think they know everything." Steve's jaw muscles tightened. "These damn Israelis won't listen to any suggestions."

Steve was a New Yorker; he didn't mince words.

My father tried to reason with Steve. "Couldn't you try it their way?"

Aghast, Steve's mouth opened wide as if he had heard a most ludicrous suggestion. He, a well-known production manager in New York, was supposed to listen to those provincial Israelis? His chin jutting forward, he glared at my father.

"*You* try to be all day long around people who tell you what to do!"

"Listen." My father pointed at Steve. "You haven't been here long. You need a bit of patience, *savlanoot*."

I could see the blood rising in Steve's face. My father hadn't been of any help to us in the difficult task of settling down with two little kids. All he did was give advice.

"Patience! That's all I hear. I'm sick and tired of it." Steve pushed back his chair and paced the room. "Look at this place—two crummy rooms for all of us." His voice rose. "I'm stuck without a car, get paid peanuts for my work, and walk around like a fool not understanding a word of the bloody language."

I went over to my husband and touched his arm, whispering, "Steve, please, don't ruin the visit." As if stung by a bee, he shrugged me off and strode toward the front door. My father, staring at Steve, held on to the edge of the table, trying to contain himself.

"Listen, you can't expect everything at once."

"No?" Steve's eyes narrowed as he faced my father. "Who the hell are you to tell me? How have you helped us? You've done nothing to make our lives easier."

"Wait a minute—"

"You're the most selfish man I've ever met." Steve raised his arm, his hand in a fist, then dropped it, whirled around, and, as if shooting a soccer ball to the goal, kicked the door. The plywood crashed and caved in, creating a gaping hole with sharp splinters.

"I'm out of here." Steve opened the broken door and disappeared.

In the stunned silence that followed, I sat immobilized, feeling as if my heart turned to stone. My father glared at me and said, "Your husband is crazy."

## ◆ Chapter 15: ◆

# Yom Kippur

We'd been in Israel for six weeks when Yom Kippur, the Day of Atonement, arrived. On that day all Jews attended services, even secular ones like me who didn't go to synagogue year-round. The air was stifling in the makeshift synagogue a few blocks away from Bet Milman. The drone of mumbled prayers lingered in the low-ceilinged room. It was interspersed with the more strident voice of the rabbi who presided over the congregants. I couldn't see my husband and son from where I was, back in the women's section, cut off from the men by a waist-high wooden partition. Most of the women wore dresses or long skirts and scarves. I refused to cover my head, though that's what was expected of a married woman, according to Jewish law. I didn't feel Jewish in the traditional sense of the word—prayers didn't mean much to me. My father, whose parents and brother died in the Holocaust, didn't believe in God. I never saw him pray in a synagogue, even when he went there to please my mother.

I tried to concentrate on the words of the prayers, but my mind kept reverting to my sweet *eema*; she brought up three children without any relatives to help her—no siblings, parents, aunts, or uncles. There I was, in my home country on the holiest day of the year, alone with my husband and two small children. One of the main reasons I came to Israel was to be with my family, yet I hardly saw them. My sister and brother were busy with their work and small children while my parents continued to keep their distance.

In a way, I didn't blame them; they couldn't stay over in our apartment and couldn't afford to book a hotel. They were busy with work and traveled very little. But maybe I was just making excuses for them, especially for my father, who made the decisions. I didn't want to acknowledge that my father was a selfish, inconsiderate person whose self-interests came before all others. It would have been too painful.

I looked around. Some women, clasping the prayer book, moved their lips silently, their eyes half-closed. Others, mopping the perspiration off their foreheads, whispered to each other or shushed the kids next to them. Worshipping God is more of a man's business, I thought; religion doesn't take women seriously. We're not allowed to pray in the vicinity of men, since we might be a temptation and distract them from their prayers. So we're assigned to the periphery, the balcony or the back of the room, away from male worshipers, the Holy Ark, the eternal light, and the rabbi.

I wheeled Shira, asleep in her stroller, closer to the partition. The rabbi, shrouded in white, prayer shawl over his head, was bending forward and backward like a willow branch waving in the wind. With his right hand he beat his chest, intoning, "*Ashamnu, bagadnu.*" We've sinned, we've betrayed. The male congregants, a sea of white symbolizing the purity and holiness of the day, chanted with their leader, "We've deceived, we've exploited . . ."

I love Hebrew, the language with which I grew up, yet those words were foreign to me and grated on my ears. Did all those men, with hands on hearts, believe what they were saying, and if so, would they change their behavior? Why couldn't we fill our hearts and minds with positive thoughts on Yom Kippur, the contemplative day? I wondered how Tal was doing in the men's section. He must have been bored stiff. How did Steve fare? Was he caught up in the sacredness of the holiday, or, since he didn't read or understand Hebrew, were his thoughts drifting away to his work? As a responsible and caring father, he probably tried to point out to Tal the various religious objects, such as the tallit they were wearing or the meaning of the eternal light above the Holy Ark. Or maybe Steve was kidding around with his son while Tal looked up at him adoringly. The latter was the more likely scenario.

Though Yom Kippur wasn't my favorite, I realized there were wonderful aspects of the High Holiday; where else in the world did a whole country come to a standstill for a day? There were no buses or cars on the streets. All stores, restaurants, cafés, offices, and public buildings were closed. Families walked together, at a slower place—with nowhere to rush to, no work to be done, no appointments to keep. A sense of awe resided in the silent streets, a feeling of solemnity.

I returned to the back of the room and sank into my seat. I marveled at my little daughter—her blond hair like a halo around her face, her dark eyelashes fluttering on her flushed, round cheeks. Was she too warm? I should have dressed her in a lighter outfit. My stomach rumbled and my tongue was coated—I hadn't eaten since dinner the previous night. An apple or a piece of buttered toast with a cup of tea sounded heavenly. I'd always fasted on Yom Kippur, even during the seven years I'd lived out of the country; it was my connection to my family, my heritage. I stifled a yawn.

All of a sudden there was a change in the atmosphere: a man came in and whispered to one of the male worshipers, who stripped off his phylacteries and prayer shawl, stuffed them into an embroidered velvet pouch, and exited with quick, purposeful strides. Two other men got up, shooting furtive glances while removing their yarmulkes, and rushed to the door. My neighbor, a woman with a lined, weather-beaten face, head covered with a black lace scarf, turned to me with questioning eyes.

"What's happening?" she whispered.

"I wish I knew."

More men headed out. A car revved up. Somebody honked. A man called out.

"Look," my neighbor pointed to the open door, "an army truck." She shook her head. "*Oy vey,* what's going on here?"

The drone of prayers gave way to whispers and hushed exclamations, which became louder and louder till the news, like brush fire, spread through the synagogue: "call up," "emergency," "attack." Women next to me started moving. Shira woke up whimpering. I pressed her to me while I searched for my husband and son. All of a sudden Steve was in front of me, moving forward as if pushing against a strong wind. His eyes pinpointed on the exit, and he dragged Tal behind.

He motioned with his chin toward the exit. "In case you haven't heard, they're mobilizing the army. Let's get out of here." How could I've known? I wondered. He probably got his information from one of the men in the sanctuary. Yet I had neither the time nor desire to be offended; I knew it was Steve's way of making a point.

"It's okay, Steve." I tried not to lose my husband while he pushed his way through the rest of the congregants rushing out. There was no way I could calm him down—once he perceived a danger to his family, he went into full alert, the adrenaline taking over. I was grateful for his concern but had a hard time dealing with his anxiety. Here he was rushing ahead, while I with Shira trailed behind. It seemed reminiscent of the day he lost me in Central Park.

We had finally made aliya—we'd immigrated to Israel—and, with my luck, a war broke out. What would happen—would they bomb Tel Aviv? And who were "they"? Egypt, Syria, or Jordan? They were mobilizing the reserves on the holiest day of the year. The Arabs were cunning, knowing full well that on Yom Kippur everybody would be at the synagogue and they could surprise their enemy. No wonder we didn't know anything about an impending war! There were no radio or television broadcasts on Yom Kippur. The attacks started while everybody was at services, praying.

I pictured the children and me sitting in a bomb shelter while Steve argued his way to the battlefront in spite of the fact that he was a temporary resident and had been in the country less than a month. However, I knew that wouldn't be an option. He wouldn't be allowed to join even if he tried. Steve had no concept of war; he was a student during the Vietnam War, and later, because he was married, he'd been exempt from the draft. Since all the able men in Israel joined the army, I was sure he'd want to be part of the action. Otherwise he'd feel left out and useless.

Pushing Shira's stroller as fast as I could, I managed to keep up with Steve and Tal. It was late afternoon; the heat shimmered from the pavement; the tamarind and jacarandas leaves drooped. I perspired under my high-collared blouse while we hurried back home. Normally, we would have left the synagogue after *Ne'ila*, the concluding prayer, when it turned dark and the first stars appeared in the sky. This day, however, the holiday was shattered. People darted about us, their question carried in the air. "What's happening?" When no answer was forthcoming, people stood around, watching with anxious eyes the formation of jet fighters streaking through the sky.

I touched Steve's arm. "Look."

A man in army fatigues and boots, a kit bag and Uzi slung on his shoulder, stood near a tarp-covered army truck. A young woman with shoulder-length dark hair, holding on to a curlyhaired child, approached the soldier. He, I assumed, had heard the coded message that a war broke out while in synagogue. He had rushed home, changed into his uniform, grabbed his kit bag, and hit the street, where he joined the other men waiting to be transferred to their army units. When the soldier spotted his wife and son he crouched, smiling, his gun swiping the ground. The little boy broke loose from his mother's grip, ran, and jumped into his father's open arms. I was so touched to see this moment—a soldier and his son.

"*Abba*," the boy asked, "when will you come home?"

"Soon; take care of *eema*," said the soldier.

Steve nudged me. "Hurry up. We better get back."

The whitewashed stucco building was in sight when a high-pitched wail blasted the air. The sound was relentless, rising and falling, rising and falling, assaulting my senses. I bent over the stroller to cover Shira's ears. My daughter's eyes were wide open, her mouth contorted, her scream obliterated by the siren. A woman shrieked, "To the shelter!" People scattered in all directions. I picked up Shira, handed her to Steve, and we ran to Bet Milman. Tal, ahead of me, looked back, motioning with his arm. "*Eema*, come, come." I pushed the empty stroller, the sound piercing my ear, propelling me forward. We gasped our way into the building and down the dark stairwell leading to the basement. It was dark with a mixed stench of mildew, stale cigarettes, and urine. Turning to Steve, I pinched my nose shut with my thumb and forefinger.

"This is awful; I don't want to go down."

"Would you rather be blown to pieces?"

Bodies jostled by us. Old women groaned. A boy hurrying down bumped into me. We huddled together on the cement floor—a bare bulb dangled from the ceiling, throwing a ghastly light on a woman and two girls next to us. We were about fifteen people, mainly women and children, squeezed into a small rectangular space where, if you walked to the back of the room, you'd have to be careful not to step on outstretched legs. A muffled, drawn-out sound penetrated the room; the even-pitched wail lasted for several seconds and then dropped to a low moan and petered out. A teenage boy ran to the door, pulled it open, and talked to somebody. "All clear," he announced, "we can go up." Upstairs in our apartment, Steve turned on the radio—Golda Meir's husky voice was somber:

"Citizens of Israel, today—October 6, 1973—around 2:00 p.m., the Egyptian and Syrian armies mounted an attack on Israel. They launched a series of air, armor, and artillery attacks in Sinai and in the Golan Heights. The Israel Defense Forces fought and repulsed the attack . . . Our enemies hoped to surprise the citizens of Israel on Yom Kippur."

Steve and I looked at each other. I had a sinking feeling in my belly, as if it were my fault that we were there at that point, that my family was in danger. Yet I knew that for Steve it was worse, unable to fight, to work— because of the war, his job would be put on hold—to do anything. He spoke first:

"What shall we do now?"

"I don't know," I sighed. "I guess we'll just have to wait this out."

"Yes? And what am I supposed to do in the meantime, sit here and twiddle my thumbs?"

A couple of days later, Steve paced back and forth in our cramped apartment.

"I can't stand it." He raised and lowered his fist as if hammering a nail. "I feel so useless—there are only women, children, and old fogies in the street."

"Couldn't you do some civil defense work?"

He stared at me. "Do I look like some cripple?"

"What about the television station? Don't they need you any more?"

Steve started pacing again, like a caged animal. "Not really. All they care about is war footage and reporting."

"There must be something you can do."

"Yes?" he faced me, lips clamped. "You tell me what it is!"

He grabbed his black attaché case and stormed out the door. I tried to suppress the lump in my throat; crying wouldn't help. He was there because of me—it was my home, not his. Yet a war wasn't something you could plan for.

I went to the kitchen to prepare lunch for Shira and myself. I took out a couple of yogurts, a cucumber, and an egg carton from our box-sized fridge. There was only one egg left—I scrambled it with non-perishable milk, sliced the cucumber and bread, and retrieved my daughter from the playing blocks in her room. In the high chair, she collected the egg with her chubby fingers and stuffed it into her mouth, her eyes beaming while bits of squished yellow-white particles dropped on the floor. I laughed.

The following morning I wheeled Shira to the grocery store down the road. A lone car passed by. A woman, holding the hands of two children, hurried along. An older man, in work clothes, crouched in front of a Peugeot, painting its headlights dark blue.

"What are you doing?" I asked.

He lifted his head up with a surprised look on his face. "Black-out regulations—it's required."

In the store, two women stood in the narrow semi-lit aisles. The shelves were half-empty—only four bottles of oil left. I grabbed one, dusted it off, and slipped it into my netted shopping bag, next to a loaf of dark bread and two rolls of toilet paper. I approached the shopkeeper, a heavyset woman who was wiping her hands on an oil-stained apron.

"Where can I find eggs?" I asked.

"Here," she handed me half a dozen, "they're rationed."

"And butter?"

"None left; nobody around to deliver food."

She spread her arms, with their soft, marshmallow-like flesh drooping, and her palms faced the ceiling. "What can you do? They need the trucks in the front."

I shook my head, looking down at my daughter. The woman leaned over the counter and touched me.

"There's margarine in the back of the refrigerator." She looked at Shira. "What a sweetie—God bless her."

When I finished shopping, the woman wrote down the

groceries on a piece of paper, licking the pencil stub after each item. She tapped up the total on an adding machine, which clanked with each entry, and handed me the slip.

As I turned to leave, she lifted up her arms, hands facing each other, fingers pointed upward like a Hasid in mid-dance. She looked at the ceiling as if addressing some unseen God and then grinned at me.

"It will be okay, *yeheye beseder,* don't worry."

That evening we gathered with other immigrants around the television in the community room downstairs. A sense of electricity pervaded the room; necks craned and ears cocked. Next to us, a high-cheekboned woman in a linen jacket, her forehead furrowed, clutched her husband's arm while staring at the anchorman. "What is he saying? What is he saying?" she asked in Yiddish. The broad-caster continued: ". . . 380 soldiers were killed today along the Suez canal, 570 wounded, and 65 taken prisoners . . ." Watching his grim-face, I shuddered.

At night, the sirens wailed again as we descended, bleary eyed, into the shelter. In the morning, Steve, his face taut, pecked me on the cheek and left for the TV station. On his return he was transformed; his eyes radiated with joy as he lifted Shira and twirled her above his head. When Tal ran up to him, he handed me our daughter and waltzed with our son around the room. Tal, catching his breath, stopped.

"What's up, *abba?*"

Steve, his face flushed, smiled at me.

"I've got a job; they commissioned me to film a documentary."

"What about, the army?" Tal blurted.

"Sort of—it's about the volunteers from abroad who come to help with the war effort."

"Great, when do you start?" I asked.

"Tomorrow."

We stood in a cluster. Steve gathered us all in his arms while I, holding Shira, snuggled against his chest and Tal hugged his father's waist.

Steve worked long hours—leaving early with the first birdcalls and returning at night when our kids were asleep. One night, after midnight, I lay awake in my narrow bed while Steve shifted in his, from one side to the other. The windows, covered with black sheets of paper, couldn't block the distant canon firing, which shattered the silence. The air in the closed room was still and humid. I turned to Steve.

"How is the filming going?"

"It's coming along . . . slowly." Steve wasn't one to admit hardship.

"Do you get any help?"

"No. I do the interviewing, filming, and editing. Besides," he paused, "they're not paying enough. I'm using up our savings."

On October 24, eighteen days after the outbreak of war, a cease-fire was declared and the blackout was canceled. Lights returned to the darkened windows, drivers removed the camouflage from their cars, and the cafés opened on Dizengoff Street. We rejoiced, but not for long. Steve, his eyes lackluster, his shoulders drooping, returned the following day from the television station. I rushed over to him.

"What happened?"

"They didn't like my film."

"What do you mean?"

"They won't show it; it's not realistic enough." He threw his attaché case on the sofa. "They said that for a documentary, it's too artistic."

I tried to hug my husband, to console him, but he turned around, went to the table, and sank into a chair, placing his elbows in front of him, hands cupping his face.

"We're leaving this bloody country," he muttered.

My heart froze. The memory of chanting rang in my ears: *We've sinned, we've betrayed . . .*

## ❧ *Chapter 16:* ❧

# The Return

In the fall of 1973, after Steve's documentary was rejected, we left Israel and flew back to New York. It was the second time I was emigrating from Israel. In Hebrew it's named *yerida*, descending, which refers to those leaving the country, deserting. It has a shameful connotation, which for years lingered within me.

Though I didn't mind moving from place to place, once my daughter was born I was getting tired of it. With two kids, the constant shifting and changing had become more of a burden. I felt like a wandering Jew moving from one continent to the other, from Europe to Asia to North America, a continuous merry-go-round. How often was I bound to repeat that cycle, I wondered. Was I condemned, like the biblical Cain, to forever roam the land? To constantly sail the seas like the *Flying Dutchman*?

Steve's uncle Lou offered to lend us his apartment near the ocean in Long Beach, New York, until we found a new home. We already knew that New York wasn't an option; neither of us wanted to bring up our children there, so Steve flew to Los Angeles in hope of finding work in Hollywood. He had our Mercedes shipped to the States from its storage in England. The kids were seven and a half and two and a half by this point, and I stayed at Lou's place for nine months while Steve moved back and forth between the East Coast and California. He worked on part-time jobs, in documentaries, while scouting for a suitable home for us.

I cherished our time in Long Beach, even though we did find a few cockroaches in the kitchen closet. When summer arrived, the kids and I spent our days swimming in the pool and the sea or playing on the beach. In the evenings we sat, the three of us, cuddled on my bed, watching movies like *Chitty Chitty Bang Bang, Willy Wonka & the Chocolate Factory*, and others that I loved as much as they did.

By the end of the summer my body was golden brown; I felt free and light, like the seagulls soaring above the waves. True, I had Tal and Shira, whom I had to feed and take care of. However, I noticed (but wouldn't admit out loud) that I thrived on my own, without Steve. Yet, thinking about it, I realized that he was the breadwinner, and without his support I couldn't have been as carefree as I was that summer.

I received a phone call from Steve. "I found the perfect place for us—a house in the woods on a mountainside, in a little town called Mill Valley, not too far from San Francisco. You'll love it." It turned out he had hated Los Angeles, the sprawling metropolis, and had gone north, where he found work on a movie set being filmed in the Bay Area. I had mixed feelings about his announcement. It came as a surprise, since he never shared his plans with me. I had no idea what Mill Valley was like or what kind of house he'd found for us. Steve was used to me accepting his plans without questioning him about them ahead of time. From my experience so far, he had always found us a reasonable place to live, so I trusted his decisions. Moreover, I was happy to have our family united while living in our own home.

Two weeks later, I arrived with our sleepy kids in the San Francisco airport late at night. Steve waited for us, and we settled into the Mercedes on the way to our new home. I couldn't discern much in the darkness. I was fatigued, and my eyelids soon closed while Steve drove into the night. I awoke to find us meandering up a narrow road ending in a steep driveway, and we arrived in what seemed to be a different world—cool fresh air, the scent of tree sap, the sound of night birds. My eyes smarting from lack of sleep, I carried Shira up the wooden staircase leading to a large shingled house. I felt as if I were in one of the Brothers Grimm fairytales—it all seemed so alien, so foreign. The large, empty whitewashed living room with floor-to-ceiling windows on three sides gave the impression of a tree house. I felt a pang of loneliness and anxiety. This was not what I had imagined. This was not a cozy home, but rather a vacant space with no furniture, curtains, or anything else that might have made me feel at ease. When I looked around, my eye caught a splash of color: a flowering red Geranium in a pot on the low partition wall near the entrance. My heart racing, I turned to Steve.

"Where'd the plant come from?" I asked.

"There's a note with it; you can check it out."

In a flash I opened the little envelope. Tears welled up as I read the words. "Good luck in your new home. With love, *eema* and *Abba*." Only my mother would think of such a surprise.

Gradually, I adjusted to my new home and environment. Tal went to Old Mill School—a small elementary school—down the hill, within walking distance from our house. Since Steve took the car to work, I ended up walking a mile downtown, pushing Shira's stroller up our hill, carrying groceries and laundry (we didn't have a washing machine). Yet I enjoyed the greenery—yellow sorrel and miner's lettuce along the road, above which towered majestic eucalyptus, oak, acacia, and laurel trees. I cherished the deer trails and the abundance of wildlife around us. I felt lonely at times, but luckily, we became good friends with our landlords, an older, childless couple who lived up the hill from us. When the kids grew older, they'd walk up to Ed and Lou's home, where they'd watch television and devour the candy Lou gave them.

Two years later, our son Ori was born in Children's Hospital in San Francisco. After completing *Crayon People*, a documentary about children, Steve ended up opening a store in Mill Valley that carried imported wooden toys. He figured it would be less stressful, while enabling him to spend more time with his family.

Ori benefitted from this immensely, and Steve adored our youngest son. He and Ori spent many hours together building Lego structures, drawing pictures, sailing paper boats in Old Mill Creek, and tide-pooling in Bolinas. Was Steve trying to make up for the fact that he'd missed Ori's birth? A few weeks prior to my due date, Steve let me know that he had to attend a toy fair in Nurenberg, Germany, and would probably miss the birth.

Of all places, he was going to the International Toy Fair in Nuremberg. I recalled Nazis, World War II, and the Eichmann trial in Jerusalem. In his new career as toy-store owner, he plunged into work with his usual gusto and intensity, brushing aside all other aspects of his life—including his wife's needs.

"Don't you realize I'm due next month?" I asked.

"It'll be fine. I've got a substitute."

"What do you mean?"

"I've invited your parents to come and stay with you." He had his hands on his waist, chest puffed out.

"But they've never been to the States."

"Don't worry; your mom can manage."

"Don't you want to be here when the baby is born?" I searched his eyes.

"Sure, but I have to attend this fair. It's important for stocking up our toy store."

"Do whatever you have to do," I said. I swallowed my tears.

I knew there was no point in arguing with Steve. He was the one who made the decisions, even if it concerned me. True, he had arranged for my parents to fly over from Israel to be with me at the time the baby was due, but it wasn't in any way a substitute for having my husband around. However, with my stoic upringing, I accepted what seemed to be inevitable. The night Steve returned from Germany, four days after Ori was born, he called me from the airport.

"Come and get me."

Leaning on our living room wall, I glanced at my watch—it was almost 10:00 p.m. Was he out of his mind? For God's sake, I'd given birth a few days ago. My back hurt, my crotch stung, and my breasts were engorged—what did he think I was, a pack mule? A sense of indignation rose like red coals within me.

"I'm not sure—"

"Can't you just hop in the car?"

"What about the kids?"

"Your parents are there to take care of them, right?"

I heard his tone and knew it wasn't a request. Hearing his voice, I regressed into an eight-year-old who avoided her father's glaring eyes when ordered to do the dishes, feed the chickens, or sell flowers in the neighboring village.

"Okay, I'll be there. What airline are you on?" Out of the corner of my eye, I caught my father and mother exchange glances. My father turned to me with pursed lips.

"You're not going to pick him up now, are you?"

"He had a long trip and he's tired."

"Tired? What about you? Don't you count at all? Your husband's a lunatic."

"*Abba*." I looked at my father's flushed cheeks. "It's done already. I have to go."

"What about the baby?" *eema* asked.

"He's okay; I just nursed him a short while ago."

My mother made a last attempt. "Couldn't *abba* drive to the airport?"

I looked at my mom, aghast. "No way!"

I knew my father would be uncomfortable driving on our steep, narrow road in the dark. Besides, he'd get lost on the way. I couldn't trust him to even make it to the airport.

My father turned his back to me and went to the kitchen. *Eema* followed. They were whispering in German, and my father was probably saying, *She never listened to us; what's the point of our being here?* I asked the same question. Since they'd arrived from Israel, I had catered to my father and, by default, to my mother, instead of having them take care of me, which was ostensibly the point of their visit. I gave them my bedroom while I ended up sleeping on the sagging living room sofa, not much of a support for my huge belly. They were helpful, however, when they stayed with Tal and Shira while a neighbor drove me to the hospital after my water broke.

Yet *abba* was right; why couldn't I say no to Steve? Why was my husband so self-centered and inconsiderate? He knew I had just given birth. And more to the point, what was wrong with me? Was I a trained dog that would jump to attention every time a male figure barked or hissed an order? It was a gut response over which I had no control. This was what had been modeled for me. It was my lot, since the beginning of time—*unto the woman the Lord God said: "And thy desire shall be thy husband, and he shall rule over thee."*

To hell with this Biblical nonsense, I thought; I was a twentieth-century woman. I tried to justify the whole situation for myself. I would soon be seeing my man, my loved one, whom I hadn't seen for two weeks. He'd hug me, telling me how wonderful I looked while I buried my face in the small of his neck, leaning against his broad shoulders.

When Steve last saw me, my belly resembled a humungous watermelon from the outdoor market in Ashkelon. Now I was four days postpartum, and my belly was still big, but not nearly as big as before with Ori now out in the world. Did it make sense to dress to impress him? I searched through my closet. I'd wear my beige knee-length skirt with my black sweater. I hoped I'd be warm enough.

I heard a little cry. It was Ori, "my light," my little baby who had slipped into the world and taken over. In the delivery room, the nurse laughed when he looked up with wide deep blue eyes under long black lashes. "He's a bright-eyed, bushy-tailed baby," she said.

Stopping in our bedroom before heading out to the airport, I rocked Ori's wooden cradle while he made sucking sounds. Tucking the blanket with the gray elephants around him, moving my pinky over his rosy cheek, I whispered: "Sleep, my little son . . . go to sleep."

Back in the living room, my father had his jacket on.

"I'll come with you, okay?"

"No, *abba*, I'll manage."

That's all I needed, my father in the car. I'd just get nervous with him next to me. I'd never felt at ease with my father, who often criticized me, and to whom I had a hard time giving a hug. Besides, it would be nice to be alone with my husband when I described the events that took place since he left.

When Steve first told me he was going to Germany, I didn't argue with him, ask him to stay, or tell him what my needs were. But that had been the pattern of our marriage—not asking or asserting my needs. Now I wished I had. If he had been with me at the birth, I wouldn't be driving to the airport in the middle of the night, feeling the way I did.

I heard steps from the kitchen. My mother came into the living room with a steaming mug in her hand. "Esther, here's a cup of tea." Her soft, hazel-blue eyes told me that she knew how I felt; her legacy was mine. My father requested that she dress a certain way, have dinner ready on time, or, because he was fed up with his job, pick up their three little children and move to a different place. She did what he said year after year after year. She'd passed her mantra along to me: don't question your husband.

"Drink the tea; it's nice and hot." She patted my hand.

"Thanks, *eema.*" I put my arm around her shoulder, kissing her cheek. She was shorter than me, and she leaned her head against my chest. Feeling slightly dizzy, I supported myself on the large desk near the window.

Once in the car, I drove down our steep driveway, catching, from the corner of my eye, a deer bounding into the woods.

Adjusting the rearview mirror, I focused on the narrow, windy road, trying to ignore the seatbelt pressing on my lower abdomen and the skirt slipping up my thighs. I wished my belly wouldn't stick out; Steve was so concerned about my figure. It didn't matter that I was only four days postpartum. I wanted to lash out at him. Let's see him carry a fetus for nine months, give birth, nurse a baby, and have a trim figure. I was the mother of his children, not some skinny, Twiggy-like matchstick model. And yet, I could see myself through my husband's eyes: roly-poly, no waistline, a veritable sack of potatoes. I took a deep breath and gave myself a pep talk. I decided he would be impressed that I showed up for him, that I was no longer pregnant, that my face wasn't round as a moon anymore, and that I could look down and see my feet. I was sure Steve would be impressed. He *better* be impressed!

On my way out of Mill Valley to the airport, I passed Tamalpais High School with its vast soccer field. I looked at the sticker below my dashboard, which read, *Breathe,* and I followed the command, filling up my lungs with air, but my mind, mulling thoughts around, whirring like a clock, refused to give up. "Are the kids all right?" "Did Ori wake up?" "What if there's an emergency? I didn't even leave a phone number my parents could call." "Is my father, fuming, arguing about me with my mother?" I stepped on the gas pedal, turning onto Highway 101. The Mercedes labored up Waldo Grade.

My parents were right about Steve: he was a bit meshuga, or crazy. I guess you *had* to be in his line of work, even though now he had a toy store and no longer worked crazy hours on movie sets. Yet, he was the father of my three children, and he was handsome—a tinge of excitement ran through my body. I'd see him soon. My fingers tingled; my pulse quickened. What would our meeting be like? In my postpartum state I couldn't run, so would *he* rush over, his eyes bright in admiration, dewy with longing? I sensed the blood rushing into my face, my cheeks flushing—rolling down the window, I inhaled the cool, refreshing night air. Something about recently having given birth made nature even more meaningful to me—the trees, flowers, and sky looked different, the colors brighter, more vivid, radiant, as if I was seeing the world for the first time, unspoiled, the way it was in the Garden of Eden, or the way a child might perceive the universe.

My back ached and my breasts felt heavy, ready to explode; the nursing pads in my bra were damp—I wished I'd been brave enough to tell Steve to take a taxi. Driving on the Golden Gate Bridge, through the dense fog, I had difficulty seeing in front of me. Shifting in my seat, trying to release my tension, I moved my shoulders up, down, and in a semicircle. Soon I recognized the box-shaped houses above Interstate 280, while on my left I saw planes ascending and descending like mechanical toys directed by remote control.

It was almost midnight, and the empty fluorescent-lit San Francisco airport glared like a football stadium. Straightening my caved-in shoulders, I stroked my belly; I had made it! I ran inside to find the first available restroom. With a relieved bladder and refreshed lipstick, I hurried to the gate's waiting area. A few people milled around. A lonely familiar figure slumped in one of the seats got up, retrieved his briefcase, smoothed his jacket, and walked toward me. We embraced. I detected the residue of his transatlantic flight: the scent of stale cigarettes, aftershave, and perspiration; the stubble on his cheek scratched my skin. We looked at each other; his eyes were dull and sunken more than usual. Was something wrong with him? I wondered. I hoped he wasn't ill.

"How are you?" I asked.

Pulling back my shoulders, my right hand on the strap of my pocketbook, the other on my waist, I looked down at my belly, hoping he'd follow my gaze. Now was the moment I'd anticipated. He'd ask me how I'm feeling, compliment me on my looks, and ask about our baby, but all he said was: "It's good to be back."

I was devastated; he didn't even ask about his new son! I felt my chest constricting while my throat choked up. Creating a forced smile, I asked: "How was the flight?"

"Long; let's go home."

In the car, Steve drove while I clasped my arms around myself. He didn't say a word about my figure, my skirt, or my makeup, and, wiping my tears, I decided I wouldn't prompt him to acknowledge the fact that we had a newborn at home. He'd see him soon enough. We were on the Golden Gate Bridge, heading north, when the deep, drawn-out bellowing of the foghorns sent shivers down my spine. The black night engulfed us—two humans trudging along, with expectations, needs, and desires we could not fulfill.

*❦ Chapter 17: ❦*

# Grand Mal

O ri was only sixteen months old in 1977 when our life in Mill Valley took a drastic turn. Steve had begun to have psychomotor seizures, during which he noticed noxious smells and experienced problems with focusing visually. The doctor thought they were a result of stress and strain and told Steve to get some rest, go on a wholesome diet, and relax in a hot tub.

This seemed an easy prescription, and the symptoms indeed subsided for six months, but then the spells increased to almost once a day. At that point, Steve consulted a neurologist, who sent him to have a CT scan at the radiology department. The results stunned us. Steve had a lesion in his brain's right temporal horn. He'd need an operation to have it removed. We were too shocked, or too frightened, to discuss what that might mean. Steve only mumbled, "I'll have the bloody surgery and get done with it."

I went on full alert, getting a babysitter for Shira and Ori, arranging a hotel for my in-laws, notifying friends and family in Israel. I functioned like a robot, not allowing myself to fathom what was happening, disconnecting my mind from the rest of my body. "Don't lose your head," I told myself, suppressing my feelings, pushing my inner turbulence deep down, keeping a lid on it that would not blow off until many years later, when my internalized fear and grief could no longer be contained.

Gussie and Milton were devastated when I called to tell them about Steve's diagnosis. Gussie reassured me with a shaking voice, "We'll fly out as soon as possible. We'll do all we can to help you and the kids."

Though they tried their best, and the children were happy to have them around, I didn't get much emotional support from my in-laws. I understood Gussie's agitation and nervousness but had a hard time dealing with it. We all feared the worst: that Steve had a malignant tumor. It turned out that our darkest nightmare became true; we found out about it after Steve's surgery on January 4, 1978, while we sat in the surgeon's waiting room at UCSF.

I sat on the edge of the chair, my fingernails digging into the upholstery. Opposite me, Gussie and Milton, their faces ashen, stared openmouthed at Dr. Hoff, who'd just come out of the operating room. With a furrowed brow, he looked at Milton and then at Gussie. His voice was flat.

"Your son has an astrocytoma of the right temporal lobe which has been partially removed . . ."

I couldn't breathe. It felt as if my body caved in. Time was frozen. What's an astrocytoma? I envisioned a bright celestial body, a far cry from the menacing mass in my husband's brain. What was going to happen to him? The doctor, reading my thoughts, turned to me.

"Steve has a 75 percent chance of living up to ten years," he said, clearing his throat, "and a 25 percent chance of living an additional five years."

The words emanated as if from a body without a face. They reverberated in my mind as if in a huge, empty cave, careening from wall to wall: *Ten years, five years, ten years . . .* I looked dumbfounded at the green scrubs, the rimmed glasses on a hawk-like nose. The words took on a life of their own, floating in the windowless room, every now and then entering my consciousness and gripping my heart with an iron fist. "My husband is only thirty-four." I tried to reason with an invisible enemy. "And Ori is just a baby. He deserves to have a dad."

"What's an astrocytoma, and how will it affect our son?" Gussie asked, her voice choking.

The doctor remained officious. "It's a nerve-tissue tumor composed of astrocytes—star-shaped cells which spread out like fingers. Since it's on the right side of his brain, it won't affect his motor abilities."

I inhaled, not realizing I'd been holding my breath. "But it might cause some personality change and affect his emotions," he concluded. I wasn't ready to take it all in, so all I absorbed was that he was going to be okay—at least for now.

The following year, in February 1979, Steve had to undergo another operation. After bouts of radiation therapy, chemotherapy, medications, and sleepless nights, Steve surprised me with the announcement that we were moving to a kibbutz in Israel. After we'd failed miserably in our first aliya, I couldn't understand why he wanted to go back.

"I've always wanted to work the land, and you'll have a chance to be near your family again," he said.

I didn't want to remind him how poorly that had gone the first time, so I pushed him on his health. Was he up to such a big step? "Did you ask Dr. Hoff if it's okay for you to go?" I asked.

"Yes, he said it's fine." He turned around and walked away.

I realized he had made up his mind. It would have been nice if he had consulted with me, but I gave him the benefit of the doubt. Perhaps he took it for granted that I'd want to return there. Much later, Dana, a close friend, confided in me that Steve brought us to the kibbutz so we'd be taken care of if the cancer killed him. I befriended Dana when she came to teach at Brandeis Day School, where I'd been a Hebrew teacher for several years. She and Steve hit it off immediately; they shared a quirky sense of humor and inquisitive minds. We ended up spending a lot of time with her and her husband, Kobi, both of them Israelis. Years later, when I heard what he had told her, I felt sad and betrayed. I wondered why he didn't trust me with such an important piece of information. I realized we hadn't discussed the future, what would happen if and when he died. He probably wanted to protect me, but then again, he was treating me like a child who couldn't be trusted with such critical facts of our shared life.

We packed our belongings, Steve sublet our house, and off we went on our new adventure. We were in Israel by that summer. Steve scouted for a place to settle down, choosing Bet Ha'emek, "The Valley Home" —a kibbutz in the Upper Galilee where green lawns dotted with ancient olive trees connected the small, whitewashed homes of the kibbutzniks. Many of the kibbutz members came from English-speaking countries, which for Steve added to the allure of the place. Though Bet Ha'emek was far from Ashkelon, where my parents and sister lived, I didn't mind. Now that I was home, I was elated to be back.

Saul, the kibbutz's secretary, a wiry American with strands of graying hair smoothed over his balding head, interviewed us upon our arrival.

"Why do you want to live on a kibbutz?" He narrowed his eyes, looking at Steve.

"I like the idea of sharing, so there are no haves and have-nots." Steve spread his palms on the table in front of him. "I've always believed in socialism."

Saul winked at Steve. "You know, socialism has its downsides as well." The interview was taking an interesting turn, yet I gulped at the next inquiry. "Do you have any skeletons in your closet?"

A shudder passed through me. What a strange question. But Steve bent over and touched Saul's arm.

"This is between us." He hesitated for a minute. "I have a brain tumor, but I'm in remission." He tightened his grasp on the table's edge. "I'm doing well."

An alarm bell went off in my mind. In a kibbutz, people lived in a tight-knit community, where gossip was part of daily life and members knew everything about everybody else. How could Steve's condition be kept secret? I knew him well enough to realize he'd be devastated if his condition became common knowledge. He believed he'd be treated like a cancer patient or an invalid. He didn't want the kibbutzniks to treat him like a leper, point fingers at him, whisper behind his back. He wanted to work, play, and live like a normal person, like everybody else. I made up my mind not to tell a soul about it.

We settled into the one-bedroom apartment assigned to us, on the lower level of a two-story whitewashed house. Shira and Ori slept in the bedroom, while Tal was assigned to the Youth Home, dorms where kids of middle school–age slept. Every night, Steve and I turned the sofa in our small living room into a bed. Surrounded by grass and trees, with open blue skies above me and no cars zipping by, it was a far cry from Forest Hills. I loved it. We made new friends: Stanley and Benita, from England originally, took us under their wings. They were our "adoptive parents," assigned to us, the standard for a new family on the kibbutz, to show us the ropes and help us get adjusted. Max and Penina—he from Poland and she a sabra—invited us often for five-o'clock tea on their lawn, where Penina served us her delicious home-baked cakes. We also befriended Hillel, a South African, and his wife, Linda, an English-woman. Hillel was in charge of the avocado plantations, where Steve was assigned. We had the love of music in common: he played the guitar while singing English folksongs in a soft tenor. I enjoyed singing and harmonizing with him whenever I could.

I hoped we'd eventually be accepted as members on the kibbutz. I was told the process took at least a year. After that, the kibbutz reception committee would give their recommendation, and the general assembly would vote whether our family was suitable to live on the kibbutz or not.

We started to adjust to life in Bet Ha'emek, though it was easier for me. Steve had a hard time adjusting, especially since he no longer was the sole breadwinner and "master of the house."

"I don't have a family anymore," he'd say to me. "I hardly get to see you and the kids." It was true. We had different work schedules, he at the avocado plantations and I at the kibbutz school. We ate, usually separately, at the communal dining room. In the evenings I was busy with various cultural activities, such as chorus rehearsals and work-related meetings. The children spent their days in their respective children's houses, where they ate all their meals, studied, and played. They only came home in the evenings.

When the first kibbutzim were founded, before the establishment of the state of Israel, the idea of the children's houses was to free the women from household chores and childrearing so they could participate, along with the men, in working in the fields, tending the animals, and defending the settlements from marauding Arabs. Kibbutz children were assigned, according to their age, to children's houses, where a *metapelet*, a woman caretaker who acted as a surrogate mother, would see to all their needs. In the beginning, they even slept in those houses, instead of with their parents. Luckily, we arrived on the kibbutz after that idea was phased out. I couldn't have handled a situation where my young children slept elsewhere, away from me.

Steve was an individualist, and a dreamer, idealistic but not in touch with what it would be like to live on a kibbutz, where you shared your life with others. Since he had volunteered for a few months at Hazore'a, he had a general idea of kibbutz life but volunteers, who served as temporary workers, weren't part of the community. Steve had no real experience of what daily life on a kibbutz entailed. I, on the other hand, spent time during my army service in various kibbutzim, so I had firsthand experience with kibbutz life. My mother often spoke lovingly about life on a kibbutz, about women's freedom and the social aspect of it. I realized what she meant; after living with Steve in our nuclear family for eleven years, I cherished my newfound freedom, friends, and opportunities. I blossomed, like a rose that had finally been given enough water.

Half a year after our arrival, in the spring of 1980, I rushed outside one dreadful morning in the early dawn; a gray-white light illuminated the outlines of the cement path, the gnarled branches of the ancient olive trees, and the flower gardens. My bare feet stepped on the wet grass covered with drops of dew. A faint scent of cow dung and silage hung in the air.

I was running to call on the nurse, Naomi. She lived in the upper apartment of a two-family house across the central lawn. I ran up the stairs and knocked on her door, which was flanked by a bloodred bougainvillea plant. Nobody answered. I didn't want to knock louder and wake up Naomi's children. Heart pounding, tears blurring my vision, I rapped again with my knuckles. I was terrified. Naomi opened the door wearing a teal baby-doll nightgown, auburn hair disheveled, the freckles standing out in her pale face.

I choked, "Naomi, please hurry, Steve had some kind of attack, and his body is convulsing."

"I'm coming. I'll just put on some clothes."

A turtledove cooed a melancholy tune somewhere behind the granary filled with cottonseeds. A rooster crowed. I shivered. Goose bumps covered my body, and my mouth was dry. As soon as Naomi reappeared, I bolted down the stairs, suppressing a scream that wanted to explode inside me: Please, God, don't let my husband die.

"What happened?" Naomi asked as we both rushed back to the house.

"I woke up and heard gurgling sounds. His body jerked, and all I could see was the white of his eyeballs."

"Did you put something between his teeth?" Naomi asked.

"Why?"

"So he doesn't bite his tongue."

"I had no idea."

Oh, my God! I imagined Steve choking, unable to breathe, his tongue caught between his front teeth with drops of blood on it!

We arrived, breathless, in front of our apartment. I recalled the horrific vision of Steve's condition before I'd left. The mattress had shook as his body leapt up and down like the severed tail of a lizard. The piqué blanket crumbled on the floor, the pillow crushed against the wall; Steve was on the bed, head tilted back, mouth open, with saliva dripping down his cheeks. I had put my hands on his shoulders trying to hold them down, but the force of his jerking body was too powerful.

Digging my nails into my palms, I steeled myself before opening our door. Then an awful thought hit me. Suddenly I remembered Steve's conversation with Saul and the implicit warning: *Don't let anybody know that I have cancer.*

"Wait a minute," I said as I blocked Naomi with my arm, "let me first see how he is."

Opening the door slowly, I willed myself to enter the room. The bed was empty. My eyes moved over the rumpled sheets, the wooden frame, and down to the floor. And there he was—lying still on the mottled, mustard-yellow rug, eyelids shut, damp strands of hair framing his gaunt face, arms folded on his chest while his legs, in cotton pajama pants, stretched out in front of him. His thin white feet looked vulnerable on the gray-tiled floor. But his face was relaxed; he looked like he was sleeping. I had no idea what to do or what that change meant. I felt my chest tighten, as if somebody had sucked all the air out of my lungs. I wondered whether he was unconscious. As if of their own volition, my palms came together in the form of a prayer. I squeezed them together until they hurt. Swallowing, pushing down the lump in my throat, I called his name gently. He opened his eyes and looked at me. His pupils were large, as though he had no idea what had transpired.

He raised his eyebrows. "What am I doing on the floor?"

"You had some kind of a fit." I retrieved the pillow and put it under his head.

I didn't realize Steve had had a seizure, or maybe I didn't want to acknowledge it. I coped with his illness by avoiding labels or names, which would have made it more real. Even if I had known what it was, I wouldn't have mentioned the word "seizure" to Steve. It seemed too ominous, too scary. I was trying to protect him.

"I don't remember anything . . . are you sure?" He creased his brow.

My words rushed out. "Steve, I ran to get Naomi to see what was wrong. She's waiting outside."

He raised himself on his elbows, eyes narrowing.

"You what? How dare you?"

"I didn't know what was happening. I was afraid."

He glared at me. An iron fist clasped my heart. I did the wrong thing; I let him down; I'd have to pay for it. It was a feeling I knew well: an angry look from my father evoked the same sensation. Yet I had no choice, I reasoned with myself. I didn't tell anybody about Steve's cancer. I had to call Naomi; it was an emergency!

"Tell Naomi to go home. I'm fine."

"What shall I tell her? I can't just send her home."

My pulse racing, I took the crumpled sheet from the bed and covered his legs. He was suffering, but I felt so helpless. I left him and went outside. Naomi was waiting, arms clasped around her waist.

"I'm sorry. Steve doesn't want you to come in. He feels better now."

"It's all right, I understand. Don't worry."

I felt such warm gratitude I wanted to kiss her on the cheek, but I knew that she'd take offense to it: Israelis, especially kibbutznicks, aren't demonstrative—they're brought up to be stoic and not betray their weaknesses; it's their mode of survival. But it could be that I was the one afraid to show my feelings, fearful that once I let my defenses down the dam would burst and I'd be flooded with emotions I couldn't handle. We walked down the path away from our apartment.

"What happened to him?" I asked her. "I'd never seen anything like it."

She looked at me with concern. "Have you seen anything similar happen to him?"

I didn't want to tell her that back in California I'd witnessed Steve's petit mal, short seizures, when he stared into space, turning ghostly white. But those had lasted only a few seconds. At the time, I tried my best not to pay attention to them. I shook my head slowly. "No, not really."

"It might have been a *grand mal.*" Naomi looked me in the eye. "It could happen to a person with a brain tumor."

My heart sank. Naomi knew about Steve's condition. Steve had tried so hard to keep it a secret; he'd be furious. The kibbutz secretary, who had reviewed our application to settle in Bet-Ha'emek, must have told her. Grand mal, or "great illness" in French—I rolled the words in my mouth as if I were an actress preparing for a role. Grand mal. Those words would haunt me for years to come; they'd pop up in the dark crevices of my mind regardless of time or space. Hoping Naomi would keep our conversation to herself, I never mentioned any of it to Steve, but I watched him closely. He didn't look well: he was pale and had lost weight; his clothes hung loose on his skinny body; and his temples were smooth and hairless where they had been radiated. My guess was that quite a few people on the kibbutz knew his secret.

To my surprise, a few months later, Steve appeared outside the dining hall with a shiny black Harley Davidson. With a big grin he parked it, unbuckled his helmet, bent his knees, and smoothed his blue denim jeans. He told me he planned to take Tal, thirteen years old now, on a motorcycle trip to Italy. I was appalled. But I also realized that he needed to believe he could still go on adventures. Kibbutz life stifled his spirit: he had to go along with what was customary, adhere to the rules, do what everybody else does. Though I recoiled from the idea, wishing Steve would change his mind, I said nothing. I knew that any objection I might have would have no effect on his decision.

Tal, who had come with me to the dining hall, stood with his mouth wide open, gazing in turn at Steve and at the motorcycle.

"Wow, where did you get it?" His blue eyes shone.

"From the dealer in Haifa."

"Can I go for a ride?"

"You bet, but not right now." Steve stroked Tal's hair. "Off to school with you."

One of Steve's coworkers, Yossi, trudged toward us.

"Hey, Steve, what's this? New transportation for the kibbutz members?"

Steve forced a smile. "Sure; it's time for an upgrade."

I knew that it was unheard of for a kibbutz member to buy a motorcycle. In the socialist community based on equality for all in which we lived, nobody owned private motorized transportation. If you needed a car to go somewhere, you signed up ahead of time for one of the kibbutz-owned cars. We both watched with relief as Yossi went up the steps to the dining room. I turned to Steve.

"We're on the list to become kibbutz members. A motorbike is not going to make the committee very happy."

Steve knew nobody was allowed to own a motorized vehicle on the kibbutz, but he always ignored the rules. Why was I surprised?

"It's okay. Come, I'll take you for a spin." He beamed at me, patting the leather seat.

"No, some other time," I hedged.

Steve didn't weigh more than a hundred and forty pounds. How could he ride that big beast?

"Come on, are you scared?"

"No, I'm not," I said, but a cold shudder ran through my body. I got on the bike. I didn't want to let him know that I feared he'd have a seizure and crash, killing us both. It was more important to overcome my fear, to help him keep a semblance of normalcy, to retain his image of being a man capable of riding a motorcycle, making love, leading a normal life. I believed that as his wife, it was my duty to keep his spirits up; that's what he had always told me. I also needed to maintain the illusion that he was fine, that he could function normally, and that he wasn't going to die.

We rode out of Bet Ha'emek, past the banana plantations, the cowshed, and the avocado groves. Holding on to Steve's waist, I adjusted my feet on the footrests. He veered to the left onto the main road, shifted gears, and lurched forward. We zoomed by the fields, neighboring Arab villages, and rows of cypress trees. My eyes smarted; squinting, I avoided the hurtling bugs. Blurs of brown, verdant, and sandy patches flew by; wooden telephone poles came at me one after the other.

Pressing my knees together, I circled my arms tighter around Steve's waist. I felt as if somebody had attached a metal rod to my spine. The wind roared in my ears: *grand mal, grand mal . . .*

We didn't last much longer on Bet Ha'emek; the effect of Steve's illness, plus his creative nature and individualism, got him into trouble with the conformist kibbutznicks. It came to a head this way: After working in the avocado plantation, he was assigned to sort out eggs. The kibbutz had several chicken coops, and the eggs were sold to the markets in the surrounding towns. On the first day on this job, Steve stood in the small cement room eyeing several straw-filled wicker baskets containing fresh eggs. Yehuda, his coworker, a Holocaust survivor whose blue work shirt and pants hung on his thin frame, pointed to a wooden template, which had holes in different sizes drilled into it.

"You take the eggs and find out into which size they fit." Yehuda held a large egg, which he gently lowered into one of the apertures.

"Isn't there a quicker way to do this?" Steve asked.

"No; this is the way we've always done it." The older kibbutznick turned his back and started sorting. Steve, the New York film-production manager, did as he was told the first day. But the next day, the members committee summoned me. Chava, her hair tied back in a bun, squinted at me through her glasses. "Your husband isn't adjusting very well to his new job."

"What happened?"

"He wanted to sort out the eggs his own way, and Yehuda said no."

"So?"

"So Steve got angry, took an egg, and busted it above Yehuda's head." Chava's eyes crinkled in laughter. "Yehuda described the egg yolk dribbling down his neck."

I repressed a smile. "So what's the result of all this?"

"Steve isn't welcome in the chicken coop anymore."

At the end of the year, sixteen months after our arrival, the kibbutz general assembly voted down our request to become members. "Esti and the kids are great, but Steve just doesn't fit in," they said. Steve and Tal accepted the verdict with equanimity, each for their own reasons. Teenagers on a kibbutz are a tight-knit group who've been together since birth. They don't accept newcomers easily. Tal, a gentle individualist, hadn't managed to become part of his group and felt like an outsider the whole time we were on the kibbutz. For Shira and Ori, four and nine, the adjustment to communal life had been much easier. They enjoyed being with other kids and spending a lot of time outdoors. Shira loved the freedom she had to roam around the kibbutz, where everybody knew her.

She was sad to leave all her friends. I was disappointed as well but aware of the fact that Steve wasn't a good fit for kibbutz life.

The verdict, plus Steve's realization that he'd be better off close to his neurologist in the US, cinched the decision to return to the States.

*❧ Chapter 18: ❧*

# The Letter

After the kibbutz, I had a hard time adjusting to life back in Mill Valley. Having to take care of the kids, cook all the meals, and manage the household on my own, I missed the freedom, friends, and social life I had in Bet Ha'Emek. We also got a new dog, a lively Australian shepherd named Stanley. Though I enjoyed having him, it was more work for me. I corresponded with a couple of friends on the kibbutz, trying to keep alive my connection to the place I loved.

"You have a letter from your boyfriend," Steve said mockingly, throwing the mail onto the dining room table. A warm glow spread through my body. I recognized the rectangular envelope, the blue and red stripes around the margins, and the slanted, ballpoint letters. It was from Hillel, my South African friend.

The letter lay on the checkered tablecloth. The table, given to us by Gussie and Milton, had been shipped from New York to London and back to the States, where it eventually occupied the dining room of our Mill Valley home. Its wood surface had witnessed many of our family dramas; arguments over our kids' diet, health, school;

accusations over shopping and telephone expenses. It witnessed Steve pounding the table while Tal, Shira, Ori, and I sat with downcast eyes as he stormed out of the house.

But it had also witnessed our family celebrations. For Passover Seders we always invited our landlords, Edward and Lou Strauss, who lived on a street above us but took a five-minutes walk down a deer path when they came to our house. They had no children and acted as grandparents to our kids. Edward, a German Jew with a trimmed white beard and twinkling blue eyes, was an opera singer who had defected from his troupe when they toured the United States in 1928. When we got to the part in the Haggadah about the exodus from Egypt, he'd sing in a resounding bass "Let My People Go," while we all harmonized. On Sukkoth, the table was transferred to our terrace, where it was part of the sukkah Steve built every year. Since getting sick, Steve had more time for his family and was more available to participate in holiday preparations. Spending time with the kids became his top priority; it was clear to me that he knew his time on earth was limited. For the holiday, I used to prepare an Israeli meal with my homemade hummus, falafel, tahini, and finely chopped green salad, to which we invited our neighbors, usually couples of mixed marriages in which one person was Jewish and the other wasn't. I prided myself on keeping the tradition alive, although we lived in a town that didn't have even one synagogue.

I sorted the mail on the table—bills, catalogues, and advertisements—making my way toward my friend's letter. Taking it, I sensed the blood rising to my face while Steve stared at me like a red-combed cock waiting to attack.

"Aren't you going to read it?"

"No, not now." I kept my head down, feeling the same way I did when my father looked at me, his eyes glaring like burning coals, whenever I did something to displease him. It seemed I was forever stuck between the two domineering male figures in my life, my husband and my father, one reflecting the other.

"It's time to pick up Ori," I said. Biting my nail, I tore away at the flesh of my ring finger, leaving a red gash.

"So you're keeping it to yourself."

I ignored him, retreating to our bedroom, shuffling along the narrow corridor, letter in hand. He was jealous, not trusting my loyalty to him. Though I liked Hillel, he was never more than a friend. There was chemistry between us, but as we both were married, it never went anywhere. I didn't want to read the letter in front of Steve because I was afraid of retribution: his anger, his withdrawal. Maybe it was his brain—the surgeon had explained that the astrocytoma pressing on the right frontal lobe affected his emotions. It took me a long time to comprehend the horrible meaning of that information. The illness aggravated his natural quick temper, and I bore the brunt of it. He'd been jealous in the past, but it got worse. I recalled the fury in his eyes when he spotted me sitting next to Hillel in a Kibbutz movie screening. The movie hadn't started yet; the lights in the hall were still on when I spotted Steve standing at the entrance door, his eyes pinpointed on me. I quickly excused myself and rushed to the entrance. We walked back in silence, but once we got to our apartment he lashed out. His face, close to mine, was contorted in anger. "What the fuck were you doing sitting next to him?" I stepped back, retreating from his fury, while I stuttered: "Nothing . . . I did nothing."

I never doubted *his* fidelity. In New York, stuck in our studio apartment with baby Tal and our German shepherd, I never questioned him when he returned from his work on film productions. He'd be gone for weeks, even months, shooting films in Mississippi, Boston, Yugoslavia, or even Nigeria. It had never dawned on me to doubt him—I was his wife, and we loved each other.

Under the surface of this usually charming, easygoing, capable man, there always lurked his desperate need to excel, to prove himself. Steve could achieve anything he set his mind on doing. He could talk anybody into doing his wishes, no matter how crazy or outlandish. However, after he was diagnosed with a chronic disease and feared losing control over his body, he became insecure and fearful. His self-image, his sense of himself as a man, plummeted.

Composing myself now with Hillel's letter folded into my back pocket, I emerged from the bedroom, my mouth a thin resolute line. "Ori is waiting. I have to pick him up," I said. I grabbed my pocketbook and fled from the house.

I ran down the steep driveway, lined with pink and white cherry plum blossoms; the air was fragrant with the scent of nectar. Six months had passed since we left the kibbutz, but I still dreamt about my friends there, especially Hillel; his white Shabbat shirt contrasting with tanned arms and neck, his shoulder-length hair and auburn beard framing his chiseled face. He managed the avocado orchards, and I loved the way he gently held an avocado between his thumb, pointer, and forefinger, turning the dark green fruit around, admiring it like a piece of art.

Steve had worked with Hillel, spending long hours under the hot sun. The veteran kibbutznick took my husband, under his wing, "I'll show you how to pick, plant, and prune the avocados; don't worry." Hillel took a liking to him, and Steve enjoyed the South African's company and guidance. Yet once Hillel and I started playing music together, harmonizing English ballads and American spirituals while we strummed our guitars, Steve would confront me afterward: "So you're spending time with *him* again."

But it was more than my duets with Hillel that bothered him. I participated in all the cultural activities on the kibbutz while Steve, not knowing the language, felt like an outsider. On holidays, especially the agricultural ones, the 250 kibbutz members celebrated together. At the beginning of May, a sense of excitement pervaded as the Pentecost holiday, Shavuot, approached. I loved this "Festival of First Fruits," when green wreaths and wildflowers decorated the tables in the communal dining hall and later, in the evening on an outdoor stage, every sector displayed its first symbolic crop—a sheaf of golden wheat, freshly picked avocados, a branch of golden bananas, a basket of powder-white cotton, fluffy yellow chicks, a spindly-legged calf, and the latest baby born on the kibbutz.

The holidays always featured music. In 1980, a week before Shavuot, Steve and I were in our little ground-floor apartment. It was late afternoon. The sun slanted through the curtains, illuminating the black-eyed Susans and blue chicory flowers on the table. A waft of cow manure blew through the open door.

I opened my guitar case, searching for the capo. "I have a rehearsal tonight," I said.

Steve pulled a monogrammed white cloth handkerchief out of his work-pants pocket and wiped the perspiration from his brow. "What are you rehearsing now?" he asked. The operation and radiation had taken their toll; his collarbones protruded below his thin neck. It was painful to see. I averted my eyes, looking at the floor. "The choir is preparing songs for Shavuot," I said, clasping the guitar neck. "There'll be a big celebration."

He spoke plaintively. "You're always out at meetings and rehearsals; you're never home. What about us, our family?" His tone became shrill. He spread his arms. "The children have their own group activities. We're not a family anymore."

I shoved my fists into my pockets. "Steve, I need to go; they're waiting for me." I felt as if I didn't have enough oxygen. Singing gave me a sense of my own worth, my identity apart from wife and mother. My rehearsals were a relief. I wondered whether Steve could understand how important it was for me to express myself, use my talents, be a person in my own right. I knew he loved my singing, often encouraging me to perform when we had guests, but it was under his guidance, his initiative, not mine. I enjoyed singing with other people, interacting with others, being out there in the world.

Now, as I walked toward Old Mill School, about fifteen minutes from our home, I tried to shake away the memories of that time on the kibbutz. I patted my pocket; the letter was in there, warm and comforting, proof of a life apart from my present life, which consisted of driving Steve to chemotherapy sessions; yelling "Quiet, please!" while teaching Hebrew in afternoon school; shopping with Shira and Ori for pants and T-shirts at J. C. Penny; or trying to figure out each evening what to cook for Steve, the only non-vegetarian in our family. I tried to compensate with special vegetarian dishes such as mushroom quiche, spinach lasagna, eggplant parmesan, cheese soufflé, or nut loaf. Still, Steve used to go at lunchtime to Marin Joe's, where he got his daily dose of meat in the form of a lamb stew, which his regular waitress kept for him, even if he came late. He tried to persuade me to start cooking meat, but I stood my ground. Whenever Ori had a cold, Steve would say: "He better start eating meat; he'll never get well eating grass all the time."

I reached the school. The neatly painted blue, purple, and yellow slides, the swings and jungle gym, were a far cry from the kibbutz "junk-yard playground," where Ori and his friends used to swing on worn tires, jump on discarded cartons, spin old bicycle wheels, turn loose doorknobs, and crawl through segments of aluminum water pipes. The kibbutz children would play for hours in their make-believe world.

Ori and I walked hand in hand up Lovell Avenue toward home. He clasped a bouquet of lemon grass, the slender stems arched under pale yellow petals, as well as miner's lettuce and wild onions he picked along the way. We played the skipping game Steve had taught him: One, two, three—skip. One, two, three—skip. We sang, "Michael, row your boat ashore, hallelujah," elongating the last syllables: "Halle-loo-oo-ya." When we got close to home, Ori raced me up our driveway. The silver Honda, the Mercedes's replacement, wasn't there. Good, I thought, Steve was out. At the time he worked as a freelance photographer, taking pictures of nonprofit organizations such as the Halleck Creek Riding Club or the Center for Abused Women. Once Ori and I got home, we headed to the kitchen where I fixed him a snack of peanut butter and jelly sandwich with his favorite drink, hot chocolate. He then walked up the hill to Edward and Lou's house to watch *Sesame Street*. Since Steve had decided that too much television wasn't good for the kids, we didn't own one.

I settled down on our living room sofa, took the letter out of my pocket, and opened it. The thin sheets of paper with dense handwriting rustled in my hands. I breathed deeply, scanning the lines—"I'm on reserve duty in an army outpost . . . I miss you . . . I miss our singing . . . I saw a volunteer girl on the kibbutz that looks just like you." I read to the end. For a moment I sat motionless, head bent, snuggling the letter to my chest.

I inserted the thin airmail pages back into the envelope and looked for a place to hide it. Where could I put it? Between the books? The plants? Add it to the pile of letters from my parents and sister? Pulse racing, I rushed to our bedroom and stuffed it into the bottom drawer of our dresser, between my cotton nightgown and sweatpants.

After dinner, while I was doing the dishes, Steve blurted, "Well, what did he say?"

"Nothing special." I scrubbed the soup pot, up and down, back and front.

Steve narrowed his eyes and stretched out his hand. "So give me the letter." I avoided his eyes, shaking my head, a sickly feeling in my stomach.

"No, I can't." I swallowed hard.

He raised his voice. "Just give it to me."

I knew that tone. I didn't dare to defy it. Heart thudding, I walked to the bedroom, retrieved the letter, and handed it over. Steve marched into the living room. Sitting in the armchair he had ordered from Sweden, feet on the stool, he proceeded to read. The black and white lines on the upholstery were as uncompromising as my husband—there were no grays in his world. How would he react when he read the signature: "Love, Hillel." Fling the letter at me? Storm out of the house? Call me vile names? I didn't wait to find out. Grabbing a flashlight and leash, with Stanley running ahead, I fled down our driveway, the melancholy stars in the black canopy over me. I always found solace in being outside, in nature, and running had a soothing effect on me.

When I returned, Steve was at his desk in the living room; the lamp light outlined his high forehead, aquiline nose, and prominent chin. Closing the door gently, I walked to the kids' bedroom. Steve didn't say a word to me. Tal, a Tamalpais High student, was out with friends; Shira and Ori were getting ready for bed. My voice breaking, I sang to them my usual Hebrew lullaby: "*Noomi, noomi*, Sleep, sleep, my little child." I kissed them good night, averting my eyes so they wouldn't notice my tears.

Later, in the darkness of our bedroom, Steve pulled me toward him and passionately caressed me. Had he finally realized that I'd chosen to be with him and not back on the kibbutz? Was he aroused by the fact that another man found his wife attractive? I didn't care—he wasn't angry with me any more; he let me back in. My frozen body thawed, and my muscles relaxed as I clung to him, tears of relief trickling down my cheeks.

## ❧ Chapter 19: ❧

# Amazing Grace

On October 17, 1983, about three years after our return from Bet Ha'emek, we landed again in UCSF hospital. Steve was about to undergo a third operation. The surgeon, citing the procedure as the latest development in technology, reassured us that "this one will do the trick." I very much wanted to believe him, but doubt gnawed in me.

In the hospital, I waited in a large hall with partitions at both ends. Above, bright neon lights glared. Nurses in trim uniforms strode purposely while other patients' family members and friends milled around, eyes downcast, talking in hushed voices. I paced back and forth waiting for Steve to come out of the room where they'd taken him to prepare for his surgery. I wished there had been someone to talk to, with whom I could share my anxiety, but I was alone. I had been on my own in many critical periods of my life: as a new bride while teaching at the Ulpan in Jerusalem—though I had a housemate at the time, I couldn't confide in her or in anybody else—when I first arrived in the States, and when I gave birth to Tal in New York, Shira in London, and Ori in San Francisco. I wondered how much of it was circumstance and how much was my own doing. My stoic upbringing had served me well in that I believed I could handle any situation on my own. But it also meant it didn't dawn on me to ask for help, or I might have been too proud to ask.

A young smooth-shaven nurse wearing a silver ring in his ear pushed a gurney out of an interior room. Steve, his head shaved, rested on a puffed-up pillow, an IV tube attached to his arm. My heart leapt. I rushed over.

"Excuse me, where are you taking him now? I'm his wife." The pounding in my chest resounded in my skull. The young man smiled at me, and the look from his soft brown eyes melted away some of my fear. He pointed to a partitioned area in the far side of the large hall. "Don't worry, we're not going far."

While walking along with the nurse wheeling the gurney, I peeked at my husband. His eyes were half-closed, sunken into the sockets below his well-defined eyebrows. His right arm was limp on top of the sheet; his slender fingers curled inward, his narrow gold band shining. Looking at his artist-like hands, I thought about all his beautiful creations: little figurines out of acorns and twigs, colorful drawings of clowns and donkeys, and elaborate puppets made of scraps of cloth and cotton wool.

At the foot of the gurney lay a large, well-worn teddy bear with rough light-brown fur, two beady eyes—one of them slightly loose—and yellow foam padding showing through where the seams had parted. Teddy wore a beige-and-brown knit sweater, which had belonged to Tal when he was a baby. It was hard to believe that he was already eighteen and practically on his own. Steve insisted on taking the teddy bear every time he went for surgery—it was his talisman.

Once the nurse stationed the gurney and left, I turned to my husband.

"Steve." I placed my hand gently on his. He opened his eyes and smiled at me in recognition.

He moved his hand over his smooth, glistening skull. "I'm so glad you're here. They gave me some pills and shaved off my hair."

He looked like a prisoner being led to the gallows. Seeing him like that frightened me. I swallowed hard. A purple triangle drawn on the right side of his head above the temple looked like a traffic signal. My hand moved forward to touch the obscene lines but withdrew as if from a hot flame.

"Is this where they'll operate?"

"I think so . . . they'll insert the radioactive seed into my brain. It will kill off those cancerous cells that refuse to die, and I'll be a new man." He grinned at me like a child.

Gosh, I thought, it's amazing how optimistic he is. But what choice did he have? If he didn't believe he'd be cured, he'd never make it. His faith helped me believe that he wouldn't die, that the surgery would cure him. Though I resented him being blasé about it, I was grateful to him.

The doctor's words from the previous day buzzed in my mind like angry bees: "Cut, seed, sew back." He was talking about Steve's brain, the same gray matter they'd cut into twice before when the radiations and chemo treatments couldn't conquer the spreading cancer. The doctor's words had nauseated me.

Putting my hand on his shoulder, I asked Steve. "What will the surgeon do?"

"He'll saw a flap in my skull, flip it open, put the seed in, and, voilá—close the lid."

Yes, I thought, it's that easy. He must be joking, though Steve believed in finding solutions—if you can *do* something about a problem, everything will be okay. I tightened my fists, pasting a smile on my face.

"You'll be fine." I stroked his shoulder gently. We were both silent, yet my stomach churned while questions shot through my head. What if the nuclear seed killed him? What if he became paralyzed?

He nodded off. His eyelids drooped, lips parted, and his breathing became shallow. I looked around. A young doctor strode past with a set of folders under his arm. He signaled a surgeon dressed in green cotton pants and shirt, a plastic blue cap on his head. His shoes were covered with the same light plastic material, pulled together with a string. Whom had he just operated on? Did the patient make it? The surgeon looked so young, maybe in his early thirties.

"Esther," Steve said softly. I bent over the gurney's metal railing, close to his face, inhaling the smell of medications and sour breath. "Did you bring your guitar?" I nodded. That was the one thing he had asked me to bring to the hospital. He loved to hear me sing—it always lifted his spirits. I recalled Steve's beaming face the times we sat with our three kids next to the fireplace, singing our favorite songs.

I picked up the guitar, which lay next to my chair with my bag on it. The bag contained my math book. I always took it with me. While waiting for Steve to complete his chemotherapy treatments or doctor appointments, I'd do homework for my math classes at the College of Marin, solving equations and logarithms, drawing graphs and tangents. I was finally going to complete my college degree. I tackled numbers and symbols, concentrating on finding the correct answer. It gave me some sense of control over my life, over what was happening to Steve and to our family.

Releasing the buckles on the guitar case, I opened the lid. My guitar had served me well over the years—in remote youth hostels in Europe, in military camps in Israel, at friends' gatherings around a bonfire, on stage in various Jewish Community Centers, and at my children's bedside when sleep eluded them. After strumming a few chords to make sure it was in tune, I hesitated. How was I going to sing and play in a place filled with nurses, doctors, patients, and their families? I felt like an intruder.

Then I remembered Steve's words: "You have to keep me buoyant. I can't make it on my own." I took a deep breath. I'd promised him I'd keep his spirits up. I'd try to alleviate his anxiety, the black tunnel he had to enter before he emerged in a stupor in the recovery room. I sighed, trying to calm the heaving in my abdomen.

Looking around, I adjusted the shoulder strap. Though we were in the middle of the hallway, nobody seemed to pay attention to us. Good. "What would you like me to play?" I asked Steve.

Steve licked his dry lips. "How about 'Amazing Grace'?" The Christian hymn was his anthem. It didn't matter that he was a good Jewish boy who went to synagogue on Rosh Hashanah, had a Seder on Passover, and lit candles on Hanukkah; he sang it with the conviction of a true believer: *Amazing grace, how sweet the sound that saved a wretch like me.*

My husband fought his cancer with any tool available. His first savior was Viktor Frankl, whom he heard on television three days after his first brain operation. He lay in his hospital bed, his head swathed in bandages, when the words of the Viennese psychologist filtered into his consciousness: "The will to survive depends on whether or not life has meaning for you." Ten days later, his bandages covered with a woolen hat, he drove to Berkeley to listen to Dr. Frankl lecture. On his return, worn out but with shining eyes, Steve had asked me, "Do you know why Viktor Frankl survived the concentration camp while the others died?"

"No, why?"

"He had a reason to live." Steve's voice grew louder, the pitch higher. "He had started to write a book before they took him to Auschwitz. In camp he reconstructed his writing by scribbling on scraps of paper so when he was liberated he could publish his manuscript."

Encouraging words, calming music, games with the children, therapy, and hot tubs—Steve tried everything in order to heal, in order to survive. I had the gift of music, which I could offer him, so I started humming the first notes of the hymn. I was still embarrassed; my cheeks flushed while I moved my thumb gently over the strings from top to bottom.

"Amazing grace . . ." Steve's soft tenor joined my wavering soprano. I took a deep breath and sang louder, with more resonance.

We were in our own world, transported by the sounds we uttered in unison. We were together on the ocean liner where we'd first met; we were in the countries where we'd traveled; we were in a nature reserve in Yugoslavia, where we'd made love hidden in the grass; we were on a sunny hill above Monaco, where we'd picnicked with three-year-old Tal. The music transcended the peaks and valleys of our life together, hurtful words and painful silences followed by red roses and little notes pleading for forgiveness.

The melody reached its peak when we heard another, different voice, a mellifluous contralto coming from behind us: "I once was lost, but now I'm found . . ." I turned around and looked into a pair of dark shining eyes above pearl white teeth set in an oval face. The woman joining our song was a nurse in a white starched uniform. We sang, Steve with a slight smile illuminating his gaunt face, and I with my head high and my fingers fluttering over the guitar strings. Our three voices floated up, over the sickness, the pain, the suffering, through the opaque hospital windows, melting away fear and resistance.

The strains of the last verse faded away. I turned to the nurse and said, "Thank you, thank you." We hugged.

"Honey, you're the one I have to thank. God bless you." Her warm words enveloped me even as she walked away through the revolving glass door. An orderly arrived and took hold of the gurney. "It's time to go." Steve's eyes were closed; the tranquilizers had taken hold of him. I pressed my palms in a form of prayer, sending him a mental message of love and hope.

"Shall I take the teddy bear?" I asked the orderly. "It's okay; he can keep it." I thanked him, my eyes tearing. His tightly woven braids swung above his shoulders as he wheeled Steve away. He halted before the double doors. "There's a waiting room on the second floor. The surgeon will let you know when it's over."

I bent over the railing and kissed Steve on his forehead. It felt clammy and warm. "Good luck," I whispered as he was wheeled through the doors. There was nothing more I could do. I remembered a childhood dream in which I was a tiny figure trying to escape as two huge rotating wheels bore down on me.

"God help him," I uttered as I walked toward the elevator. It was as though a rock were lodged in my solar plexus. The elevator lights blinked. The door opened, and I stepped in. The air in the elevator reeked of ammonia. Standing in the back while people pressed in, I could hardly breathe. It was silent except for the whirring of the belts and the metallic *ping* when we passed each floor. In my mind's eye I was on a high diving board, dazed by the blinding sun and water, my knees shaking while the coach, way down on the pool's edge, monitored the countdown. I focused my gaze on the elevator's numbers: nine . . . three, two, one. Thank God, I thought, I'm out. "Excuse me," I blurted as I brushed against a woman's arm.

The phone booth at the end of the corridor was dimly lit. I could barely see the numbers on the dial as I called my babysitter. My heart pounding, I clutched the receiver. Swallowing my saliva, my head spinning, I realized I didn't know what to tell the kids if they came to the phone and asked how Steve was. I didn't want to scare them, so I decided to reassure them in any way I could.

Tal was away at college, so I'd talk with him when it was all over.

The babysitter answered, and I asked, "Are Shira and Ori okay?"

"Fine," she answered. There was a moment of silence. Then, "Ori wants to talk to you."

"*Eema*, when are you coming home?" His sweet eight-year-old voice rang through the line. I forced my vocal cords to utter an even, normal sound.

"I'll be back before you go to bed, don't worry."

"Can you bring me some candy?"

"Sure, as much as you like." I swallowed hot tears and hung up. A hand touched me softly on my shoulder. I looked back. The nurse who had sung with us was smiling at me. "Honey, don't cry. Everything is going to be just fine." Her mellow voice again enfolded me, caressing and reassuring.

Steve's operation was termed a success, but we had no way of knowing whether it would beat the cancer. At home, he searched for ways to keep up his spirits. One day he asked the kids and me to come with him to the variety store in downtown Mill Valley. I was amazed when he asked the woman behind the counter, "Do you have some white face paint?" After paying for it, he proceeded to smear the paint over his cheeks, forehead, and chin.

He passed the paint to Tal. "Okay, your turn."

Tal, who was home for the weekend, complied, knowing better than to ask questions. Ori let Steve whiten his face, but Shira was adamant: "This is crazy. I am not going to paint my face." When Steve handed me the paint, I shook my head. "No, thanks, I don't like paint on my face." I looked at him quizzically. "What are you up to?"

"We're going to Hillhaven to make the old people happy." Hillhaven was a local convalescent home, a last stop for many elderly patients. He then turned again to the sales person: "Do you have helium balloons?"

She smiled at him. "Sure . . . how many do you want?"

He looked at us as if counting the numbers of balloons. "How about ten white balloons?"

Why all white? I wondered. Maybe he thought it was a festive color or the symbol of peace. Steve was always interested in the peace movement. He handed a couple of balloons to each of us, after which we headed out the door. Steve was the boss, so it didn't dawn on the kids or me to refuse to go with him. Besides, I would have done almost anything to make him feel better.

Hillhaven's dimly lit corridor reeked of medications and urine. One man and several old women sat in wheelchairs, staring at the wall in front of them. A shriveled woman, her head slumped on her chest, mumbled, "I want to go home, I want to go home."

Steve marched on, Tal and Ori lagging behind. Shira stayed outside, and at first, I hovered at the entrance, trying to hide the balloons behind my back. But then, with some trepidation, I walked in. I wasn't sure how the residents would react. I doubted whether he had even contacted anyone to ask for permission. I thought the idea was sweet but a bit unnerving. It was strange; it reminded me of a Fellini movie. Yet that was Steve: impulsive, flamboyant, and irreverent. In a way he was also naive, believing that a simple gesture could alleviate others' suffering and pain.

"Here, have a balloon," Steve said as he handed one to a woman with white frizzled hair, her two front teeth missing. She took the string in her gnarled fingers and said nothing. Another woman grumbled, refusing the offering.

When we left, we still had several balloons. At the plaza, near the bus stop, a big black guy with wiry gray curls grinned at us. Steve handed him a balloon.

"Thank you, sir." The man took the balloon and chuckled.

When we got home, Steve let the remaining balloons float to the ceiling, where they remained, strings dangling, for over a week. Five days after the Hillhaven episode, I walked into our living room, where the hovering balloons still lingered. They had shrunk, sinking closer to the floor. Just like Steve, who was trying so valiantly to stay buoyant.

I thought wistfully about my husband's desire to make the old people feel better, to bring some fun into their lives. What he did was endearing, but I felt irritated as well; he didn't share his plans with me or with the children. He went on a whim and expected us to follow, whether we liked it or not. I often felt like one of the kids, not his wife. When Steve acted this way, childlike and fun-loving, I felt as if I were the only adult in the family. I felt anger, pity, and compassion all at once, and in light of his illness I wondered whether his actions were his way of making the most of life, of connecting with others, of expressing his humanity. Perhaps it was his way of deterring death.

*❧ Chapter 20: ❧*

# Commonweal

For eight years, the word "cancer" hovered like a dark monster, overshadowing our lives, yet we pretended it didn't exist, telling our well-meaning friends, "No, it's not cancer. Steve has a brain-tumor." The word "tumor" was somehow less frightening. Cancer evoked for me a clawing animal tearing Steve's body apart. During the time Steve battled his illness, if any of his family or friends uttered the forbidden word, his eyes would turn into two mean slits. He refused to talk about it; we didn't discuss his situation or what he was going through. Though the secrecy was difficult for me, I honored his decision, knowing that it was his way of coping with the illness. Actually, the "head in the sand" approach suited me, since I wanted to believe that the cancer would somehow disappear.

In 1985, the eighth year of his illness, Steve's doctor finally gave up on him, saying, "I have no more tricks in my bag." Steve had so many hopes for the last surgery in which they planted a nuclear seed in his brain. But it didn't work. Steve was devastated; there was no reason for him to fight anymore. I racked my brain for ways to help him. And then, as if by a miracle, in the October issue of our local paper, I saw an article about a cancer retreat. I read it several times. It was an interview with Michael Lerner, director of Commonweal, a cancer retreat center on the cliffs above Bolinas. I felt my blood pulsing. Here was an answer to my prayers.

When I got home, Steve was resting on his bed reading a photography magazine. Waving the paper, I rushed to our bedroom. "Look," I tried to catch my breath, "this might work; it might be a solution."

I wasn't sure what I was talking about, how the retreat could save him, but I wanted to believe it would help, make him feel better, even prolong his life. The article mentioned holistic treatments: special diets, meditations, massages, group therapy. I had always believed in alternative, natural healing methods. All the poisons they poured into his body hadn't cured him, so why not try something new?

Steve was less enthusiastic. He looked at me with tired eyes. "How can they help me? Nothing works."

"But that's the point; you've nothing to lose, and who knows? Maybe a different approach will help."

Steve must have heard the desperation in my voice. He considered my suggestion. "Will I have to go there on my own?"

"No, spouses of patients can come along as guests." I held my breath, hoping for him to agree to go.

"Can you make arrangements for the kids while we're there?"

Elated, I came up with a quick answer. "Shira is old enough to watch Ori for six days. Besides, we're not that far from home, and she can always call us."

Shira, who had started high school, was happy to be in charge of her younger brother while we were gone. With an eager look in her round blue eyes she promised, "We'll be fine. I'll take good care of Ori."

I called Michael Lerner, who encouraged us to come as soon as possible. We signed up for the second week in November. Steve and I packed our bags and drove up Mt. Tam, then down, past the lagoon to Bolinas. Before entering town, after driving along a narrow road flanked by towering eucalyptus trees, we passed an uncultivated field with a small sign on the road that read, *Commonweal.* We turned left toward the ocean, and, on a bluff, we spotted several wooden cabins amid wind-blown pine trees.

Michael Lerner, a soft-spoken elf-like man in his forties, in faded brown corduroy pants over woolen socks and Birkenstock sandals, welcomed us. He pointed to one of the cabins. "You'll have your own cabin. And over there," he pointed in the other direction, "are the dining room and communal hall. Please, make yourself feel at home. Lunch will be served soon."

I felt let down when we entered the cabin. It was austere, with two twin beds flanking a nightstand, a small wooden table and chairs, and a bathroom with a shower. However, I reasoned, we wouldn't spend much time in the room, and this wasn't a vacation. After a short rest, which Steve needed since he was tired from the drive, we walked about five minutes along a dirt path to the dining hall. We sat next to a man and woman who both looked thin and pale. They welcomed us and pointed to a buffet. Steve took one look at the various salads and grains in shades of green and brown and exclaimed, "What the hell is this?" He had never eaten vegan food.

I hadn't thought to inquire about the food or the daily schedule. I was so relieved that someone could help Steve that I didn't care about details. I was dead set on going to the retreat; I went on an impulse, in the belief that the retreat would save him. That was all that mattered to me.

The following day had a strict schedule: we sat in the retreat with eight other cancer patients while we meditated, inhaled deeply in a yoga session, listened to each other's pains and fears during circle time, and visualized fierce dragons breathing fire, eliminating white cancerous cells. Among the eight guests, I was the only partner and the only one without cancer. I was considered a "participating support person." I felt out of place, an intruder. Most of the people there were in the process of dying, so absorbed in their own problems that it was hard to tell what they felt about my presence. Were they resentful, jealous, or apathetic? Probably the latter sentiment. I knew how all-consuming cancer was.

By the morning of our third day in Bolinas, I went to Michael's office. Wringing my hands, I exclaimed, "I can't participate in the circle today; I need to get out." The heavy atmosphere in the retreat was getting to me. Listening constantly to heartwrenching stories about living with cancer and trying to cope with it was suffocating me. I needed to get some fresh air.

Ten minutes later I rode his old bicycle on the dirt road out of Commonweal, pedaling hard, pushing down one foot after the other, ignoring the jolts in my groin as I bumped over potholes and rocks below me. Would all this visualizing, arranging figures in a sand box, and smearing red and black lines on drawing pads really help Steve? Was I at risk of becoming sick like them? They were all normal people with regular lives, so how did they contract this horrendous illness? I shook my head to dispel an image of a wild beast lurching in my chest. The wind in my face felt good as I sped down the hill, tightening my fingers over the handlebars. After passing teal manzanita bushes and maroon madrone trunks, I inhaled the pungent scent of pitcher sage as I approached the sea. I left the bicycle on the sand, peeled off my shoes and socks, folded up my jeans, and ran along the pounding waves, circled by seagulls and pelicans.

When I returned, riding the bicycle to Michael's office, he stood in front, as if waiting for me. I got off the bike and leaned it against a tree.

"We have to talk," he said.

I looked at him, puzzled. Was it about Steve? Had he been acting up? Steve wasn't one to follow prescribed timetables and activities. "Okay . . ."

"You know, Steve is going to die," he said, putting his hands on my shoulders.

His words stung me. They were the last words on earth I thought he'd say. I jolted back, sensing the bile rise in my stomach.

"No, it's not possible," I choked. "You're lying."

"I'm afraid it's the truth."

I fought back tears. "He can't die. He's too young. He lived with cancer for eight years. He'll continue to live!" I looked up at him. "I thought this place is supposed to help him."

"You'll have to accept it, for your own good."

"No, never." I bolted away as if a scorpion had bitten me. I ran down the chaparral-lined path, sobbing.

It wasn't possible; he couldn't disappear. My thoughts swirled; I couldn't fathom the meaning or reality of death. I couldn't visualize the nothingness it entailed. I'd never had to confront death, since nobody close to me had died before. Steve, whom I had lived with for almost twenty years, was the only man with whom I'd shared my life. Though he wasn't always present, I knew he'd return home. He couldn't suddenly vanish and leave me alone with our three kids. It seemed unnatural, like coming home and seeing that the whole house had collapsed.

That night at 2:00 a.m., I woke up to Steve groaning. He pressed his palms against his head, eyes bulging, complaining of a headache. I ran to Michael's room. He arrived a few minutes later with codeine-laced painkillers. Steve took them with a shaking hand while Michael put his arm around him. I looked at the two men, my heart filled with agony and compassion for Steve, gratitude and admiration for Michael. I was also resentful that my husband had been selected by some higher force to suffer so much while others were free of pain.

The following morning as the first streaks of pale light filtered into the room, Steve and I lay awake in our beds.

"I've had it here," he said. "All we get to eat and drink are different kinds of weeds."

"It's meant to heal."

"I hate wheat grass and chicory." He stuck out his tongue in disgust.

"You should give it a chance."

"I have. I don't want to any more."

"What do you want?" I asked.

He gave me a wan smile. "Some coffee and a juicy burger."

"You can't leave in the middle. You haven't given it a try."

He spread out his arms, palms up, his thin wrists sticking out from his striped pajamas. "Oh yes I have. I've slept on a hard bed, shuffled to meals on dirt paths, eaten seeds and grass that pass for food."

"This is our last hope." I said.

"Why do you think so?"

"I don't know, Steve. What else is there?"

An old twinkle came back into his eyes. "Look, if I've got just a short time to live, let me enjoy it." This was the first time he'd ever mentioned the fact that he might die. Just saying it aloud gave me permission to feel a bit more at ease about his decision to leave—if that's what would make him happy, why not? Still, I felt we shouldn't leave in the middle. I begged him to stay at the retreat, to give it a try, to change his carnivorous diet into that of an herbivore, to cleanse his systems, to stop, for once, trusting doctors, and to put his faith in healers: yogis, therapists, psychologists—enlightened human beings who could possibly prolong his life. But he didn't believe in alternative healing, and it was too late. The cancer had taken over.

When I told Michael that Steve wanted to leave the retreat, he looked at me softly. "I'm sorry to hear that, but I understand. Steve needs to do what he wants right now."

That night we checked into the Clarion Hotel in Terra Linda.

He might be right, I thought, as I slid next to him under the starched, crisp linen sheets, feeling their cool stiffness, hoping he'd relax and get a reprieve from his suffering. The television light flickered, lighting up his gaunt face, the one I knew so well for the last nineteen years and which now began to resemble a smooth skull: sunken eyes, hollow cheeks, bloodless lips—lips that once created a fire within me. No, I thought, I can't let myself drown in self-pity; it won't help either of us. But I couldn't fight back a deep sense of despair, which overwhelmed me, freezing my limbs, numbing my mind while I moved closer to my husband in search of warmth, realizing, second by second, that the flame was flickering on the verge of extinction.

I pulled at the sheet, wondering if I'd manage to sleep sharing Steve's bedcovers. At home we each had our own down comforter; I needed my space. I hoped the stale central-heated air wouldn't keep me up all night. I had an awareness of impending doom, that there is no way to escape fate, the way a dung beetle, slowly pushing its ball of manure, hears the thud of a heavy boot along its path but cannot swerve in time. I nudged closer to my husband—his limbs were cold and rigid as he lay on his back, mouth open, slightly snoring. Why did I think he'd feel better in a hotel than in a cancer retreat center?

The following morning, supporting Steve, holding on to his elbow, we exited the elevator and headed to the dining room, which looked deserted. Heavy brocade curtains kept out the sunlight, the air smelled musty, and Lara's song from *Doctor Zhivago* droned in the background. A waitress with a black apron, thick ankles, and tired bleached-blond hair came over and handed us two large plastic menus on which appeared glossy pictures of breakfast dishes in various shapes and colors: stacks of dripping pancakes, dirt-brown sausages, flesh-pink slices of ham accompanying pale-yellow circles of fried eggs. No wonder people suffer from strokes, obesity, and heart attacks, I thought. But Steve was much more comfortable with this menu than he'd been with the food at Commonweal.

He scanned his menu and looked up.

"I'll have eggs over easy, a short stack of pancakes, rye bread, and a cup of coffee."

The waitress took the order and stared for a second at Steve's felt hat, which didn't quite cover his shaven temples. Did she realize he had cancer? I averted my eyes.

"I'll have the same with wheat toast and no pancakes." I nodded to the waitress, who wrote it down and walked over to another couple who had just come in, the only other people in the whole place.

When his breakfast arrived, Steve dug into it with the glee of a man for whom Yom Kippur had just ended. I smiled as he cut a piece of the egg and brought it to his mouth, but soon my smile froze—the egg yolk slid down his chin and dripped onto his burgundy flannel shirt, where it left a mustard-yellow trail. I felt embarrassed for him, and for some reason for myself too. I looked sideways hoping nobody else noticed, thinking he'd take out his handkerchief and clean it up, that he'd smile and apologize for the mess, but no; he kept eating, unaware, while I sat motionless, not daring to tell him for fear of humiliating him. I had a horrid sensation of sinking into the ground like the dung beetle.

Back in our room getting ready to leave, I collected my toiletries when Steve called out, "What day is it?"

"It's Wednesday." I folded my nightgown, adding it to the pile of turtlenecks and T-shirts in my valise.

"What's the date?" he asked.

"It's November eighteenth . . . I think." I picked up my diary, stuffing it in the spare space behind the clothes.

"What day is it?" he repeated, a strange edge to his voice.

"It's Wednesday, I told you." Why does he keep on asking? I pressed down on my suitcase and zipped it in one quick movement.

"What *day* is it?" The question shot into the air.

Turning abruptly, I dropped my hairbrush. Steve lay on the

ruffled blankets, arms crossed behind his head, staring at the ceiling, unblinking.

"Steve." I tried to catch his eye. A palpitating, ominous fear crept up my spine. I kept my voice as calm as possible. "It's Wednesday."

The air in the room felt heavy. The wall-length mirror reflected the picture above the headboard: an opaque vase of irises in faded blues and grays perched on a shroud-white tablecloth.

"Esther." His voice was shrill. I jumped up, my heart beating like the old water pump in the dark orange groves of my childhood, *pom-pom, pom-pom.*

"What is it?"

He clasped and unclasped his hands, the whites showing in his wide-open eyes, his tongue moving over his dry, cracked lips. He turned his head slowly, facing me.

"Can you tell me what month it is?" He enunciated with deliberation, as if his life depended on my answer.

I picked up a corner of the bed sheet, twisting it tighter and tighter. An arrow of fear pierced my body. His mind was gone; it was the beginning of the end; he was slipping away from me. Words floated up from a deep, murky well, a reverberating echo of Doctor Lynch's husky voice: "The tumor will move. If it presses on the brain, it will affect his memory and speech." My chest felt hollow while I laid my hand on Steve's frozen fingers, talking to him like to a child.

"It's November." The low, muffled alto voice seemed to emanate from some other body, not mine. "Come, I've finished packing, let's go down."

I tugged at his hand, but he remained motionless, his head turned up, his eyes turned inward into his own world.

That week, after we returned home, hospice stepped in to help me cope with Steve's dying. The doctor's words that he might live a few more months meant nothing to me. It was as if someone announced that the world would vanish or that I'd get up the following morning without my eyesight. Steve had undergone three operations, radiation, and chemotherapy, which he either drank or had dripped through a needle into his vein. I insisted to myself that he wasn't going to give up, that he'd survive. I couldn't acknowledge the obvious: that Steve had gradually stopped functioning.

At the end of November, a couple of weeks after our return from Commonweal, I walked into our bedroom and found Steve leaning on one elbow trying to push himself up. He greeted me with a crooked smile; the muscles in his mouth didn't function anymore.

"I'm going to eat breakfast at Fred's; come help me get up."

"You're what? No way!"

Fred's, in Sausalito, where a colorful group of ex-hippies, artists, and boat people from the anchor-outs on Richardson Bay gathered, was Steve's favorite breakfast hangout. He beckoned to me, his thin neck protruding. I stared at him in disbelief. Was he out of his mind? He could barely make it to the bathroom.

I held my right palm up in a stop motion. "Steve, you can't. You can't walk." I laid my hand on his shoulder, feeling the shoulder blade jutting out under the flannel cloth.

"Help me," he whispered while straightening his legs, slipping one foot into his plaid cotton slipper.

I had to go along with him. He still had a will to live; he couldn't give up. Pressing my lips, I inserted my shoulder under his arm, heaving him up. His shaky body felt heavy on mine. He stood up for a second and then collapsed, as if somebody let go of the strings of a marionette.

I inhaled deeply, fear numbing my limbs. "Steve, it won't work."

Tightening my belly muscles, I tilted him back onto the bed. Gently, I moved his thin pale legs back under the blanket and covered him.

Michael Lerner's warning—"Steve is going to die"—began to sink in. Death, though I couldn't fathom it, was becoming a reality, a black-cloaked figure that was going to rob me of my husband, to extinguish the last breath of my lover, my friend, and the father of my children. I had never witnessed death; I didn't follow the aging and dying of grandparents. Mine were murdered in the camps. I didn't know what to expect; Steve was forty-two years old. Nobody dies that young, I thought. At least nobody *I* knew had.

Looking back at Steve, his head resting on the pillow, chin pointing upward, translucent eyelids half-closed, I slowly left the room. I didn't want to think what would happen after he died. I didn't function that way. I protected myself by dealing with the present, by coping with disasters as they arrived. I survived by acting like the proverbial ostrich. I didn't try to project or plan anything for the future. Steve was still alive, he could still talk, he could still breathe, and he was still with me. That was all I cared about.

## ❧ Chapter 21: ❧

# Morphine

B y the end of the first week in December, Steve was bedridden. He lay in our bedroom propped up on pillows in the hospital bed provided by hospice. A urine-collection bag dangled from the end of the bed, a tube protruding from under his down blanket. Emptying it into the toilet, I puckered my mouth, trying not to look at its yellow-brown contents or inhale the acrid smell. This is what our relationship had been reduced to; instead of functioning as his wife, I turned into his caregiver, his nurse. We both were in the middle of our lives, far from old age, when this scenario would more likely have taken place. When Steve signed the *ketubbah*, I couldn't have foreseen, even in my worst nightmares, that nineteen years later he'd be on his deathbed.

The weak December light shone through the corner window-panes, alighting on a box of Kleenex; a hardcover book, *The Healing Power of Laughter* by Norman Cousins; and a small bronze bell. The ringing of the bell—Steve's summons when he needed help—caught me in the kitchen washing breakfast dishes. I resented the ring; it reminded me of Steve's helplessness. But more than that, each time I heard it, I felt like a soldier having to obey a command, or I had a flash of my mother always being at my father's beck and call. I couldn't blame Steve; he was the one suffering while I was healthy. Yet deep inside me, like lava bubbling under the surface, waiting to erupt, I felt my anger with Steve's illness. It was an opponent I couldn't see or fight back against. All I could do was be there for Steve, help him in any way I could while keeping a lid on my frustration and despair.

I removed my orange latex gloves and rushed to the bedroom. "I'm coming, I'm coming." I accelerated with each additional ring. The wooden floor echoed as I ran along the narrow corridor, barely missing the cat's litter box in the corner. Steve's face was pale and gaunt, his eyes fixated, as if pulled by magnets on some invisible point in front of him. Stretching out his index finger, he pointed with jerky movements, mumbling incoherent sounds like a wounded animal. He couldn't talk anymore. I followed his gaze to the top of the dresser opposite his bed. Amid a small bronze sculpture of a mother and daughter lighting Sabbath candles, a photo of three smiling kids in snowsuits, and a rose in a bud vase stood an opaque green-tinted glass bottle.

A month earlier, when he could still talk, he had confided in me, whispering like an enemy informer, that he had made a deal with Doctor Lynch to give him a prescription for morphine pills in case he needed it at the end. Seeing my quizzical look, he added, "I'd rather jump from the bridge than end my life like a vegetable."

At the time I didn't question or challenge him. I had no time or energy to figure out what was really going on with him. Life didn't slow down for death; I was busy being wife, nurse, mother, chauffer, cook, and house cleaner. I couldn't afford the luxury of dwelling on the reality of my situation. Plus, what would I do if my suppressed resentment and anger surfaced? How would I function? So I kept it all deep down and tucked away. Steve and the kids needed me, which was what mattered. Beneath the torrent of activities laid a deep fear, a dark, lurking monster I couldn't, and wouldn't, face: the possibility that the father of our three children was dying.

"Steve." My eyes met his. "I can't do it. I can't give pills that will end your life."

I wanted to clasp him in my arms, soothe his trembling hands, tell him I loved him but that I couldn't possibly help him end his life. I walked toward him, my arms outstretched, but then I froze. His mouth twisted, his eyes narrowed, and the veins in his temples bulged. I could hear the unspoken words: *How dare you disobey me?* I stood a few feet away from the dresser, my arms limp at my sides. I looked up at the ceiling. In the corner, a gangly daddy longlegs spun its web, sliding up and down along an invisible thread. "No, Steve, please . . ." I turned and escaped from the room.

I racked my brain, thinking of someone who could advise me what to do. I thought of his friend Paul Roebling who had come out to California to be with us two weeks earlier, after our return from Commonweal. On the second day of his visit, Paul, obsessed with his diet, returned from the local health food store carrying two plastic bags of grain. I peered at the black and ochre contents.

"What is it?"

"This is organic wild rice, and this is Wehani rice." Seeing my raised eyebrows, he added, "It's very healthy."

Great, I thought, why was he so boisterous? Was he planning to feed Steve nutritious rice? Was he going to save him? Steve couldn't eat solid foods anymore, so it didn't matter. I was with Steve day and night, watching him eat less and less, becoming thinner every day.

The evening after I refused to give Steve the pills, I called Paul in New York. "Help me; I need your advice."

Paul's soft, refined voice thundered through the phone line. "Just give him the morphine. You have to consider him first."

In mid-November, a few days after Paul's visit, Steve's red-headed cousin Rich arrived from the East Bay, carrying a carefully wrapped package. In our bedroom, beaming, the dimple in his left cheek deepening, he peeled one layer of paper after the other.

"Here, all the way from Florida. Aunt Evelyn made it." He produced a large mason jar containing a yellowish liquid in which objects in muted colors of beige and green floated. My vegetarian soul grimaced as he offered it to Steve.

"Grandma Katie's chicken soup will make you feel better."

Steve, who could still talk then, smiled—the right side of his mouth turned up while the left side remained immobile, producing a crooked grin. Seeing his ravaged face, I felt a twinge in my heart; that's what was left of his fine features.

"Thanks, Rich, it's my favorite."

Steve focused his right eye on his cousin, his left eye turning sideways as he wiped his brow with a thin pale arm.

"Will you have some with me? You know Esther doesn't eat this stuff."

"I'll be right back," I said. I went to the kitchen, the jar in my hands, palms pressing against the glass until my knuckles turned white. Did Rich think the soup was going to cure Steve? I heated the soup, pureed it, and returned to the bedroom with two steaming bowls. Steve's eyes lit up as he gingerly brought the spoon to his mouth, hand wavering, lips parted in anticipation. Closing his eyes, he paused a few seconds as if to utter a blessing. Then, sipping the soup, he uttered a contented "Mmm . . . ," the liquid dribbling down the side of his mouth. He took a few more sips and put the spoon back on the tray.

"Hey, Rich," Steve cleared his throat. "It's delicious—I'll finish it later."

Richard gulped down his aunt's soup while Steve laid his head back on the pillows, his chest rising and falling with labored breath.

The rest of the soup remained in the refrigerator for a week until I poured it down the disposal, and then I scrubbed the oily patches it left on the sink's bottom.

Even at the end, Steve was trying to be his charming self. He didn't want to offend Rich by not eating the soup, but he also needed to pretend that he was still capable of enjoying food, thereby keeping a semblance of normality.

The morning after Steve requested the morphine, I opened a drawer in his desk in which I found a small hardcover notebook. I swallowed hard as I read the precise, clear black-ink lettering: "I can't eat the food I like, I can't play with my kids, and I can't make love to Esther, what's the point of living?" When I turned the page, Jack London's words jumped out: "I'd rather go out a bright meteor than a slow burning candle . . . the proper function of Man is to live, not to exist." That's why he had asked his physician for the pills! With Steve, life was either being alive or dead but not in between.

Steve was bedridden, mute, and powerless; he'd lost most of his ability to function. My obligation was to help him. But help him do what? Die? How could I? I believed in life, in nature taking its course. I even saved the spiders in our shower and the ants on the kitchen counter. There was no way I'd give him the morphine pills, which he had collected in an amount that would do him in.

Since Paul wasn't of much help to me, I decided to call Buddy, another cousin of Steve's, who lived in Berkeley. He and Steve grew up together in New York. Buddy would have the answer, I thought. He wrote books for a living.

"What shall I do?" I pleaded with him.

"You have to make it easier for him." His voice was soft. "You'll do him a favor."

I put down the receiver. Covering my face with my palms, I shook my head. An ice-cold sensation crept up my legs. "No, I can't . . . I can't kill him."

I thought, why do they all want me to give Steve the morphine to help him end his life? Who am I to decide when he'll die? Don't they realize that it's not something I want to do? They weren't listening to me, to my needs. I felt as if I was held in a large pair of pliers with the air being squeezed out of me. The bluish morphine pills, those harbingers of death, haunted me. The voices of Paul and Buddy rumbled in my mind: "You have to do it. You can't let him suffer." My nerves were on end, my head pounded, and I couldn't sleep. I couldn't come up with a solution.

The day after I had called Buddy, when our friend Bill, the Jungian analyst, came to visit, I clung to him, my face wet against his jacket. I first met Bill and his wife, Maria Alex, when I was pregnant with Ori. I taught them Hebrew in preparation for their immigration to Israel. After ten years, they returned to their home in Mill Valley.

"Bill, I don't know what to do."

Bill smoothed his white moustache with thumb and forefinger. "I'll talk to Maria. She has good common sense, and besides," he smiled, "she's a woman."

An enormous sense of relief, like a warm blanket, overcame me. It was the first time somebody had listened to me, didn't just tell me what to do.

"Thanks, Bill." I stood on my toes and kissed his cheek.

That evening, I was folding laundry in the kids' room when the phone rang. Maria's lilting Austrian accent, pronouncing my name with a sigh on the first syllable, came through the phone.

"Esther, Bill told me . . . now listen." I clutched the receiver, pressing it against my ear. "Don't give him the morphine. If you do, you'll have to live with it for the rest of your life."

"But I can't just let him lay there," my voice quivered, "and suffer."

Maria's voice was soft but stern. "Talk to his physician; he can prescribe a controlled morphine drip to alleviate his pain. I'm sure he'll calm down."

My hand shook as I gently replaced the receiver. Blinking through tears, I stepped out onto our curved wooden terrace and breathed in the cool night air laced with the scent of pungent eucalyptus and pine. Looking up at Venus's bright light, I took a deep breath. There was a way out; it wasn't all on my shoulders. I was so grateful to Maria. She was the only one who thought about my dilemma, not just Steve's. It dawned on me there was another way of functioning besides doing what I'd been told to do. It was my first recognition that I might be set free from Steve's demands and expectations.

I took a deep breath while pressing my palms together in prayer, before returning to our bedroom to check on my husband.

# Chapter 22

# The Broken Promise

Hanukkah arrived early in 1985. Usually it coincided with Christmas, but that year, it began at the end of November. I liked it better that way; I didn't have to compete with red-nosed reindeers, jingling bells, and mounds of toys on display. "*Eema*, can we have a Christmas tree?" Tal, Shira, and Ori had asked me over the years. I dreaded that question. "We are Jewish; we have our own holidays," I answered, my heart heavy when I saw their disappointed eyes and pouting mouths.

How could I explain to them that their grandparents were branded "enemies of the people" just because they belonged to the Semitic race; that my father's parents were last seen in the death camp Theresienstadt; that my own parents were penniless refugees in wartime England; that being a Jew, an Israeli, was as important to me as breathing.

I thought of my mother's oft-repeated story. I could hear her clear voice and bright eyes while relating the episode that had changed our lives: "You were five when you attended a small country school in the Scottish highlands. You liked the teachers and got good grades, but one day . . . " My mother would then lower her voice as if something ominous was about to happen, " . . . you came home with an art project—green, cutout paper with serrated edges, stuck in a wooden spool. You proudly showed it to me. 'What is it?' I asked, and you answered with bright eyes, 'It's a Christmas tree.' That night *abba* and I discussed your education, finalizing our resolve to immigrate to Israel."

My mother's story haunted me now in the States, with the storefront windows sprayed white to look like frost and tinsel crowning the fake fir trees inside.

"No, we can't have a Christmas tree," I told nine-year-old Ori that year. "We celebrate Hanukkah. You'll get lots of presents."

I had already purchased the gifts for the first night: warm socks for each kid, plus pick-up sticks for Ori, Monopoly for Shira, and Albinoni and Bach sheet music for Tal.

A few weeks before the holiday, when he could still function normally, Steve was sitting in his favorite Swedish armchair. The wintry morning sun lit up our living room, accentuating his sunken cheeks and stooped shoulders. The logs burnt in the fireplace emitting a tangy, woodsy aroma. He wore a stocking cap, which covered the crescent-moon-shaped patches of pink skin above his ears, the places where the technicians at UCSF zapped his brain.

On my way to the kitchen, I heard him call me: "Come here." He stretched his arms, in which he held a piece of clothing. "Look what I got for Shira." He handed me a forget-me-not-blue turtleneck, which felt soft and cuddly like a teddy bear.

"It's 100 percent cotton," he said.

Steve had picked the perfect size and color for our blue-eyed daughter. He always did. When Shira was seven, he'd delighted her with a T-shirt that had her smiling face on the front and the words "Super Girl" printed on the back. Now she was a high school freshman already, and an avid soccer player. I knew she'd adore the sweater.

"You know," he looked me in the eye, "I might not be in shape to give it to her."

My throat constricted. "Don't worry, *you* will give it to her, and she'll love it."

But looking at him, I wasn't so sure. Would he even make it to Hanukkah? Would he survive? I shook my head, as if a swarm of mosquitoes attacked me. Of course he'll be okay, I thought, he's made it so far; why wouldn't he pull through this time?

But Steve persisted. He had a look of desperation; his sunken eyes seemed even deeper. "If I can't, do you promise you'll give her the present?"

Appearing to be cheerful, I put my hand on my chest in the form of an oath. "I promise."

I wrapped the gift in white tissue paper. My eyes watering, I picked it up and gently carried it to our bedroom, where I deposited it on a shelf in the closet where I kept all the gifts. I made myself believe he'd be well enough to hand it to Shira. I could picture the big smile and hug she'd give him.

For the next couple of weeks, we anticipated the Festival of Lights. I phoned Tal, now a freshman at UC Santa Cruz. "Make sure you come home next weekend."

Tal, who shared my love of music, was studying classical guitar. On Friday nights after Shabbat dinner, we often sang and played music together with the rest of our family. Steve's face would light up with joy when we sang Pete Seeger's "Garden Song" or "Amazing Grace," which we harmonized, Tal singing the bass line, Steve, not able to keep a secondary tune, sticking to the main melody.

When Tal arrived for Hanukkah, I stood on my tippy-toes and gave him a big hug. I hadn't realized how much I had missed my tall, handsome son, so similar to Steve with his high forehead, deep-set eyes, and cleft chin. Tal held my arms, looking at me with his warm smile: "How are you, *eema*? Managing all right?" I knew I could count on him to help me around the house and be there for Shira and Ori. I breathed a sigh of relief.

Two years earlier, in July, I presented Steve with a banjo for his fortieth birthday. He'd always wanted one, ever since he'd befriended John "The Walker," the tall, wiry-haired guy who vowed a year of silence, demonstrating for world peace. John had walked up the coast from San Francisco to Oregon and passed through our home a few months earlier, leaving the playful, melodic strains of his banjo reverberating in our living room. When John visited us, the lines between Steve's eyebrows vanished while he sat, his eyes closed, the corners of his mouth raised in a half smile, listening to the dancing notes of bluegrass and country songs.

I had gone to Magic Flute, a music store in San Rafael, to inquire about a second-hand banjo for Steve for Hanukkah. I couldn't afford a new one. The salesman came out of the storeroom with a long-necked instrument. "A guy came in here to trade his banjo for a smaller one." He moved his thumb across the strings. "It has a great sound." I felt my pulse quicken; the tinkling sounds were those of John's banjo. With the instrument in my lap, my fingers circled the copper frame overlaid with taut scroll-like skin. Holding the slender neck, I struck a few notes. There was no mistake; this was the banjo that had belonged to The Walker. "I'll take it," I said. Clutching the present, I rushed to the car, anticipating my husband's joy.

Steve had learned to strum a few chords and was delighted when he could join us in the fireside hootenannies. The cancer, however, worsened; the side effects of his medications kept him up at night and made him listless during the days. During that time, I drove him twice a week over the Golden Gate Bridge to his chemotherapy sessions at UCSF. There he lay fully clothed on a narrow hospital bed, a drip-bag suspended from a metal rod next to him. On our last trip, a white-capped nurse had entered the room.

"How are you today?" She smiled at Steve while preparing the syringe.

"Fine, thanks." He rolled up his sleeve, exposing a thin pale arm, the dark hair seeming out of place on the white skin. I turned my head away when the nurse stuck the needle in his vein; Steve emitted a low groan.

Her voice was soft. "Sorry, hon, you haven't got many good veins left."

I peeked as she tapped the flesh in the crook of his arm. The blue and black blotches looked like a Rorschach test. When she had to prick his skin again, I ran out of the room, racing to the end of the corridor, where I plunked down into a gray upholstered chair in the fluorescent-lit room. I covered my quivering mouth with my palm. I couldn't handle it anymore.

In these months leading up to Hanukkah, Steve hadn't played, sung, or horsed around with the kids. When the holiday came around, he was lying in our bedroom, his eyes half-closed, arms limp on the down comforter. The smell of Canola oil permeated our narrow kitchen, where Shira helped me prepare the traditional latkes, potato pancakes. She grated russet potatoes into an ice-filled bowl while I sautéed onions, which I mixed with grated potatoes, eggs, flour, sesame seeds, and salt. I then spooned the mush into the sizzling oil, creating palm-size patties with golden-brown edges. I loved to nosh the first crisp latke straight out of the pan.

Ori set the table, placing the ornate silver *Chanukeeyah*, which Steve inherited from Grandma Katie, in the center, flanked by two smaller chrome-plated ones. Steve came by the menorah honestly; his grandma had announced that the silver menorah would go to the first grandchild who married a Jewish partner. Marrying an Israeli was just a bonus.

Ori entered the kitchen looking for candles. He touched my arm.

"*Eema*, is *abba* going to light candles with us?"

I put down the spatula and, taking a deep breath, wiped my hands on the checkered apron.

"No, he's not feeling well."

"When will he be okay?" Ori's large eyes pleaded with me.

I didn't know how to answer. I had asked the same question, over and over.

I squeezed Ori's shoulder. "Soon he'll be better." A lump rose in my throat as I turned to the frying pan to flip over a burned pancake.

Tal entered the house with an armful of logs he had gathered in our front yard. A couple of shallow-rooted acacia trees keeled over during the heavy rains the winter before, so we had a supply of wood. He built a fire and stacked the rest of the logs under the stone shelf in front of the fireplace. Ori ran over and tugged at his sleeve. "C'mon, Tal, let's light the *Chanukeeyah*."

Tal, his lanky frame towering above Ori, took his brother's hand as they headed to the table. When Ori was born, I told Steve, "They're ten years apart; they'll never play together." Little did I know. Over the years they flew kites, sailed paper boats on the creek, and hung around with each other quite a lot. Watching them walking together, I felt a warm glow of gratitude spread throughout my body. I raised my eyes and silently thanked God, or whoever was there, for the love between my two sons.

I checked the table—it looked festive with a blue tablecloth, *Chanukiyot*, colorful napkins, and fragrant latkes piled on an ornate ceramic plate from the old city of Jerusalem. The kids were all sitting at their spots now, but something was missing. I tapped my forehead—the presents! How could I have forgotten them? I rushed to the hall closet and retrieved the gifts wrapped in blue paper, where silver Stars of David vied for space with gold Menorahs. Next to each present I placed a little bag of Hanukkah gelt, chocolate coins wrapped in silver foil engraved with the profile of Theodor Herzl.

"What about Steve?" Tal asked. He was fond of calling his father by his first name. "Can we give him some latkes?"

Steve's health had deteriorated rapidly; just two weeks ago he had been able to sit in the living room, whereas now he couldn't get out of bed. He slept most of the time. Tal, who'd been away, wasn't aware of the situation.

I didn't know what to tell my gentle nineteen-year-old son, who was afraid to face reality, who could not accept his father's condition. Steve couldn't eat solids anymore. Surely Tal had noticed.

"No, Tal." I strode over to the table. "We'll talk about it later."

Tal faced me. "Can't we just wish him a happy holiday?"

"Okay," I answered.

The four of us stood up and gathered before the bedroom's half-open door. Turning to my children, motioning to be quiet, we tiptoed into the room. Steve's eyes were closed, his mouth slack.

"Maybe he'll wake up soon," Shira whispered as we turned to go back out. I gently closed the door behind us.

We gathered round the living room table, the flame flickering on the slender candle as we passed it to each other, lighting the Menorahs. "Rock of Ages, let our song praise thy saving power," we recited. Our hushed voices gathered momentum as we sang the stanzas, first in Hebrew, then in English. I wanted our children to enjoy the holiday even though Steve couldn't join us. I wanted our lives to continue as normal, not comprehending how impossible that really was. While eating latkes with applesauce, I pushed away the image of Steve lying immobile on his bed. If I acknowledged that Steve was in the bedroom close to death, I would have choked on my food. Above all, I wanted to protect the kids (and maybe myself), to spare them the agony of watching their father dying. It wasn't a conscious decision; it was my way of survival.

After eating and opening the presents, we played with the dreidel, a quadrangle top with four letters—*Nun, Gimel, Hay, Shin*—standing for the words "A Big Miracle Happened There." We spun the wooden top, gambling with walnuts and M&M's, each letter indicating how much we put in or took away from the kitty. Shira moved Ori's hand away from the colorful chocolates. "Don't cheat." Her eyes danced with mirth. I smiled at her; I hoped I could keep the pain and sorrow at bay.

The wax dripped from the candles, creating red, yellow, and blue puddles; the bright flames turned a ghoulish blue before they expired with a hiss in a pool of wax, leaving charred, black wicks. Shira's laughter and Tal and Ori's banter sounded as if it were coming through a blanket of fog. I needed a small miracle of my own, one that would get my kids' father up on his feet, joining them in their revelry. I wanted to believe that Steve would bounce back, the way he always did over the last eight years since his diagnosis. But I knew better—the hospice people arrived each morning. I wanted to throw them out; they were intruders. I wanted to scream at them, "Steve isn't going to die!" Yet I needed their help. They turned Steve over in bed, emptied his urine bag, and changed the sheets. I couldn't accept the finality of it; if I did, I believed I'd fall apart.

"*Eema*, it's your turn." Ori handed me the dreidel while stuffing two chocolates in his mouth.

In one of our last conversations before Steve lost his ability to talk, I'd broached the subject of his burial. It was a rare quiet morning. Steve, propped up in his bed, leafed through a film magazine with our cat, Ambush, curled up at his feet. I sat on a wooden chair next to him, my heart racing. How was I going to raise the question, approach the subject of death? How could I phrase it? How could I express the words without breaking down? I cupped his hand.

"Steve . . . what do I do when it's over?" He looked up at me; the fine laughter lines at the side of his eyes deepened.

"Do whatever you like." He spread his fingers, palms upward.

"But, Steve, I need to know."

"Just throw me in the garbage can." His lips curved up in a smile, but his eyes darkened.

"How can you talk like that?"

Is this how he was helping me out? I knew he couldn't deal with death; joking was so much easier. But how was I supposed to cope with it? I knew he cared about our future. He'd taken out the largest life-insurance policy he could. He even told me, "You'll be rich when I die." I didn't want to be rich. I wanted him to be near me, to be my mate, to continue being the father of our children. I walked out of the room stifling a sob. I felt sad and frustrated; even now, at the end of our life together, he wasn't listening to my needs, wasn't trying to make it easier for me. Yet once again, I realized he couldn't deal with his dying and preferred to joke about it. My tears weren't much of a help.

At the beginning of our married life, Steve would get furious when I cried. "You are just like my mother," he'd tell me, explaining how she would cry so she could get what she wanted from his dad. My tears would dry up on the spot. Later, when the cancer spread and the white blood cells overtook the red ones, Steve would glare at me if I whimpered. "You're supposed to be buoyant and keep my spirits up if there's a chance I'll survive."

How could I be buoyant? On one of our trips back from a chemotherapy session, Steve was nauseous. "Slow down," he told me as we crossed the Golden Gate Bridge. He rolled down the window, stuck out his head, and heaved. My face flushed as the driver to my right frowned, turning his head in disgust. I reached out my hand to stroke Steve's back but then retracted it, overcome by resentment and loathing. I wished things were the way they'd used to be when Steve sat in the driver's seat, handling the car with assurance, as if it were an extension of him. Looking forward, I continued to drive, clutching the steering wheel.

That night, following the failed conversation about what I'd do after it was all over, I was in the kitchen cooking dinner. Steve woke from his nap on the living room sofa.

In a weak voice he called out, "Can you come a minute?"

"Sure." I put down the kitchen towel and tucked in my shirt. I wanted him to see me at my best. I still hoped he'd notice me—what I was wearing, that I was taking good care of myself.

"You know," he smiled, his white teeth contrasting with his ashen cheeks, "you shouldn't stay alone after I'm gone."

"What do you mean?"

"I mean . . . when I'm not around anymore."

I felt as if a snake slithered down my spine, jolting me upright. This was the first time he'd ever talked about his own death.

"You're not going to die." Rather than a statement, this came out as a plea, a desperate attempt to ward off the unimaginable.

"I am, and I want you to find somebody else."

I covered my face. I couldn't fathom being with anybody else. "No, I'll never marry again."

"With a figure like yours, it'd be a waste not to."

He hadn't lost his sense of humor, and he was complimenting me in his way. Still, he'd hardly complimented my body during our marriage, so I was taken slightly aback. And at the same time I was touched by his words. I knew it wasn't time to analyze what he said, though. He was dying. I moved close and hugged him. "I love you."

"It's all right." His eyes reddened. "You'll always remember me. I'll come back as a chipmunk or a . . . gopher. When you see one, you'll think of me."

I trembled, holding his thin, emaciated body in my arms. I felt as if I'd tasted a bittersweet potion. I was grateful he cared about what would happen to me but was exasperated by the jovial manner in which he talked about his death. Yet thinking about him as a little furry animal did bring an inner smile, which softened my eyes and curled up the corners of my mouth.

On the eighth day of Hanukkah, the last day of the holiday, I stood at the head of Steve's bed while I searched his immobile face, trying to resurrect his former features, but I couldn't. His closed eyelids, their translucent skin crisscrossed with spidery blue veins, fluttered in sunken hollows. His thin mouth twitched in his pale, withdrawn face.

When Hanukkah was over, I opened our closet and looked up. To my horror I saw Shira's turtleneck, untouched, on the shelf. I grabbed it and pressed it to my shaking body. A fierce, dagger-like pain pierced me while I emitted a sharp cry. I broke my promise to Steve. I forgot to give his present to Shira. I betrayed him! I felt dizzy, as if a dark cloud had settled over me, obscuring the light, eliminating any hope for the future.

# Chapter 23

# Death

The vision of the blue turtleneck haunted me. I finally gave it to Shira, explaining that Steve had gotten it for her. With contorted lips and a sarcastic smile she said, "So, why didn't *he* give it to me?" She then tossed the turtleneck onto the dresser in her room. I felt as if she had thrown it in my face. "I'm sorry," I muttered as I quickly exited the room. What could I say to her? That her father was dying and there was nothing I could do about it?

By the end of the first week of December, Steve fell into a coma. I refused to believe it was the end; I'd heard about cases where people came out of a coma and survived. But finally, the hospice nurse convinced me he was dying, that he wouldn't wake up. My mouth felt dry, with a bitter taste in it. Not looking at the nurse, my voice breaking, I asked her, "But how will I know when it's the end?"

"He'll stop breathing—"

Looking up at her, I cut her short. I was dumbfounded. "But how will I *know*?"

She laid her hand gently on my arm. "You won't hear him breathing."

That night, I lay in my bed next to the hospital bed provided by hospice, listening to Steve's belabored breath—in, out, in, a long pause. I didn't dare breathe; I wanted to make sure I could hear him. Steve had been in a coma for five days. It was the middle of the night now, and I was waiting up just in case. After what seemed like an eternity, I heard a loud wheezing and knew that the air was still squeezing through his nasal passages down into his fluid-filled lungs. I lay in a fetal position, every muscle awake, my ear straining. It was dark except for a soft light from the night-light coming through the slightly open bathroom door. I was grateful to my sister, who'd come from Israel two days earlier to be with me. At least I wasn't all alone; there was another adult in the house. Milton, who'd come out from New York to be at his son's side for the last few days, was around too, but he stayed at the Tiburon lodge, not far from Mill Valley. Gussie, unfortunately, was bedridden with a broken hip. She couldn't even come out to California to see her son for the last time.

I eyed my husband—a pale gaunt face, soft, matted light-brown hair, sunken eyes under arched eyebrows. I wondered how many more hours or minutes he had on this earth. Would I remember him the way he was before his illness, with long sideburns, full lips, and a radiant smile? Despite the difficulties in our marriage, I loved him, and I felt all the more nostalgic knowing I was about to lose him forever.

The infusion bag hung from the stand above the bed, the cold metal glinting in the streak of light, a slight smell of ether pervading the room. Maybe if I visualized hard enough, his lungs would clear up. Closing my eyelids, I saw an image of my husband inhaling and exhaling, the unobstructed air flowing, distributing oxygen. My reverie was broken by an enormous gurgling breath followed by complete silence. No, that couldn't have been the end, I thought. My heart pounded; its beat became louder and louder. My pulse grew more erratic. My eyes wide open, clenched fist on my mouth, legs rigid, I stared at the little bumps in the textured ceiling, looking for a clue, an answer from somewhere, some higher force I hadn't reckoned with.

The silence continued. Was that it? I thought. Had Steve died? Clutching the pillow, my hands in fists, I muttered the ancient Jewish prayer: "*Shma Yisrael Adonai Elohaynu, Adonai Echad.*" My lips moved of their own accord, as if I'd been practicing that moment for years. Jews had recited those words for ages before death and martyrdom, but I'd never realized they meant anything to me. From what part within me did those sacred words come—was it the language of my soul?

Then I heard a faint exhalation. He was still breathing, he was alive, and he was still with me! Inhaling deeply, I closed my eyes, trying to relax, but my wired nerves resisted. My ears were ringing. I held my breath and listened. Again, I couldn't hear a thing—the heavy silence weighed on my chest. I counted: one, two, three, four, five; nothing, no sound, a void, emptiness. He had stopped breathing, just like the nurse had said. For real this time. The inexpressible words entered my mind: he's gone. What did that mean? Where was he? Where was Steve, my husband, my mate, my lover? My hand over my mouth, I lay immobile, unable to utter a sound.

I was afraid to look at his face. I had lived with him for almost twenty years. His body was as familiar to me as my own—the silky brown hair on the backs of his fingers, the mole at the bottom of his nape, his bony round kneecaps. But at that moment he became a stranger. I couldn't touch him. His body was there, near me, but *he*, Steve, wasn't. It was settling in that he was really dead.

I inhaled deeply and peeked at the clock on the dresser—the time was 3:20 a.m. Suddenly, my mind cleared. I didn't want to wake up Shira and Ori; I didn't want to scare them in the middle of the night. I pulled myself up from the bed and rushed over to the living room, where Rachel was fast asleep on the sofa. Swallowing hard, I choked on my words as I woke her up to tell her what had happened. I was shivering.

"Rachel," my voice sounded high and thin. "I think Steve's . . . dead. What do I do?"

She sat up, and I clung to her, feeling like a hollow frame that could collapse any moment. The fireplace next to the sofa gaped at me with its large opening, the spikes of the grate forming black lines over the pile of gray ashes. Rachel, soft and warm in flannel pajamas, soothed me. After a minute, my shivering subsided.

"Let's go to the bedroom and take a look," she said. She had always been the practical, matter-of-fact one.

We tiptoed through the long corridor, past Ori's bedroom and the children's bathroom. I didn't dare enter the room. Rachel went to the hospital bed, leaned over, and placed her ear near his nose.

"Yes, I think you're right, he's dead." She shook her head back and forth. I bit my lip. How could he disappear, turn into nothing?

With great effort, lifting one leg after the other, I walked toward his bed, my palm outstretched. No, it wasn't him. His spirit was truly gone. I withdrew my hand. I couldn't get myself to touch him.

"Rachel, what shall I do?" All my willpower had been drained out of me: I felt like a floppy ragdoll.

My sister closed the bedroom door softly. She took my hand, drawing me back to the living room. "Let's light a fire," she said. She started tearing up newspapers and piling twigs and logs on the empty grate.

Soon the wood crackled while we sat huddled, close to each other, watching the leaping flames. Looking into the fire, I didn't see a thing. Nothing in the room—sofa, paintings, lamps—existed. It was all a big blur. Tears trickled down my face and along my neck. I turned to Rachel and kissed her, leaving a wet mark on her soft cheek.

"I'm so glad you came, that you're here with me."

She squeezed my shoulder. "Yes, I'm really lucky I arrived in time."

I shuddered. "Can you imagine if I'd been here all alone with the kids?"

We sat near the fire for a long time, holding each other. I felt numb; if someone had poked a needle through my arm I wouldn't have felt it. Rachel looked at me with creases in her brow. Standing up, she pointed outside.

"Look, it's almost daylight." She turned and poked the fire. "And the fire is dying out." I didn't respond. It didn't matter if there was daylight, if the fire died, if the world continued to exist. Steve was gone. Everything should have died with him. How come *I* was still alive? My sister's voice filtered through my thoughts.

"How about a cup of tea?" she said.

I nodded, staring at the crimson-tinted white fog sitting on the tree line on the ridge across the valley. A new day was about to begin, whether I wanted it to or not.

"What about the kids?" my sister asked.

The kids! My God, what should I do about them? I didn't want them to see Steve immobile, with no life in him. It would be too painful, especially for Ori, who was just nine. And Shira, my fourteen-year-old teenager, shouldn't have to face her father . . . dead. Maybe I'd have Steve's body removed, and then I'd tell the kids he had died. I turned to Rachel, who was pouring hot tea into mugs.

"I'll call hospice and Dr. Posner. Somebody has to take him."

She nodded. "Yes, I guess so." Rachel seemed bewildered by the fact that I had to do everything myself. In Israel, if a family member dies, the whole community gathers immediately to help and support the bereaved.

I dragged myself to the phone, not sure how to tell them, not *wanting* to tell them. I lifted the black receiver. With a shaking hand, I dialed hospice's number. I received the answering machine.

"Hello, I . . . ," I swallowed hard, my eyes brimming. "I think Steve is . . ." I took a deep breath and finished, "dead." I couldn't say any more. I felt as if I couldn't breathe. I shuffled away from the phone, my hands covering my face.

Rachel came over and hugged me. After a while I regained my breath.

"What about Tal?" she asked gently.

My heart sank. "Tal! I have to call him straight away. He has to come home."

I dialed Tal's number. "Tal," my voice was thin, urgent. "You need to come home straight away . . ." My voice trailed off.

My son's deep voice came over the phone: "What is it, *eema*? I can't come home right now; it's the end of the semester, and I have finals." Tal hadn't been able to face his father's illness. He couldn't fathom his father dying.

"Tal, *abba* just died," I said softly, my hand on my belly, massaging the cramp in my lower abdomen.

It was silent on the other end of the line. After a few seconds I heard his voice, clear and decisive, trying to reassure me.

"Of course, *eema*, I'll be home tomorrow." Then, in a pleading, softer tone he added, "Hang in there, will you?"

"Yes. Thank you." Relieved, I hung up while warm tears streaked my cheeks.

"Come here," Rachel said. She walked over and held me, her arms tight around my heaving shoulders. "It's all right; you'll be okay."

No, I wouldn't be okay—nothing would be okay. Steve was gone, and I was alone with my three children. Rachel would go back to her family in Israel. Milton would return to Queens, to Gussie.

The phone was ringing. It was the nurse from hospice. She was so sorry; she let Dr. Posner know, and a hearse was on its way. I heard Shira in the shower. She got up every morning at seven, gobbled down a bowl of Honey Nut Cheerios, and rode her bike to Tamalpais High School. How would I tell her that she had no father anymore? As it was, her life wasn't easy. She was sandwiched between two brothers, who had received most of Steve's attention. She was a shy girl, with few friends, and I wasn't always available for her. Once I gave birth to Ori and the doctors discovered Steve's illness, I didn't have much time and energy left for my daughter.

I heard the sound of a car laboring up our steep driveway. From our high veranda, I saw it—an enormous black entity. Death had come to take my husband away. People were at our front door, knocking. No, I thought, I won't open the door; I can't face Steve's lifeless body. A sliver of fear shot through me like an arrow. I felt like screaming, He's not dead! Go away! The knocking persisted. Defeated, my head down, I opened the door. I pointed to our bedroom and went quickly to the kitchen, where Shira was pouring milk into her cereal. She looked at me, her eyes narrowing.

"What's going on?"

"Shira . . ." My voice trailed off. I felt as if a stone had lodged in my throat. My daughter's blue eyes grew large with fear. She understood.

Her voice was harsh. "When did he die? Why didn't you wake me up so I could say bye to him?"

"I . . . I wanted to protect you."

She moved back as if I posed a threat to her. Her lower lip trembled while she swallowed, her mouth forming a narrow line. "How could you do this to me? You don't understand. I wanted to give him a kiss. Now he's gone."

I wanted to hug her, but there was an invisible wall around her. My sweet Shira, who had trusted me. I let her down. The whole world had let her down.

"Please, Shira, I didn't mean to—"

"I don't care. Leave me alone."

She turned around, bumping into the kitchen doorframe, and dashed into her room.

"Shira, wait a minute." I ran after her.

We met in the narrow corridor after she came out of her room. Her fist was tight around the strap of her backpack as she squeezed past me. I heard the front door slam, and she was gone.

After Shira ran off to school, I went looking for Ori. I needed to get out of the house as soon as possible. I didn't want to witness the people taking Steve away; I couldn't handle it. I was sure they knew what to do, but my mind couldn't process what was happening, and I needed to escape. Ori was in the kitchen, where Rachel prepared his breakfast. As soon as he finished his cereal, I grabbed his hand and said, matter-of-factly, "Let's go." We climbed the deer path in front of our home up to Tamalpais Street. I heard the revving of an engine, and looking through the trees I saw the hearse carrying my husband's body away. My stomach churned; I couldn't handle the sight. I walked fast, pulling Ori along. After a few minutes, I paused.

"Let's run." I said, trying to sound cheerful. I had decided, albeit unconsciously, to protect Ori by pretending life continued as usual.

After racing each other, I stopped and, catching my breath, turned to Ori.

"You don't have to go to school today; you can play." I was hoping against hope to stall the inevitable.

His dark blue eyes peered at me from under long, black lashes. His solemn look made him appear older than his age.

"What about *abba*?" He wanted to know.

"*Abba*?" I hesitated, trying to figure out what to say. "We'll have a funeral and bury *abba* tomorrow, when Tal is home. Okay?" I only realized weeks later how clumsily I had handled this. Ori never brought up our conversation, but I knew I did a lousy job of relating the situation to him. Yet I couldn't do any better; I was deep in my grief, barely aware of my surroundings, functioning like a robot while I dealt with everyday life.

Ori didn't react, or didn't know what to say. Doctors had discovered Steve's cancer when Ori was just nine months old. Since then, sensing there might not be much time left, Steve had devoted most of his energy to his youngest son. In fourth grade, Ori came home one day announcing that his class was studying New Zealand and he'd love to go there.

"Okay, start saving," Steve told him, and he gave him a little piggy bank.

A few months later, the two of them traveled for ten days to Christchurch, Queenstown, and Mt. Cook in the South Island. Steve never told Ori about the migraine headaches and seizures he had during the trip. When they returned, Ori reported seeing "thousands and thousands" of sheep.

Ori didn't say anything about the funeral. Reaching out, he hugged me, arms around my waist. Holding his body close, I could feel his heart beat. My warm tears dripped on his smooth, black hair. I'd do all I could to take care of him, to make sure he'd weather this enormous loss. I wanted him to have a secure, safe life. I had no idea how I'd manage to act as mother and father to my three children. All I knew was that I'd be there for them, any moment they needed me. A surge of relief, a sense of lightening, passed through my body. Steve hadn't disappeared; he was here, in our three children. His genes, his spirit, were in each one of them. Something shifted for me with this recognition. I knew then I'd be able to go on, with Tal, Shira, and Ori giving meaning to my life.

I wiped my eyes and took hold of Ori's hand. "Shall we?" And we resumed walking up the hill, the sun in our faces.

## ❧ Chapter 24: ❧

# The Burial

A day before Steve died, the night of December 11, I still had no idea where to bury him. I didn't want to consult his parents; I never felt close enough to confide in them, though I did have a soft spot for Milton, who doted on me. Besides being worlds apart—an Israeli woman versus New York Jews—I didn't want to add to their burden. Steve was their first-born, handsome, talented, and successful son. I couldn't imagine how they felt about losing him. I didn't even try to imagine it. I was immersed in my kids and my survival.

Gussie and Milton were frustrated living so far away from their son. We had frequent phone conversations, and when the tumor grew and Steve lay in bed comatose, they called me daily.

On the second day Steve lay unconscious, Milton was on the phone. "Have you made arrangements?"

"Arrangements? What do you mean?" I scribbled black lines on a pad.

"You know. Where will Steve be interred?"

The word "interred" grated on my ear. I knew Milton wasn't the only one who used euphemisms for the painful events of life.

"Interred" was less painful than "buried." "Passed away" was easier to accept than "died." But if other people, especially those close to me, accepted it, they'd have to deal with Steve's death as well. Then I wouldn't be alone in that terrible mess.

"Do you mean where will they *bury* him? I . . . I don't know." I couldn't get myself to say out loud that *I* would have to bury him.

All I heard on the other end of the line was the sound of Milton's raspy breath. I had no choice; I had to deal with Steve's dying. I was the one who had to make decisions.

"I'll make a few phone calls and let you know."

"Bury him in Colma," Elaine, Steve's cousin, told me on the phone later that day. "It's a Jewish cemetery. They'll take care of the grave," she said. I remembered the cemetery, located on the way to the airport, rows and rows of white slabs. No, Steve wasn't going to be part of the masses. He was too much of an individual, too special; he didn't fit in there. Besides, I needed something close by so the kids and I could visit him.

As Steve lay in a coma for several days, I tiptoed in and out of his room, grimacing at his immobile face, feeling my stomach churn. According to the hospice nurse, he could die any minute. I had no choice. I had to figure out where to bury him. On the morning of the fourth day, while Shira and Ori were at school, I paced our living room. Through the large windows, I could see the large eucalyptus tree Ori had named "Charlie." Whenever I'd lose my patience or Shira would yell at him, Ori would run to Charlie and put his arms around his friend. When he was four, Ori could hug half of Charlie's trunk. Now, at age nine, his tree-friend had grown so tall and its trunk circumference so wide that he could embrace only part of it. I was glad Ori found his refuge. He was Steve's darling, and I was sure Steve's illness wasn't easy for him, though we never discussed it.

My eyes wandered around the room. On the shelf next to Viktor Frankl's *Man's Search for Meaning* lay the big yellow phone book. I looked up "Cemeteries." There was Home of Peace, Hills of Eternity, and then, in small letters, Daphne Fernwood, Cemetery and Mortuary, Tennessee Valley Road, Mill Valley.

When I dialed the number, the manager listened to my situation and then asked, "Do you want him embalmed?"

"No, we'll need to bury him within forty eight hours."

"Will you have an open casket? Will there be a viewing in the mortuary?"

"No." I cringed at the thought. "We're Jewish. We'll get a simple coffin and go straight to the burial site.

A day after Steve's death, we had the funeral. On a brisk sunny morning, a convoy of cars trailed behind a black hearse climbing up a winding narrow road. I followed the hearse with Tal, Shira, and Ori with me in the car. I wore black pants and an overcoat and asked myself questions: Did I let everybody know? Would the rabbi be there on time? Was I dressed appropriately? As long as my mind was busy, I wouldn't have to feel anything.

Shira, in the seat behind me, turned her head back. "*Eema*, look at all these cars. We can have a party up there."

Ori giggled. "Yes, *abba* always wanted to have fun. I know, let's invite him."

Shira nudged Ori. "He can ask God to let him come down for an hour."

Tal, in the passenger seat, turned around.

"Come on, guys, we're going to *abba*'s funeral."

Shira pouted mockingly, bringing her fists to the corners of her eyes. "So what do you want us to do? Cry the whole time?"

I parked the car at the bottom of the hill. "Okay, we're here; you can get out."

Shira and Ori ran ahead. Tal offered me his arm while we walked up the grassy slope. I tried not to step on the flat gravestones or on the yellow daisies that had sprouted up after the rain. At the top, I saw a mound of reddish earth piled up next to a rectangular pit. I didn't dare to go and look. Car doors slammed and black-clad figures climbed up, gathering in small groups. Rabbi White, standing near the grave, adjusted his tallit around his shoulders. Spotting us, he walked over, attaching a bobby pin to the skullcap on his dark curls.

He put his arm around me and asked, "Are you all right?"

I stiffened. Was he trying to console me? He wasn't a person with whom I felt any closeness. I didn't want his pity.

"Yes, thanks." Turning away, I pulled out a tissue.

The wind picked up, and the leaves of the eucalyptus trees behind us rustled; above, a lone turkey vulture circled, dipping up and down on the currents like a drunkard.

Rabbi White touched my shoulder. "Looks like everybody is here; shall we start?"

It was strange that he asked me. It should be Steve who gave his permission; he was the head of the family.

We huddled together, staring at the ground: Tal and Shira on my right, Ori to my left, my arm around him. "*El Male Rachamim*, merciful God," the rabbi chanted from the gray prayer book. I peeked at the kids. Shira and Ori's eyes were red; Tal's head was turned so I couldn't see his face. Milton, his short legs balancing his stout body, held onto Mike, his surviving son. I heard the prayers and saw the people but I couldn't *feel* anything. I was hollow inside, like an empty shell of a crab tossed up on the beach.

When the service was over, the caretaker handed Mike a spade, and he shoveled some dirt into the pit, on top of the coffin. The rest of the family followed suit. I had a strong urge to flee, but I picked up a lump of clay and threw it into the grave. When I turned to leave, the world in front of me was a blur—friends and neighbors approached somberly, muttering condolences.

"I'm so sorry."

"Take care of yourself."

"Steve was a great guy."

People dispersed. The caretakers filled up the pit. A woman, a script girl from one of the movies Steve had worked on, slipped a white handkerchief trimmed with lace in my hand. "Here, I want you to have this," she said, and she vanished. She didn't know what to say. Maybe that was her way of saying goodbye to Steve.

"*Eema*, look," Ori said and pointed to a small animal peeping from the earth just a few feet away. "Let's see what it is."

Ori's hand in mine, I walked closer to the little rodent.

"I think it's a gopher," I said. Finally, my tears welled up. I hugged my son, rivulets streaming down my cheeks. Choking, I faced Ori. "He promised me he'd come back."

Without saying a word, Ori put his small arms around me and squeezed me as tight as he could.

A few days after the funeral, Shira and Ori collected some of their father's belongings to erect altars in their rooms in his memory.

"Can I have *abba*'s ring?" Ori asked me. It seemed like a strange request from a nine-year-old child.

I looked into his eyes. I felt a twinge of guilt—I wished I could have given it to him. When it came to burying Steve, all I had to rely on were my instincts. I had no idea what was "right" or "wrong," I didn't know about a protocol for burials. I'm not religious, so I didn't adhere to a strict Jewish burial. I'd been asked if I wanted his ring when they came to take his body, but I'd said no, "Just leave it on him." I felt it would dishonor him to take it off his finger—and couldn't get myself to keep a ring off his dead hand.

"I'm sorry, Ori, I left it on *abba*'s finger. Will you forgive me?"

"It's okay, *eema*."

The next day Ori asked me for Steve's silver cufflinks, the ones with the "theatre masks," a smile on one and a frown on the other.

"What will you do with them?" I asked.

"Could I just have them, please?"

A few days later, his eyes shining, Ori stretched out his palm, on which lay a thick silver ring with an uneven surface.

"Tal melted the cufflinks to make this for me."

I felt my heart swell with love for my young son. Drawing him close to me, I thanked him silently for his sensitivity, ingenuity, and smarts. I lifted his chin and looked him in the eye.

"Orilè, I'm so grateful you are my son." My eyes tearing, I stroked his soft cheek. "*Abba* will always be there for us. He hasn't vanished." I pointed at my heart. "He's within us."

"*Emalè* . . ." That's all he could utter. Trying to hold back his tears, his lips quivered, and his face twisted in agony as he flung his arms around me. And then the dam broke. If a bird had flown overhead, it would have witnessed two human figures, a small and a larger one, clinging to each other, intertwined in an embrace, attempting to soothe their pain, fear, and loneliness.

# Epilogue

Returning to normal life was impossible. Each of us dealt with the loss in our own way. Every morning I ran the two-mile Lovell Avenue loop, downhill, along Cascade Creek to the Coffee Roastery in downtown Mill Valley. I ran fast, elbows bent, knees lifted, fists clenched, feet pounding the pavement, forward, faster, faster, escaping the hollow, empty feeling within me, the gaping void within my soul, the place I didn't dare to look.

When I reached the Roastery, I downed a large glass of steaming caffe latte. Adrenalin and caffeine pumping in my body, I'd run uphill, back home. I grew infatuated with Norm, the café owner. I was so needy, I'd fall for any eligible man I encountered, any person who would say a few kind words to me. After my morning routine, I felt alive for a few hours. But the pain, loneliness, and despair soon crept back in.

After school, when Shira and Ori vented their anger on each other, unable to cope with their father's death, I yelled deafening, high-pitched screams. They fought constantly. Shira slammed her younger brother against the wall, and Ori protected himself by punching and kicking. I wasn't used to being the disciplinarian—that was Steve's job. When I couldn't handle the turmoil anymore, I would scream and run out of the house, escaping my kids' despair. I felt totally inadequate.

The bills, the insurance forms, the unbalanced checkbooks overwhelmed me. There were the cartons of professional photographs Steve shot. I knew he used to send them to a photo archive in New York, but I had no idea how to organize the piles of eight-by-ten photos or sort out the hundreds of slides. Finally, our neighbor Ellen saved me. She took over, filing the photos and sending them off to New York for me. Before Steve died, he'd handled all the paperwork. He was the head of the household and saw it as his job.

One afternoon, when Shira came home from school, she found me slumped at the dining room table, head on my arms, ready to give up. She tossed her backpack on the couch and walked over to me. Her voice was soft, but I could sense her alarm.

"*Eema*, what is it?"

I raised my head, aware of my red eyes and disheveled hair. "I can't handle this; it's too much for me."

All of a sudden, Shira changed into an efficient young woman who took matters into her own hands. "Come, show me where all the bills are."

I pointed to the papers strewn all over the table. "There."

She started to collect the bills and envelopes. "Okay, where is your checkbook?"

I gave it to her. She sat at the table and started writing checks, one after the other. She tore out one and handed it to me. "Here, *eema*, all you have to do is sign your name."

The lump in my chest began to dissolve. I felt enormous relief, as if I had been dehydrated and liquid was being injected into my veins. I put my arm around Shira's shoulders. Her unruly long hair brushed my face as I bent over to kiss her. "Thank you, Shirale, you're my saving angel."

I had mixed feelings. I was so grateful to my daughter, yet

ashamed she had to do adult work, work I should have been able to do. I was the parent; I didn't want her to take care of me. Yet this reversal of roles might have helped her, showing her that she was needed, instilling in her a sense of pride.

After that, I did my best to keep up everyone's spirits, but I could not assuage their grief. Once, while cuddling Ori, he said to me, "I'd rather not have known him at all, that he had died when I was born, so I wouldn't have the pain now. I miss him so much."

His warm tears, mingling with mine, dropped on my arm.

Shira, who was dealing with puberty on top of the devastating loss of her father, walked around with a grim face, refusing to express her feelings. I tried to get her to talk but didn't succeed. When she got her driver's permit, I bribed her into seeing my psychotherapist. With her at the wheel, we drove fifty minutes each way to Point Reyes. There she sat each week for an hour opposite the therapist without uttering a word. Frustrated, we were at a loss what to do. Shira wouldn't talk about her father's death. This went on for six months.

Defeated, I sent her, during her sophomore year, for a semester to my sister Rachel in Israel. Later I found out that Shira had threatened to jump off the roof of my sister's house and had once swam deep into the Mediterranean without heeding my sister's desperate calls. Still, she came back a saner, more relaxed person. She wasn't so angry and was more willing to accept the fact of her father's demise.

I searched for a meaning to my life, a reason why I remained alive after my husband's death. Though living with Steve was never easy, he left a huge void in my life. After endless therapy sessions, hours with a psychic who examined my auras, and primal scream sessions, I was still lost.

In March 1986, a few months after Steve died, I went to a widows' retreat in San Rafael. Five women gathered in a room as the late-afternoon light filtered through a high, rectangular window barely illuminating a somber black-and-white photograph of some austere building. The facilitator introduced herself. "I lost my dear husband twelve years ago, and I'm still devastated." I was aghast. Steve had just died. *Her* husband had been gone for many years. How dare she compare our losses? Mine was recent. I felt raw, confused, angry, completely overwhelmed, unable to accept or internalize what had happened, and there she was, talking about *her* devastation. I heard her say, "And now we'll share our stories." I tensed up. How could I tell these strangers about Steve? How could I relate the horror of the weeks and months prior to his death, the surgeries, chemo, radiations, and nightmarish days of watching him in a coma?

Then Rena, a small woman with a narrow face, wavy black-gray hair, and brown, expressive eyes, started to talk: "My husband was in a coma before he died . . ."

The tight coil inside me started to unravel. I wasn't the only one who had seen her husband in a coma. I could feel her pain. I knew she'd understand mine. All the women talked. Overcoming my fear and hesitation, I shared my story as well. I didn't elaborate. I spoke in an even, monotone voice. Yet after I finished, I was relieved. As the light in the room dimmed, our leader lit candles and placed a record on a turntable. She asked us to get up, listen to the song, and dance to it. We did—each one of us twirling around in our own space, our own world of grief and joy of living.

As time went on, I started to count everything in terms of "before" and "after" Steve's death. I developed severe stomach pains accompanied by diarrhea and vomiting. The cramps in my abdomen felt like an animal gnawing at my intestines. For hours I lay in bed, unable to eat or move. The kids, frightened out of their minds, didn't know what to do. Ori, the most outspoken of my children, talked for the three of them when he said, "*Eema*, are you going to die too?"

In one journal entry I wrote, "I'm so sick of my illness. I feel like an invalid, dragging my feet, without the capacity to function, to exert myself. I'm so lonely and scared."

Several tests revealed nothing. The doctors, not knowing what was wrong with me, diagnosed my sickness as a virus, bacterial infection, giardia, sensitive stomach, whatever. Dr. Friedman, who came on a house visit, found me writhing in bed, a hot water bottle on my belly, my feet moving like scissors, up and down, to distract me from my pain. After checking my abdomen and listening to me sob for ten whole minutes, he said I had gastroenteritis accompanied by extreme stress.

When I went to my psychotherapist to get some relief, she had me lie down on a massage table and inhale deeply.

"Point to the area in the body which you filled with air," she said.

"Up to here." I pointed to my diaphragm.

"Can you inhale deeper?"

I followed her instruction.

"Where is it now?"

I touched my collarbone.

"Can you try a bit more? What will happen if you breathe into your head?"

Through choking sobs I managed to mumble, "I can't. I . . . I'll die."

The therapist, eyes moist with consternation, stroked my hair lightly.

"It's okay. You'll get through this."

I couldn't allow myself to connect my head with my body. For so long my feelings had been numb, as if shot with novocaine. I didn't react most of the time; I couldn't bear the consequences. I wouldn't let myself acknowledge the pain and fear during Steve's illness, the suffering after his death.

My illness was a process I had to go through to release the toxins of submissiveness, giving in, acquiescing. It was repression concentrated in my vulnerable organs—my stomach and my digestive system. I couldn't "stomach" the years of suppressed feelings, stuffed-down emotions—rage, resentment, frustration, fear—held-back screams, and clenched fists.

I worked hard to free myself, to regain my identity, my will, now that I was out of Steve's orbit. I wrote words I never dared tell him:

"This time I'll do all the talking, and wherever you are, you'll indulge me and listen. You treated me like a child, a person inferior to you. I'd always wanted to be an equal in our marriage, something you never permitted. We would have been so much better off if you hadn't insisted on imposing your will, making decisions on your own, if you had shared with me your work, concerns, and fears.

If I could reverse the clock, the hours, months, years, I'd say to you: "I have as much right to think and express myself as you have."

I hated your temper—you slammed doors, gave me the silent treatment, screamed at me, our children, my parents. You threw a pencil at Shira when she interfered with your writing at the desk. You tossed the television off the deck because Tal watched a soap opera. What message did that convey to our son?

Yes, you wrote apology notes, formal letters printed on your typewriter—what good did they do? You'd already inflicted the pain and humiliation. At the time, I couldn't say no to you—I was afraid of your demonic anger, your wrath. Nobody will ever dictate to me again how to live my life; it's too precious, too short."

I didn't know how many years I had left, but I resolved to make the most of them: teaching Hebrew, doing yoga, swimming, hiking, spending time with family, savoring the connection with my women friends.

I would eventually learn to share life with a man without forfeiting my own. I would meet Elan, a kibbutznick, thirteen years younger than me, who studied Hebrew literature at UC Berkeley. In the year he took off between his bachelor's and master's degrees, he decided to complement his gardening work with Hebrew teaching. He hadn't a clue how to teach, so when he couldn't handle his class, the principal told him, "Go to Esti's class and learn from her." I would spend my time at teachers' meetings, speaking in Hebrew with Elan and laughing at his jokes. It would take living with

Elan for ten years before I signed my second *ketubbah*, believing I wouldn't repeat my mistakes. By that time I would finally feel that I could trust Elan, that he'd respect me as a unique human being with intellect, capabilities, needs, and desires.

A friend would tell me that after a loved one's death we cut thousands of threads that tie us to the departed. I would continue to sever those ties, snipping the cords, for many years to come.

There would come a time when I'd look at Tal, grown up, an editor and film teacher with a family of his own. He'd move his head sideways, hands gesturing, palms upward—just like Steve, I'd think. Ori's intense looks and Shira's mischievous playful manners would mirror my late husband's. Their love, caring, and concern for me, and the joy I derived from my grandchildren, would enrich my life and give it meaning.

In rural India, after the husband dies, his widow takes a year off, going from village to village to tell her story. When she returns home, she can continue with her life; she's released from the bond and can face the world without her mate. In time I will not be angry with Steve anymore. Looking at his photograph on the desk, I will smile back at him. I will be free to remember my husband's crazy, wonderful, tormented soul. I will be free to go on with my life.

# Acknowledgments

I would like to thank my teachers at the MFA program at USF, where the seeds of my book were first planted: Deborah Lichtman, Kate Brady, Lewis Buzbee, Jane Anne Staw, Lisa Harper, Margo Perin, Michelle Richmond, and Lowell Cohn. They encouraged and cajoled me to write, prompting me to dig into my emotions and unearth hidden scenes of my life, while providing me with tools to put it on paper.

My appreciation to Abby Wassermann, writing teacher and editor of my first draft, whose knowledge of the craft of writing guided and inspired me. My thanks to my writing buddies, Bronni Galin, Brenda Foster, and Antonia Van Becker, whose comments and insights enriched my story, giving me faith to continue writing.

My gratitude to Floyd Skloot and Bud Roper, who read my manuscript with keen writers' eyes and gave me invaluable feedback that helped me revise my story.

My heartfelt thanks to Brooke Warner, who helped me smooth out the kinks in my manuscript, connect the dots, and express more of my feelings. Brooke gave me the strength to realize my dream of publishing my book.

I would like to give thanks to my wonderful children and grandchildren, who bring so much joy into my life, and express my gratitude to Steve, my deceased husband and the source of inspiration for this book, whose life was cut too short.

And last, *todah rabah*, thank you, to Elan, my mate, who was the first to read and critique my writing; who rallied to my SOS calls when the computer played tricks on me; and who accompanied me along the arduous journey of creating this book.

# About the Author

Esti Skloot is an adjunct professor of Hebrew at the University of San Francisco. She was born in England to Jewish refugees who escaped Nazi Germany, and grew up in Israel where she received her teaching credentials from the Hebrew Teachers' Seminary in Jerusalem. After serving in the IDF as a singer in an army entertainment troupe, she married an American and immigrated to New York and later California, where she received her BA in music at Sonoma State University and her MFA in creative writing at the University of San Francisco. Skloot loves nature, music—she is now learning to play the flute—and books. She lives in Mill Valley, California with Elan, her Israeli husband, and their pit bull, Laila. She has three children and four grandchildren, all of whom live in the Bay Area.

*Author photo © Shira Skloot*

# SELECTED TITLES FROM SHE WRITES PRESS

She Writes Press is an independent publishing company founded to serve women writers everywhere. Visit us at www.shewritespress.com.

*Loveyoubye: Holding Fast, Letting Go, And Then There's The Dog* by Rossandra White. $16.95, 978-1-938314-50-6. A soul-searching memoir detailing the painful, but ultimately liberating, disintegration of a twenty-five-year marriage.

*Not Exactly Love: A Memoir* by Betty Hafner. $16.95, 978-1-63152-149-2. At twenty-five Betty Hafner, thought she'd found the man to make her dream of a family and cozy home come true—but after they married, his rages turned the dream into a nightmare, and Betty had to decide: stay with the man she loved, or find a way to leave?

*The Full Catastrophe: A Memoir* by Karen Elizabeth Lee. $16.95, 978-1-63152-024-2. The story of a well-educated, professional woman who, after marrying the wrong kind of man—twice—finally resurrects her life.

*Naked Mountain: A Memoir* by Marcia Mabee. $16.95, 978-1-63152-097-6. A compelling memoir of one woman's journey of natural world discovery, tragedy, and the enduring bonds of marriage, set against the backdrop of a stunning mountaintop in rural Virginia.

*Lost in the Reflecting Pool: A Memoir* by Diane Pomerantz. $16.95, 978-1-63152-268-0. A psychological story about Diane, a highly trained child psychologist, who falls in love with Charles, a brilliant and charming psychiatrist—ignoring all the red flags that will later come back to haunt her.

*The Buddha at My Table: How I Found Peace in Betrayal and Divorce* by Tammy Letherer. $16.95, On a Tuesday night, just before Christmas, after he had put their three children in bed, Tammy Letherer's husband shattered her world and destroyed every assumption she'd ever made about love, friendship, and faithfulness. In the aftermath of this betrayal, however, she finds unexpected blessings—and, ultimately, the path to freedom.